Can You Believe It?

30 Years of Insider Stories with the Boston Red Sox

Joe Castiglione with Douglas B. Lyons

TRIUMPH
BOOKS

Library of Congress Cataloging-in-Publication Data available upon request.

This book is available in quantity at special discounts for your group or organization. For further information, contact:

Triumph Books LLC
814 North Franklin Street
Chicago, Illinois 60610
(312) 337–0747
www.triumphbooks.com

Printed in U.S.A.
ISBN: 978-1-63727-343-2
Design by Patricia Frey
Photos courtesy of the author unless otherwise indicated.

Contents

Foreword

I MET JOE WHEN I CAME TO THE RED SOX IN 1991. My parents felt a connection with Joe on a daily basis as they listened to him broadcast the Red Sox games on the radio when they weren't at the game. My dad thought, *if you treat my son well, you're a good man.* And Joe did. That was the start of the friendship between Joe and my parents which continues to this day. Joe and I took a liking to each other. During my eight years with the Red Sox, I did many interviews with Joe and we spent a lot of time together in the clubhouse, behind the batting cage, and traveling with the team.

When I got to the Red Sox, I asked for No. 44. My coach at Seton Hall, Nick Bowness, sat me down and told me about the struggles that Jackie Robinson had gone through as the first black man in the major leagues in 1947. Bowness had worn No. 42 during his own career. I knew about Robinson, but Nick helped me put Robinson's career in perspective. I switched and asked for No. 42.

My parents thought, and I came to agree, that Joe was always a positive person. He reported the facts, not his opinion. He could see the forest for the trees. If I had a good day, he'd report that. If I had a bad day, he'd report that, too. Straight and honest, whatever the issue, Joe always gave me a fair shake. He told the story right down the middle. He treated everybody that way. That's the way he is. I'll always be grateful for that.

It was tough being a Red Sox player for eight years (1991–98). Boston had a history of great players such as Cy Young, Harry Hooper, Ted Williams, Bobby Doerr, Joe Cronin, and Carl Yastrzemski, and I was honored to be part of that tradition.

But everybody on the team, in the front office, in Boston, and throughout Red Sox Nation knew that the Red Sox had not won the World Series since 1918. I know that I worked extra hard during my years in Boston to win it all for the Boston fans. I'm sorry it didn't happen while I was a player. When you wear that uniform, you try to achieve that goal.

Through all their struggles, their years of not winning, coming close and falling short, Joe was always positive. Many in the media became cynical and negative. But Joe never did.

When I had a contract dispute with the front office in '98, Joe told it straight. Joe and I still talk about our eight years together. He felt some genuine sadness about my leaving Boston. So did I. Joe told me I should never have left Boston.

I was very fortunate to have had a pretty solid 12-year baseball career. I was the American League MVP in '95 and was selected for the All-Star team three times. After my playing career ended, I was able to get into another business: rehabilitating older buildings. I call it my second life.

Joe and I have stayed very close.

When Boston finally won it all in 2004, I felt a tremendous weight had been lifted from my shoulders. I felt great for everybody associated with the Red Sox.

As soon as you get to Boston, you learn about the Jimmy Fund. But there is a difference between knowing about the Jimmy Fund and working with it. One of the first questions for most players in Boston is, "How can I help the Jimmy Fund?"

Jason Leader was my impact person. Because of Jason, I had a much closer relationship with the Jimmy Fund than I or anybody else ever expected.

We were in the clubhouse in Anaheim when Joe asked me to call a Jimmy Fund patient named Jason Leader. Joe tells the whole story later in this book. I got on the phone with Jason and tried to give him some encouragement. I took the phone around the corner so we'd have some privacy. I told him that I would try to hit a home run for him. Later, during the game, when I came up to bat, I really wasn't thinking about that conversation. I was just trying to hit the ball. But I connected for a home run. When the ball went over the fence, I remembered what I had said to Jason, but I didn't think that anybody else had heard me. Joe put the story on the air and was very happy with all the media attention the story got. I became very close to Jason, his siblings, and his parents. So did my parents.

I didn't really know how the Red Sox felt about me after my departure. I was very proud to be inducted into the Red Sox Hall of Fame in 2008. It's a great feeling. The Red Sox have had so many great players. But to be included in that history at Fenway is a great thing.

On August 31, 2011, I went back to Fenway to participate in the Jimmy Fund radio-telethon. My parents and I reconnected with Jason's parents. That was also the first time I had the honor of throwing out the first pitch at Fenway Park. My seven-year-old daughter, Grace, was with me. I had her out on the field. She'd never been to Fenway Park and is too young to have seen me play.

Joe Castiglione means a great deal to the Red Sox, especially to the fans. Players come and go. Some stay in Boston for a year or so, some longer. I was there for eight seasons. But Joe is always there. Good season or bad, you can always count on Joe Castiglione's positive and straightforward attitude and reports. His voice is a constant throughout New England.

—Mo Vaughn

Introduction

WHEN PEOPLE IN NEW ENGLAND TURN ON A GAME, THEY WANT TO FEEL LIKE THEY'RE LISTENING TO A FRIEND, NOT SOMEBODY JUST SPOUTING OFF NUMBERS. Joe has that relationship with fans, and he really makes it special for them.

We did the *Manager's Show* every gameday. We were on the buses and the planes and in the clubhouses together every day. Joe's not just a person I worked with; Joe's a friend.

I grew up outside of Pittsburgh, so I listened to Bob Prince broadcast Pirates games a lot. In St. Louis I listened to Harry Caray and Jack Buck do the Cardinals games. I actually had a record album of highlights from the 1964 Cardinals World Series narrated by Harry Caray. I used to play it every night in my room. Vin Scully of the Dodgers was also one of my favorites.

Joe Castiglione has his own unique style. When people turn on the radio to hear Joe broadcast a game they feel as if they're sitting in their living room listening to their friend talk. And I think that's what they enjoy. Joe goes back to my dad, Tito, who was a major leaguer.

People tell me that even though Joe is not a "homer," they can tell whether the Red Sox are winning or losing by the tone of his voice. This is what's so special about our game. It's not just numbers and batting averages. It's relationships and stories.

—Former Red Sox Manager
Terry Francona

CHAPTER 1

"Magical Mystery Tour"
30 Years of Red Sox

2012 WILL MARK MY 30TH YEAR AS A BROADCASTER FOR THE BOSTON RED SOX. My friend Tom Shaer, longtime TV sports anchor at NBC Chicago and an Agawam, Massachusetts, native, calculated that I have seen more Boston Red Sox games than anybody else. Here's the math:

1983–2011: 4,718 regular season games.

In addition, I've see 469 spring training games, plus eight Red Sox games I broadcast when I worked in Cleveland (1979 and '82) and Milwaukee ('81).

That brings the total to 5,033. That number includes four midseason exhibition games, two Jimmy Fund games against the New York Mets, and one against the Cincinnati Reds sometime in the '80s.

Now add 93 postseason games: 30 American League Division Series games, 48 American League Championship Series games, and 15 World Series games.

Grand total through 2011: 5,288 Boston Red Sox games.

That's certainly a lot of games. But every game is different. That's why I'm excited every time I leave home to go to work. Who's pitching tonight for Boston? Who's pitching for the other team? Will there be an exciting play like an inside-the-park home run or a triple play? A no-hitter? Will some rookie make his debut? Will he swing at the first pitch and slam it for a home run? A walk-off home run?

Sometimes I hear people use the expression "meaningless game." Sometimes they are referring to the last two or three games of the regular season after a team has either clinched a playoff berth or been mathematically eliminated. But I've never used it. Every major league pitcher, in any game, is trying to get the batter out. Every batter is trying to get a hit. Every outfielder wants to make the catch or make the throw to keep it to a single. Every infielder is trying to field that bunt. I've never seen a player lay down on the field and not try his hardest just because the pennant race has been decided. And when a team misses the playoffs by just one game that 1–0 loss in April where somebody took a called third strike to end the game seems even more important.

Over the years I've been to a few minor league games. In 2007, I saw the St. Paul Saints, an independent minor league team, play the Grand Prairie AirHogs when the Red Sox had a night game in Minnesota. I've also seen the Ft. Myers Miracle play the Bradenton Marauders in the Florida State League on an off day in June 2011. The Miracle play at the stadium the Twins use for spring training games. And on four occasions I've watched the Chicago Cubs play day baseball while I was in Chicago to do a Red Sox–White Sox night game. People always ask me what it's like to sit and watch a game without broadcasting it.

It's a little different.

I was born in New Haven, Connecticut, on March 2, 1947, the oldest of eight children, and I grew up in nearby Hamden. My father, Frank, the son of Sicilian immigrants, grew up in New Haven and walked to Yale University, which he attended on a full scholarship. He then went to medical school in New York City and later worked as a general practitioner in his old New Haven neighborhood. After serving in World War II, he decided to specialize and became a dermatologist, practicing until the age of 85, three years before his death in November 2003. My mother, Pamela, attended the Yale School of Music and played the organ at many New Haven churches before her marriage to Dad.

Dad taught me to read baseball scores and box scores before my ABCs. He was a Yankee fan back then. New York was much closer to Hamden than Boston.

I loved to play sports, especially baseball, but realized by the age of 10 that being a professional athlete was not in the genes. I became a baseball card collector and flipper, a fungo hitter, and a Wiffle ball player. Today I play in the Over-60 Winter Softball League during spring training and for the Silver Foxes of Rhode Island in the Roy Hobbs National Tournament, both in Ft. Myers.

Although my friends and neighbors thought I was crazy, I would pretend to broadcast my backyard fungo games daily. Even then, I knew my life's ambition: to be a major league broadcaster.

I went to Colgate University, where I majored in history. I walked into the school's radio station, WRCU-AM, as a freshman, and got a job doing a rock 'n' roll show. I was "Joey C, the Big Cheese!" More importantly, I got the opportunity as a freshman to broadcast Colgate football and basketball games. I did every football game, home and away. In 1965, we beat Army, and in '66 the Colgate team was 8–1–1. But Colgate baseball games were not broadcast. The games were considered too long and too dull. Also, the baseball field had no electricity for our equipment.

While I was at Colgate, I worked at WRUN in Utica. My first job in commercial radio was doing the third quarter of each Colgate football game, thanks to the kindness of Lloyd Walsh, the station's play-by-play announcer, who wanted to give a student a break. During the summer of '65 I did news at WELI in New Haven. But I never listened to WELI because they played only "middle-of-the-road" music. Then I did a morning rock 'n' roll show on WADS in Connecticut, where I was known as "Joe Anthony."

I started listening to Red Sox games on the radio in '67 when their broadcasters were Ken Coleman, Ned Martin, and Mel Parnell. That was the year I went to my first game at Fenway Park, standing in the bleachers to watch the Washington Senators beat the "Impossible Dream" team on a late-inning double by Hank Allen.

I was aiming toward a broadcasting career, either in sports or as a disc jockey. But even though I loved rock 'n' roll—especially Motown—and the '60s were a great time for rock 'n' roll music, I decided that being a disc jockey would quickly get repetitive and boring. I concentrated on a career as a sportscaster and I sent out lots of audition tapes. But when I got no good responses, I got a job broadcasting high school and then semi-pro football games and doing a sports-talk show in Meriden, Connecticut. Then, when no other job offer came, I went to graduate school and earned a Master's degree in TV and radio at Syracuse. I also worked at WSYR-TV Channel 3 in Syracuse, where I started out doing commercial tags and station identification. Later, I became a super-utility announcer doing spot duty on sports and news, and as a TV movie host. I also was a color analyst on Syracuse University basketball games. This was my first TV job and I enjoyed it. I was there for almost a year, earning $2.25 per hour.

After Syracuse, I moved to Youngstown, Ohio, where I did sports on WFMJ TV for $140 per week. Five nights a week, I did the 6:00 PM and 11:00 PM sports wrap-ups. I also covered Youngstown State football games and high school basketball and football games. I was making $15 per game.

Youngstown is about halfway between Cleveland and Pittsburgh, and I covered several games of the 1971 Pirates-Orioles World Series. The Pirates' public relations director, Bill Guilfoile, welcomed me as if I were part of Pittsburgh media, inviting me to spring training and even to postseason games. I would go to Pittsburgh to do interviews and stories on the Pirates when the Youngstown station would let me have a cameraman. But my station was very cheap, so I continued to send out audition tapes to stations in bigger cities.

In November '70, I went to a ski club function where I met Jan Lowry. Neither one of us skied. Jan didn't like me at first because she thought I acted like a TV star, but Jan became my wife in '71.

One of my audition tapes went to KDKA in Pittsburgh, the Pirates' flagship station as well as the first station (in 1921) to broadcast a baseball game. They had an opening for a reporter to do sports updates and news. My tape got me an interview, and it also got me excited. Pittsburgh had four major league teams (Pirates, Steelers, Penguins, and Condors of the American Basketball Association). It would be quite a step up from Youngstown. But they never filled the position. Of course, if I had taken that job in Pittsburgh, I would not have met Jan.

Two years later, KDKA-TV offered me a job filling in for two weekends. I went to my station manager in Youngstown to ask his permission, which he refused to grant. He was afraid I'd be hired full-time and leave Youngstown. I should just have done the shows without asking. This only strengthened my determination to move out of Youngstown.

In August '72, I moved to Cleveland's Channel 3 WKYC-TV, as the weekend sports anchor. While I was overjoyed to get out of Youngstown, where there was no room for advancement, the friends I made there lasted forever, including, of course, Jan and her family.

We moved to Broadview Heights, Ohio, just outside of Cleveland in '72. At WKYC (which was owned by NBC) I made about $150 per week for just two days' work, about what I had been paid in Youngstown for five and a half days. Also, in Cleveland I joined the union (AFTRA — the American Federation of Television and Radio Artists), through which I have continued to have health and pension benefits. The station paid 10 percent of my salary to AFTRA's pension and welfare fund. My benefits stay with me no matter which AFTRA station I work for.

Just down the street from our apartment in Broadview Heights was the headquarters of radio station WJW. I filled in there on weekends. Roy Wetzel, who hired me at WKYC, said that he liked my work because I didn't shout. I still don't…unless the Red Sox win.

In addition to my sports duties at WKYC, I also worked on the NBC news desk, answering the phone and listening to fire and police radios. I was working from 11:00 PM to 7:00 AM.

Jan and I were still living in a $150 per month apartment when our first child, Joe Jr.—whom we always called Duke—was born in '73. After two years in Broadview Heights, Jan and I bought our first home in Mentor-on-the-Lake. Four years later, I turned down a job offer in major league baseball as the public address announcer for the Cleveland Indians. The pay was terrible—just $15 per game—but more important, it would interfere with my job at WKYC.

On March 25, 1975, I was covering the heavyweight title fight pitting Muhammad Ali against Chuck "The Bayonne Bleeder" Wepner at the Richfield Coliseum in Cleveland. As we were heading back to the station at 2:00 AM in the WKYC "newscar," I got a call that Jan was in labor. I was supposed to do a piece for *The Today Show* that morning about the fight but I canceled and went to the hospital in Willoughby, Ohio. Thomas Frank Castiglione was born at 12:30 PM. I was there.

Over the next few years, with changes in station management, I was demoted from a broadcaster to a producer, but I stayed with it because we needed the money. Football Hall of Famer Paul Warfield was hired for my on-air job. I also did news at a rock station, WGAR radio in Cleveland, for $5 an hour. In '76, I was on the air on the 4th of July, the nation's 200th birthday.

1978 brought more changes at the station. I was back on the air. I was also doing some events for the NBC network at $33 per report. That doesn't sound like very much money, but at the time it was pretty good. During one Cleveland Cavaliers–Indiana Pacers Thursday night mid-season game, I sent in six reports. That's $198 for one night's work. Not bad.

In '79, I did a series with Paul Warfield called *Superstars to Superstars*, for which I was paid about $10 per hour. Meanwhile, I'd applied for the job of television broadcaster with the Cleveland Indians. I submitted an audio tape, and I got an interview with Bill Flynn at Channel 8 in Cleveland, which was going to broadcast 40 Indians' games. Flynn, who answered his own phone, interviewed me on a Monday. He told me to call him the following Wednesday, February 14, at 2:00 PM to find out whether I got the job.

Paul and I flew to Florida and Texas to film episodes of *Superstars to Superstars* with Cypriot placekicker Garo Yepremian, pro-bowler Don Carter, and Roger Staubach, the quarterback for the Dallas Cowboys. At precisely 2:00 PM on Valentine's Day, I called Bill Flynn, who told me that I had the job. He was going to make the official announcement in an hour. My salary would be $300 per game. That would be $12,000 per year, since his station would do only 40 games. I called Jan, my parents, and the rest of my family.

More than 100 letters and notes awaited me when I returned to our home in Solon, Ohio. Everyone who knew me knew how long I had dreamed of and worked toward a job broadcasting major league baseball.

In '79, I went to my first spring training as a major league broadcaster. The Indians trained in Tucson, Arizona, a city I had never visited. Although for economic reasons my station was not going to broadcast any spring training games, my family and I spent two weeks in Tucson. Jan was pregnant with our daughter Kate.

My first game as a big-league broadcaster, with my partner, 26-year-old Fred McLeod, was on April 5, 1979, prophetically from Boston's Fenway Park. During my first year with the Indians, their manager was former catcher Jeff Torborg. We have remained friends for more than 30 years. The Indians' starter was Rick Wise, who faced Red Sox starter Dennis Eckersley, a future Hall of Famer (primarily as a relief pitcher) and a future broadcast booth partner. My father and my Uncle Charlie were in Boston for my first game.

After one game in Boston, we flew home to Cleveland. Our plane was hit by lightning, a scary experience that reduced one player to tears. Because many of the Indians games were not televised, I watched but did not broadcast a lot of games, familiarizing myself with the players' names, numbers, talents, and tendencies. Unfortunately, the Indians also had a tendency to lose. They lost 10 in a row in June.

I had been present when our sons Duke and Tom were born, and I wanted to be there for our third child's birth. But we were in Chicago and United Airlines was on strike. Once I got word that Jan had gone into labor and that a neighbor had taken her to the hospital, I made other travel arrangements and arrived at the hospital just after 11:00 AM. Mary Katherine (Kate) Castiglione arrived at 3:35 PM. I was there. Jan was not very happy that while she was in labor, the doctor in the delivery room wanted to talk baseball with me.

I rejoined the Indians in Seattle, where reliever Sid Monge saved a game for Cleveland. He handed me the ball, on which he had written: "This is in honor of your new daughter. To Katie. May she live to be 101." Katie, now married and the mother of two, still has the ball.

One of the Indians' games in '79 was rained out and fortuitously, as it turned out, not made up. The team finished the season 81–80, their second winning record since '68.

Toward the end of the season, Channel 8 was awarded a three-year extension on its contract to broadcast Indians games. But the two sides disagreed over money, and the extension was canceled. This was a severe blow to all the people who worked on the games: producers, cameramen, engineers, and me. Broadcasting Cleveland Indians games was virtually all I did at Channel 8. But after the season, the station found some other work for me as a sports reporter and a weekend anchor.

Meanwhile, the Indians did not have a TV outlet for the 1980 season. They eventually signed with Channel 43, which hired its own broadcasters. I continued to work at Channel 8 through '82, anchoring and reporting on sports. But in '80 I did manage to broadcast two Indians–White Sox games with Nev Chandler when Herb Score, the regular broadcaster, had to attend a funeral. The two games I broadcast were well received, but I was still trying to get back to a regular baseball broadcasting job.

In '81, I applied to be the TV play-by-play broadcaster for the Milwaukee Brewers. But I didn't get it. Although Milwaukee was not wired for cable TV, a number of Brewers games were broadcast on SelecTV, a pay TV system that required a box on top of the TV set. On St. Patrick's Day of that year the executive producer for SelecTV offered to pay me $300 per game plus $30 per day meal money. He also offered to fly me back and forth from Milwaukee to do Brewers games. I'd be working with Tom Collins.

I went to the library to find out about the Brewers—who were then in the American League—and about Milwaukee. I flew to Milwaukee the night before Opening Day, a game we didn't broadcast, and had dinner with Tom Collins. We really hit it off. Everybody I worked with in Milwaukee treated me very well, even though I was sort of an outsider. The Brewers' director of broadcasting,

Bill Haig, was very supportive of me and gave me a fine recommendation later which helped me get hired to do games for the Boston Red Sox. Bill and I are still quite close.

SelecTV put me up at its corporate condo in Waukesha, Wisconsin, but I usually stayed with Tom Collins.

1981 was the year of a players' strike, so Tom and I did only 10 games. The Brewers won the second-half title and a playoff spot. My call when Rollie Fingers struck out Lou Whitaker in the clinching game: "The Brewers win the second half! The Brewers win the second half!" Not quite Russ Hodges', "The Giants win the pennant! The Giants win the pennant!"

Tom's mike failed during his postgame interviews, so unless you could read lips, you had no idea what the players were saying. After the game, Tom and I celebrated at Ray Jackson's restaurant near County Stadium, a hangout for Brewers players and broadcasters.

All in all, '81 was a good year for me financially. In addition to the money I was making in Milwaukee, I was still working as a freelancer for Channel 8 in Cleveland, making about $36,000 annually. The station offered me a full-time job, but I rejected it. It was still my dream to be a full-time baseball broadcaster.

The Sports Exchange, a regional cable network, was started in Cleveland, and I was the first person hired. They were going to broadcast Indians games. The cable network was owned by Ted Stepien, who the year before had given me an exclusive: he was going to buy the Cleveland Cavaliers in the NBA, which I broke on TV-8 on the 11:00 PM sports. Ted was a pioneer, forming a regional sports channel, though he was never taken seriously by the Cleveland media.

During my first year with The Sports Exchange I earned $65,000 and the station bought me a car. We went on the air with the Indians in spring training. My broadcast partner was one of the greatest pitchers of all time, Hall of Famer Bob Feller, a Cleveland legend.

The Sports Exchange was paying the Indians $20,000 per game in rights fees, but the only cable system that picked up our games on a paying basis was in Ravenna, Ohio. So we went off the air in September. All but two of the employees were laid off. Luckily, I was not. I looked for another job. Since I had to report for work at the Richfield Coliseum to get paid, I spent most of my working day playing basketball in the Cavaliers' practice gym.

In '80–81, I broadcast games for the Cavaliers on pay-TV, but did not get to do any games the following year because of the financial troubles of The Sports Exchange. I was still looking for a new job.

One of the commentators at Channel 8 was Casey Coleman, with whom I helped produce special features for the station. I'm not claiming any credit for his success. He did that himself. I just opened the door for Casey. He told me that Red Sox broadcaster Jon Miller was leaving to go to the Baltimore Orioles. That meant that Ken Coleman was looking for a new partner. I'd met Ken a few times over the years and had followed his career.

I sent Ken an audition tape including an inning of radio play-by-play of an Indians game that I'd recorded from the stands, and a videotape of an aircheck of an Indians-Brewers TV game. I also sent a tape to Jack Campbell, who ran WPLM, which was to be the new flagship station for the Boston Red Sox. WPLM had been the flagship station for the Boston Bruins for a year, but '83 would be the station's first with the Red Sox. It was rather unusual then, but quite common now, for an FM station to be the flagship. I flew to Boston to meet Jack at the station in Plymouth, Massachusetts, which he dubbed "America's hometown."

The next day, a Saturday, Jack called to tell me that I got the job: radio broadcaster for the Boston Red Sox. Up to that point I'd done only 70 games on television and two on the radio. But Jack wanted the Red Sox to make the announcement. He warned me that if the news got out before then, it wouldn't happen. I was elated, and called Jan immediately with the good news. But first, I swore her to secrecy.

Once I was introduced as the new Red Sox broadcaster, I had to call Ted Stepien, the station owner in Cleveland, to let him know. He was upset because we were supposed to meet that morning to discuss our Indians telecasts and I was to bring the donuts. Ted initially refused to take my call. Joanie, his secretary, told me, "Ted doesn't want to talk to you. You missed the meeting. Ted had no donuts!" I said, "Joanie, tell Ted he will like what I am about to tell him. He won't have to pay me anymore." Reluctantly, Ted got on the phone and accepted my resignation, but later told people that I "ran out" on him.

I had a lot to do to prepare for my new job. First, I had to sell our home in Cleveland. Next, I had to look for a place to stay in Boston. I also had to get ready to go to spring training in Winter Haven, Florida. There were going to be a lot of changes ahead for my family. Duke was 10, Tommy 8, and Kate was just 4.

I had been to Winter Haven, Florida, where the Red Sox had their spring training camp, previously, when I was freelancing for NBC. But this was different. Now I was the new Red Sox broadcaster. I realized that six weeks ahead of Opening Day I didn't know anybody besides Ken Coleman and his wife, Ellen.

The next day I went to the Boston clubhouse and met manager Ralph Houk. He was called "The Major" because he had reached that rank in the army during World War II. I was invited to dinner with *Boston Globe* writer Larry Whiteside, who took me under his wing (Larry won the J.G. Taylor Spink Award from the Hall of Fame in 2008) and Mike Shalin of the *Boston Herald*. By the time our first spring training game arrived, I was still pretty nervous. The Red Sox played the Tigers at Joker Marchant Stadium in Lakeland, Florida. Since Jan and the kids were still in Cleveland, they couldn't hear the game. I remember the 10th inning: the Red Sox threw out the tying run at the plate. Ken Coleman told me that I had done a good job.

That spring we broadcast 20 games. But it wasn't until the roster had been cut down for Opening Day that most of the players got to know me. You really get to know people—even that many—when you travel together.

One of the people I met was Johnny Pesky, who was a Red Sox coach at that time. I also started long friendships with TV broadcaster Ned Martin, traveling secretary Jack Rogers, and public relations directors Dick Bresciani and George Sullivan.

As Opening Day approached, Jan and the kids were able to spend some time with me during spring training. But as the start of the season approached and we had not yet sold our home in Cleveland, they went back to Cleveland, and I went to Boston with the team.

My first regular season game for the Red Sox was in Boston on April 4, 1983. Future Hall of Famer Dennis Eckersley started for Boston against Toronto's Dave Steib. In '79, Eckersley was the pitcher in the first major league game I ever broadcast, when his Red Sox beat my Cleveland Indians. Now, in '83, Eckersley lost my first game as a Red Sox broadcaster.

The next day was an off-day, so I used it to move into the Susse Chalet Inn for $26 per night when I was in Boston. When the Red Sox were on the road I packed up my stuff and put it in the hotel's basement. Saving $26 per night was a big deal at the time.

My father came to Fenway for our second game, also against the Blue Jays. Then we flew to Texas where the Rangers beat the Red Sox in two out of three games.

The reaction to me in the media was pretty good. Ken Coleman was very supportive. Jack Craig, the *Boston Globe* sports media critic, wrote nice things about me at first, but later criticized me for the same things he had praised me for earlier.

In June, there was a reunion of the '67 Red Sox "Impossible Dream" team which won the AL pennant in Carl Yastrzemski's Triple Crown year. The reunion was a benefit for Tony Conigliaro, who had been in a coma after a heart attack three years before. On June 6, the '67 team gathered in the dining room at Fenway Park when Buddy Leroux entered the room. He and general manager Haywood Sullivan, a former catcher, ran the team with Jean Yawkey, who had a controlling interest. Leroux, the former team trainer, announced that he was taking over the team himself. Sullivan was out and former manager Dick O'Connell was back as general manager. This announcement—the "coup Leroux"—overshadowed that night's game against the Tigers.

Sullivan and Yawkey went to court to regain ownership of the team and they won. Now Leroux was out, but the legal battle took a long time. Meanwhile, the '83 Red Sox finished in sixth place (78–84), their first losing season since '66.

Every chance I got I flew to Cleveland to see my family. Our house there was not selling. This was all very hard on Jan. But Duke, then 10, got to spend some time with me in Boston. The visitors' clubhouse attendant put him to work shining shoes for players like George Brett and Robin Yount. How was Duke to know that both would wind up in the Hall of Fame?

My first year with the Red Sox was also the final year for future Hall of Famer Carl Yastrzemski. I'm very glad that we got to know each other that season. We spent many hours on the team plane and on buses together. Yaz was always cordial and enjoyed talking about young hitters in the system. He did not enjoy reminiscing about his own career. I will never forget sitting with him on a bus in Toronto, discussing different brands of beer.

In the eighth inning of Yastrzemski's final game on October 2, 1983, he went out to his usual spot in left field. Manager Ralph Houk then sent Chico Walker out to left and Carl got a tremendous ovation from the crowd as he ran off the field for the final time.

That weekend the *Boston Herald* ran a story citing unnamed sources that said I would not be back with the Red Sox in '84. We had finally moved into our new house near Boston and it was Jan's birthday. Even though station owner Jack Campbell denied the story, it was cause for concern.

Duke and Tommy started in their new school in October, and with the end of the season I had nothing to do. I helped with the unpacking. Jan and I, frequently accompanied by four-year-old Kate, drove around New England getting to know our new home region. In early '84, our flagship station, WPLM, asked me to call on the smaller Red Sox affiliates who had not yet paid their fees for the '83 season and collect it from them. I felt like a collection agency, but it was a much-needed paycheck. I was glad to have the extra off-season work because I had taken a pay cut to move to Boston, and money was tight.

1984 was a little easier for me. I was no longer the new guy. I knew the players and they knew me. The team finished in fourth place, but with a winning record of 86–76. At the end of the season, Ralph Houk retired as the Red Sox manager and was succeeded by John McNamara. Boston beat the Yankees on Opening Day '85, but that was the highlight for the season. The Red Sox finished in a dismal fifth place, 81–81.

Chapter 2

"The Tracks of My Tears"
1986

During spring training in 1986, the Red Sox traded Mike Easler to the Yankees for Don Baylor, a trade that worked out very well for Boston. Roger Clemens, recovering from arm surgery, didn't start until the fourth game of the season, which he won. On April 29, Clemens struck out an incredible 20 Seattle Mariners without a walk before 13,000 at Fenway. After a performance like that, I was very glad that Roger appeared on our postgame show.

Besides the final two games, '86 was quite a wonderful season. The Red Sox took over first place in the American League East in May and just kept winning. They clinched the AL East pennant on September 28 with an Oil Can Boyd 12–3 victory over the Toronto Blue Jays at home before a capacity crowd of 33,000.

On October 7, the battle with the California Angels for the AL pennant began. It was a very hard-fought series that went the full seven games.

Mike Witt of the Angels pitched a complete-game victory in Game 1 at Fenway Park, beating Roger Clemens 8–1. The Red Sox could manage only five hits to the Angels' 11.

Game 2 was a different story. Although Bruce Hurst surrendered 11 hits in a complete-game victory, Boston gave up only two runs as the Red Sox tied the series with a 9–2 victory. The game saw five errors and 17 men left on base. One key play was when Angels starting pitcher Kirk McCaskill, a former hockey player at the University of Vermont, lost a ground ball in the sun.

After the game, we got on the team bus to Logan Airport for the five-hour flight to Anaheim with the series tied at one.

In Game 3, Boston out-hit Anaheim 9–8, but the Angels outscored Boston 5–3 and went ahead two games to one. Oil Can Boyd gave up home runs to Dick Schofield and Gary Pettis.

The Red Sox were leading Game 4 3–0 in the ninth when the Angels tied it on a hit batsman. The winning run came in the bottom of the 11th inning on a single by Bobby Grich that scored Jerry Narron. Roger Clemens started the game for Boston, but was gone by the ninth inning and didn't figure in the decision. Now the Angels were ahead three games to one. Boston's back was up against the wall.

Game 5 in Anaheim was one of the most exciting games I have ever seen or broadcast. If it had been a midseason game it would have been a great game. But with the AL pennant on the line, the game—played before a crowd of 64,000 hysterical fans—was really one to remember.

Bruce Hurst started for Boston and went six innings. He opposed Mike Witt who had won Game 1. Rich Gedman homered in the second inning with Jim Rice aboard to give the Sox a 2–0 lead. Then Bob Boone homered in the third for Anaheim. 2–1 Boston. That's the way it stayed until the bottom of the sixth inning. Doug DeCinces doubled, and Bobby Grich hit a long fly ball that backed Dave Henderson up to the center-field wall. The ball glanced off his glove and went over the fence for a two-run home run. Angels 3, Red Sox 2. As good as Grich felt, that's how terrible Dave Henderson felt. He might have cost the Red Sox the pennant— just another way to lose to add to the list of Red Sox late-season disasters.

But the game was not over. The Angels scored two more in the seventh inning to take a 5–2 lead. In the top of the ninth inning, Don Baylor homered with Dave Stapleton aboard to narrow the Angels' lead to 5–4. Then Rich Gedman was hit by a Gary Lucas pitch—the only time he had hit a batter all season—and Dave Henderson stepped up to the plate with two outs. Henderson hit a Donnie Moore pitch into the left-field stands to give the Red Sox a 6–5 lead as the game went to the bottom of the ninth. As Henderson rounded the bases, he was jumping as high as he could, as if the weight of his earlier mishap had been removed.

(On July 18, 1989, Moore committed suicide at his home in Anaheim. His agent said that he never forgave himself for giving up that home run to Dave Henderson, but he had problems far greater than that.)

In the bottom of the ninth inning, California scored a run and tied the game at 6. They had the bases loaded with the winning run at third base and one out.

Reliever Steve Crawford got Doug DeCinces on a shallow fly ball to right and Bobby Grich on a soft liner to the mound to end the threat. The game went into extra innings. In the top of the 11th inning, the Red Sox went ahead 7–6 on a sacrifice fly by Dave Henderson. In the bottom of the inning, the Angels went down 1–2–3 and the Red Sox won. Steve Crawford got the victory, Calvin Schiraldi the save. This was one of the most thrilling games I ever saw. The Red Sox were still behind three games to two, but an elated team flew back to Boston. The players thought that their incredible extra-inning victory had given them that elusive momentum they needed to win the next two games at home.

Nearly 33,000 filled Fenway Park for Game 6, a 10–4 Boston win behind Oil Can Boyd. Now the series was tied at three wins each and there would be a decisive Game 7. Few events in sports are more exciting than a seventh game to decide a league championship. This was my first Game 7 as a Red Sox broadcaster.

Roger Clemens started Game 7 for the Red Sox and went seven-plus innings. In the bottom of the second, Boston scored three runs on an error, a hit, a walk, a fielder's choice, an intentional walk, and a hit. The Red Sox pulled away in the fourth, scoring four runs, three on a Jim Rice home run. Dwight Evans homered in the seventh to make the score 8–0. California got three hits and scored a run in the eighth, but that was it. The Red Sox won the game 8–1 and the AL pennant. They were going to the World Series for the first time since 1975, when they lost to the Reds in seven games.

I'd always dreamed about broadcasting a World Series, and now, thanks to this great comeback, I would be getting that opportunity.

The Mets were favored, but Game 1 went to the Red Sox, 1–0 at Shea Stadium on an error by Tim Teufel. Roger Clemens faced Dwight Gooden in Game 2, but Steve Crawford got credit for the victory as Boston won 9–3 to take a 2–0 lead. Now the Series shifted to Boston. The Red Sox lost games 3 and 4 at Fenway Park and the Series was even at two. Boston beat New York in Game 5 to take a 3–2 lead.

Game 6 was played at Shea Stadium on October 25, 1986, before a crowd of more than 55,000. The Red Sox and all of their fans were extremely excited. A victory would give Boston its first world championship since 1918.

Boston's ace, Roger Clemens (a league-leading 24–4 during the regular season), started for the Red Sox. He faced the Mets' Bobby Ojeda (18–5). The lead seesawed. First it was 2–0 Boston, then 2–2, then 3–2. Clemens left after the seventh inning with a blister, replaced by Calvin Schiraldi in the eighth—one of the most controversial decisions in Red Sox history.

The Mets tied the game in the eighth, neither team scored in the ninth, and Game 6 rolled into extra innings.

I was doing the play-by-play in the 10th inning when Dave Henderson's home run off the *Newsday* sign in left field to put the Red Sox ahead 4–3. I waited a second before calling it to make sure that it really left the park.

After Wade Boggs doubled to left, Marty Barrett brought him home with a single to center field. Now Boston led 5–3.

It was still my "turn" to do the play-by-play, with Ken Coleman doing color commentary. But Ken had been with the Red Sox for 17 years and I thought he deserved to be on the air when the Red Sox won the game, which they surely would. I offered to go down to the clubhouse for the postgame interviews and the champagne celebration. Ken left it up to me.

I went down to the Red Sox clubhouse, ready to do postgame interviews with the giddy world champions. The champagne was ready and the protective plastic sheeting was up in the Red Sox clubhouse. I waited with a guard who had a radio, but I couldn't see the field.

As I listened, Wally Backman and Keith Hernandez flied out. One out to go for a Red Sox victory. Then Gary Carter singled, pinch-hitter Kevin Mitchell singled, and Carter scored when Ray Knight singled. 5–4. *Okay,* I thought, *Boston is still ahead with two outs.*

John McNamara brought in Bob Stanley in relief of Schiraldi. Mookie Wilson danced out of the way of a wild pitch which allowed Mitchell to score the tying run and Knight to go to second. This was the most pivotal play of the World Series. Was it a wild pitch or a passed ball? To this day, Stanley says it doesn't make any difference: "We lost."

Then Wilson hit a ball up the first base line that went through Bill Buckner's legs at first base. Knight scored from second and the Mets won Game 6; one of the most memorable in World Series history. The champagne was wheeled out. There would be a Game 7. After the wild pitch that tied the game, I started to run up toward the booth at Shea Stadium to do the 11th inning. I was on a ramp where I couldn't see the field, but I heard the crowd and knew the game was over. It wasn't until I got back to the hotel hours later that I saw the video of the ball getting by Buckner on *SportsCenter.*

It rained the next day and the game was postponed. So Jan and I had dinner with Joe and Dot Morgan. Joe was then the Red Sox bullpen coach. We went to Rusty Staub's restaurant, owned by the former Met.

Boston got homers by Dwight Evans and Rich Gedman to lead 3–0, but in the sixth inning Keith Hernandez came up to bat, facing Bruce Hurst with the bases loaded. I was doing play-by-play. I thought, *If Hurst gets him out, we win. If Hernandez gets a hit,* they *win.* Hernandez hit a two-run single to get the Mets on the board and they tied the game a batter later. The Mets went on to win the game 8–5 and the Series 4–3.

The Red Sox had been one out away from victory. As we prepared to get on the bus to the airport, some idiot in the upper deck at Shea Stadium threw a glass bottle that hit Jack Rogers, the Red Sox's traveling secretary, right in the head. Nobody knows if it was intentional. But Jack had a deep cut. He was taken to the clubhouse where the medical staff gave him stitches. He remained stoic. What a way to end the season.

There wasn't much to do during the off-season but try to put '86 behind us and prepare for the '87 season as the defending AL champions. But defending a title is very hard. The Red Sox haven't won back to back pennants since 1915–16, though they did win the AL wild-card in 1998 and '99, 2003–05, and '08–09. In my view, the wild-card, which began in '95, is necessary to keep interest in the pennant races alive in more markets.

Rich Gedman and Roger Clemens were holdouts in '87 because of the collusion of team owners. Clemens did not sign until near the end of spring training. Despite his late start and getting off to an 0–2 start, Clemens finished the '87 season 20–9 and won a second consecutive Cy Young Award. Clemens' success was one of the few highlights of the '87 season.

One of the others was the emergence of rookie Ellis Burks, who hit 20 home runs and stole 20 bases. The Red Sox were out of the pennant race early, finishing in fifth place, 20 games behind the Detroit Tigers.

Chapter 3

"It's Magic"

1988

THE RED SOX STARTED SPRING TRAINING IN 1988 WITH HIGH EXPECTATIONS. The pitching staff was led by two-time Cy Young Award–winner Roger Clemens. But '88 was the year that the story of Wade Boggs' long affair with Margo Adams came out. That led to an altercation at the old Hollenden House Hotel in Cleveland. After a day game in Baltimore and a long wait for a commercial flight to Cleveland, what started as kidding with some of those involved led to angry shouting and then some pushing and shoving in the hotel elevator between two players, neither of whom were involved in the original controversy. A few players were quick to report the story to the newspapers and the incident perhaps helped seal the fate of manager John McNamara.

After the last game before the All-Star break, we got on the team bus at Chicago's Comiskey Park for the drive to the airport. McNamara made what turned out to be a fateful comment to reporters after the game. He said that considering all the problems and injuries that the Red Sox had suffered, finishing the first half of the season one game over .500 wasn't that bad. Johnny Mac was fired when the season resumed four days later, replaced by third base coach Joe Morgan.

Morgan set a major league record by winning his first 12 games as manager, then 19 out of 20, and 24 straight at home (a club record). He turned things around and brought the Red Sox home in first place. The Boston media started referring to Joe's managerial style as "Morgan Magic."

It was one of the most exciting times of my 30 years with the Red Sox, and not only because we had been such close friends with Joe and Dot Morgan. There were so many exciting finishes during the streak, which started with a Roger Clemens gem versus Kansas City and included a walk-off home run by Kevin Romine, the first home run of his career and a 10th inning walk-off home run by Todd Benzinger against Minnesota.

But the Sox were swept 4–0 by the Oakland A's in the ALCS. As Morgan later said, the A's were a better team.

The Red Sox's '89 season was forgettable. They finished in third place, six games behind the Toronto Blue Jays. That was also the year that the broadcast booths at Fenway Park were redone. The old booth was hard to get to, cramped, hot in the summer and cold in the spring and fall. Now they were larger, easier to get to, had a better view of the field, were air conditioned, and more comfortable

1989 was also my final year with Ken Coleman. He suffered a heart blockage and missed part of spring training. During his absence, Johnny Pesky filled in, as did Bill O'Connell, a longtime Boston sportscaster.

Ken returned to do a spring training game against the Dodgers, but had to rest after just three innings. That spring training game wound up going 15 innings. I worked the last 12 alone, although Hall of Famer Don Drysdale came by to call half an inning so I could take a restroom break. Eddie Romero won the game with a walk-off home run.

Jack Campbell's contract as the radio-rights holder for Red Sox games expired. None of us knew whether he would be renewed. If not, Ken Coleman and I might need new jobs. General manager Lou Gorman was on the phone when I walked into his office that day in July when a new contract for the broadcast rights was awarded. I knew that Lou knew. He gave me a thumbs down signal, meaning that Jack had lost the rights. Lou told me later that Steve Dodge, owner of Atlantic Ventures, was the new rights holder.

I found out that Steve was a native of Hamden, Connecticut, where I grew up. I didn't know him because he went to prep school and I went to public school. I also found out that he was a Red Sox fan and listened to many of our broadcasts. He liked my work. I was lucky. Frequently, when the rights holder changes, so do the broadcasters. But in late July, Joe Winn, the chief financial officer at Atlantic Ventures, called to tell me not to worry. He said we'd meet after the season.

Steve Dodge's favorite player was Gary Geiger, who was with the Red Sox from 1959 to 1965. Geiger was diagnosed with a collapsed lung—the first time I'd heard that expression. I thought that only a true fan would have Gary Geiger as his favorite player.

On the next to last day of the season, I ran into John Harrington in the players' parking lot. John said, cryptically, "I guess you know how things are going to turn out." I wasn't sure. But I hoped I'd be back in 1990. I'd been with the Red Sox for seven years. We'd bought a house in the suburbs. Duke was 16, Tommy 14, and Kate 10. If the new rights holder wanted to change broadcasters, it's not like I could go and work for the other team across town.

I went to a meeting at the radio station around the corner from Fenway Park two days after the season ended. I had been up half the night worrying about my future, which was in someone else's hands. At the meeting I was told that I would indeed be returning to broadcast Red Sox games on the radio. But Ken Coleman would not. He was going to retire for reasons of health and I would have a new partner.

As salaries for experienced major league broadcasters go, I was underpaid. So I asked for a significant raise. And I got it!

That afternoon, I went to visit Ken. He was very happy for me and my new contract. He said that he'd been worried about me, not himself. He would continue to work for the Jimmy Fund.

Later that day, I got a call from Steve Dodge congratulating me. He also told me that he could visualize the games while listening to my broadcasts. I could tell that he listened closely to each pitch I called.

Steve also said that he had been considering three broadcasters to succeed Ken.

One of the finalists was Bob Starr, the voice of the California Angels and the Los Angeles Rams. Dodge asked me who I thought was the best. I wanted to say that after seven years I thought *I* should be the lead broadcaster. That meant more air time, more innings, and more money. But I was happy with my new contract and new salary, no matter what they called me.

I asked Rangers broadcaster Mark Holtz for advice. He thought Bob Starr would be a good fit, and said we could work well together. So I told Dodge that my choice was Bob Starr. After Bob was hired, I called him to get acquainted. We really hit it off, and worked well together for three years. Bob and I started working together in spring training of '90. It seemed like we had been working together for years.

CHAPTER 4

"Good Times Bad Times"
1990–2002

1990

ONCE THE LOCKOUT ENDED AND THE SEASON STARTED, THE RED SOX, LED BY MANAGER JOE MORGAN, BATTLED TORONTO ALL SEASON FOR THE AL EAST TITLE.

On Wednesday, October 3, the final day of the season, the Red Sox were in first place but only by a game. To win the division, they needed a win or a Toronto loss. Boston hosted Jeff Torborg's Chicago White Sox, which wound up finishing second in the AL West. Boston led 3–1 in the ninth, but Chicago got the tying runs on base with two outs and Jeff Reardon on the mound. Future White Sox manager Ozzie Guillen came to bat.

Meanwhile, I obviously hoped that Boston was going to win, and I wanted to be ready. So I went down to field level to do postgame interviews. I was near Dot Morgan, sitting in a field-level box seat. Guillen drilled one down the right field line, but Tom Brunansky made a sliding catch in the corner to end the game and give the Red Sox the AL East crown. They finished two games ahead of the Blue Jays and 21 games ahead of the last-place New York Yankees.

The elated Red Sox ran off the field right by me and my microphone. I went into the clubhouse to do some interviews and to get soaked in champagne as the celebration started.

But, just as in '88, the Red Sox were swept in four by the Oakland A's in the ALCS. (The A's were themselves swept in four in the World Series by the

23

Cincinnati Reds, who had been in first place in the National League all season.) A disappointing end to a very exciting and upbeat season.

1991

1991 was a very disappointing season for the Red Sox. In July, Red Sox middle reliever Jeff Gray suffered a stroke right in the clubhouse. He recovered, but never pitched again in the big leagues. The Red Sox were swept by the Royals in a three-game series in early August, leaving the team seven games under .500. There were strong suspicions that manager Joe Morgan's job was in jeopardy. In fact, at one point the Red Sox sought out Whitey Herzog, who declined the chance to take over as manager.

Then the team started to turn things around. They swept a four-game series in Toronto in mid-August. By September 22 they were just a half game behind the division-leading Blue Jays. The Red Sox faced their traditional rivals the New York Yankees at Fenway Park. With two outs in the ninth inning and the Red Sox ahead 5–4, Boston pitcher Jeff Reardon (who saved 367 games in his 16-year career) hung a pitch out over the plate which the Yankees' Roberto Kelly hit over the left-field wall to tie the game at 5. In the 10th, 23-year-old Bernie Williams hit a double off Matt Young—a poor free-agent signing—that scored Mike Humphreys and Alvaro Espinoza, putting the Yankees ahead 7–5. That was the final score as Boston failed to score in the bottom of the 10th when Jack Clark, the tying run, struck out with Mo Vaughn on second. This was one of the most crushing moments I have ever experienced in baseball.

The Red Sox were now a game and a half behind the Blue Jays as the team flew to Baltimore. Roger Clemens won the first game of a doubleheader, but in the nightcap Dwight Evans, who had spent nearly two decades with the Red Sox and was now finishing his excellent career with the Orioles, walked with the bases loaded to win the game for Baltimore. Joe Morgan tried to take some of the blame for the loss, saying that he left reliever Greg Harris in too long.

That was pretty much the end of the season for Boston, even though there were still 10 games remaining. The Red Sox ended the season at 84–78, which put them in second place in the AL East, seven games behind the Blue Jays.

Two days after the end of the season I went to get my lawn mower repaired. When I returned home, I learned that Butch Hobson was the new Red Sox manager. Joe Morgan, my best friend in baseball, had been fired.

1992

1992 was an awful season for an awful team. Wade Boggs, a five-time batting champion with a .328 career average, and a future Hall of Famer, was in the final year of his contract. He was pressing and hit just .259, the lowest in his career. I kept track of how many times during the season he smacked one off the Green Monster in left field. He usually hit the wall 20–25 times each season. Not in '92, when he failed to hit the wall after May 22.

The rest of the team lacked power, speed, and the ability to score runs. What they did have plenty of was injuries. The team won 73 games, lost 89, and finished dead last in the seven-team AL East. It was Boston's worst finish in 60 years.

1992 was also my last year working in the booth with Bob Starr, with whom Jan and I had become very close. Our station tried to cut expenses that year by barring us from flying on the team plane, for which they had been paying the Red Sox a fee, roughly the equivalent of first-class airfare. They made us fly coach on commercial flights. "Burly Bob" sometimes had a tough time fitting into the narrow coach seats. By the end of the season, he'd had it. He was going back to the Angels, even though he had a year left on his WRKO contract.

After the last out of the final game of the season, Bob and I shook hands, and he was off to the airport and California. I did the postgame show and a brief wrap up of the miserable '92 season.

Also in '92, Jean Yawkey, who had owned the Red Sox with her husband Tom since 1933, passed away.

1993

After Bob Starr returned to Anaheim, Jerry Trupiano was selected as my broadcast partner. Jerry had broadcast games for the Houston Astros and the Montreal Expos. He was a pro. He was also my first broadcast partner who was about my age. He's only seven months younger than I am. Jerry was devoted to his family and he liked rock 'n' roll. We got along very well right from the start in spring training.

1993 was the Red Sox's first spring training in Ft. Myers, Florida, on the Gulf Coast, after 27 years in Winter Haven in central Florida. The spring games were to be played at a beautiful brand-new ballpark in nearby City of Palms, where all the palm trees were imported.

The '93 Red Sox were similar to the '92 Red Sox: they couldn't run, they couldn't hit, and they couldn't pitch much either. Even Roger Clemens, one of the greatest pitchers in history, had a losing season (11–14), the first of his career. When the season ended, Lou Gorman was relieved of his duties as general manager, but he stayed with the team as a senior advisor. Dan Duquette was named the new general manager for the '94 season. There were other changes too: Haywood Sullivan sold his interest in the team to John Harrington, who took over the team on behalf of the Yawkey Trust.

The Red Sox had another sub-.500 season: 80–82, 15 games behind the Blue Jays but not the worst in the AL East. That dubious honor went to the Milwaukee Brewers (69–93, 26 games back).

1994

Then came '94. What a disastrous year!

At the start of the season, the team was short on pitching, power, and speed (not an auspicious combination).

In early August, there was a family trip to Minnesota. I took Tom, 19, and Kate, 15. We visited the Jesse James Museum in Northfield and went to a casino. Tom and Kate had a great time. Then we flew to Baltimore. Midnight, August 11 was the strike deadline. The game was stopped and then canceled but not by the strike. It rained. After midnight, with no agreement, the strike was on. As far as getting home, players were on their own. No traveling secretary to make flight arrangements, no team bus, no team plane. That went for Kate, Tom, and me, too. Everybody hoped that the strike would be brief.

I rented a car and drove to Bethesda, Maryland, to see my sister, Pam Potolocchio, and her family. We spent another night there, hoping that the strike would end soon. It didn't. I began to worry. Under my contract, if the strike lasted more than 10 games I would no longer be paid. I was powerless to affect the outcome of the strike, but I was going to be hurt by it.

After two days in Bethesda, we flew home to Massachusetts. The strike dragged on. WRKO asked Jerry Trupiano and me to do a radio talk show, which we did daily for two weeks, 10:00 AM to 2:00 PM. The show was fun, but four hours is a long time. And there weren't that many calls. We were glad when some of our baseball friends called in. Jeffrey Lyons even called from New York to talk with us about the movies for an hour.

Toward the end of August, our radio talk show ended. I went to some minor league games, but without major league baseball, September seemed very strange.

And boring. I went to a Colgate football game and another at Holy Cross, where Tom was a sophomore.

In September, my father had heart bypass surgery in New Haven and I was glad to be able to spend time with him. But baseball commissioner Bud Selig's announcement on September 14 that there would be no World Series was shocking. 1994 would be the first year since 1904 without a Fall Classic.

On October 15, after a day of golf, I came home to find messages from the radio station and from Trup informing me that my salary would be reduced because of the number of games that had been canceled. By that time, the strike was two months old. I didn't understand. The chief financial officer of American Radio informed me that, except for the two weeks Trup and I did the radio talk show, I would not be paid. Virtually all the other TV and radio broadcasters were being paid in full. Our radio station decided to save about $25,000–$30,000 on me! Why? Trup and I were not on strike. We were ready, willing, and able to work. In fact, we wanted to work. Meanwhile, the radio station got its rights fees back from the Red Sox and put other programs and commercials on the air, so it was not really losing any money during the strike. The team's TV broadcasters continued to be paid in full. Just not us. At the time I was paying college tuition for Duke and Tom, nearly $60,000 per year. I really couldn't afford a $30,000 pay cut. It also seemed very unfair. Although American Radio had always treated me well, I resented this pay cut during the strike.

The '94 season came to a very unsatisfying end. There was no finality to it; no last games, no "see you in spring training," nothing. It just sort of petered out. And the issues of the strike had not been settled.

1995

When the '95 season started, the strike was still on. The owners declared that they would use "replacement" players: men who had some professional experience, perhaps in the independent leagues, or unsigned college players. Now they could tell their grandchildren that they played in the major leagues.

But I knew that the Major League Players Association (the players' union) was so strong and so united that the owners' threat to use replacement players would simply exacerbate the tension and feelings of ill will and distrust sweeping through the sport.

Some of the replacement players, like Randy Kutcher, were former big leaguers trying for a comeback. He'd played briefly for the Red Sox and Giants.

When spring training started, while we didn't know who the players would be, we did know who the new manager and coaches were: Kevin Kennedy was the new manager, assisted by Tim Johnson, Herm Starrette, John Cumberland, and Dave Oliver. They were all seasoned professionals.

I remember a spring game in which general manager Dan Duquette sat with us in the broadcast booth. When Don Barbara, a lead-footed first baseman tried to run to first base, Duquette said he looked like Fred Flintstone trying to start his car.

To call these replacement players "Boston Red Sox" players was a joke and everybody knew it. They just didn't have the talent. The runners were slow, the throwing arms were weak, the batters were off, and the pitchers were about 10 miles per hour slower than the regulars. It was embarrassing.

My friend Bill Gould, at the time the chairman of the National Labor Relations Board, issued an "unfair labor practice" decision against the owners. As a result, shortly before we were to break camp to open the season in Minnesota, Judge Sonia Sotomayor of the U.S. District Court in New York (later a justice of the United States Supreme Court) issued an injunction ending the strike. There would be a new spring training while the "real" players worked themselves into shape. So we went home for a few weeks and planned to return when games with the regular players started.

I was not used to being home in April. I got to see some of Duke's games at Stonehill College in Easton, Massachusetts. Because of the delayed schedule, Jan, by then teaching second grade, was on the school's April vacation. She flew down to Florida with me. We broadcast four or five spring training games, but the stands were quite empty. The New England fans who planned their spring training trips to Florida to see Red Sox spring training games had missed the real players by a few weeks.

We opened the regular season at home against the Twins, but it was not part of a series. Just that one game. The schedule was most unusual. But we had patched things up with the radio station, and Trup and I were paid for the games missed in '95.

The '95 season started well for the Red Sox. They won 20 of their first 31 games through May. I remember a game against the Yankees on May 14 at Fenway Park. In the bottom of the ninth inning, with the game tied and one out, Mike

Macfarlane, Boston's catcher, sent a Steve Howe pitch into the bleachers for a walk-off home run. In fact, Macfarlane was the first person I ever heard use the phrase "walk-off home run," and he may have originated it. In my opinion a walk-off home run is the most exciting play in baseball.

The next day, in an effort to draw fans back to the ballpark after the long and divisive strike, after fans had found other things to do, the Red Sox staged a rally by the left-field wall. I remember that two of the team's stars, Mo Vaughn and José Canseco, were there. The team was hot. They stayed in first place for the rest of the season and the reason was a pitcher, but it wasn't Roger Clemens. Clemens missed much of the early part of the season with a sore shoulder. The pitcher who was carrying the team was Tim Wakefield. Knuckleballer Phil Niekro, a Hall of Famer, had worked with Tim in Ft. Myers. He told the Red Sox that he liked what he saw. In '95, Wakefield started the season 14–1.

Mo Vaughn had a terrific season and was named the AL MVP. José Canseco had a pretty good year too, smacking 24 home runs. But Clemens did not have a Roger Clemens year. He finished just 10–5.

What was missing, the front office decided, was a top closer. So during an early July game in Minnesota, Rick Aguilera left the Twins' bullpen in the seventh inning when the trade was finalized and was in the Red Sox's bullpen the next day. It worked. Aguilera saved 20 games for the Red Sox down the stretch and Boston won the AL East title.

For the first time since 1954, the Indians made it to the postseason and Boston opened up the best-of-five ALDS in Cleveland on October 3. Kevin Kennedy selected the ace of Red Sox staff, Roger Clemens, as the Game 1 starter. He pitched well through the seventh, but Boston had a tough time scoring. When Clemens left in the bottom of the eighth, the score was tied at three. It stayed tied through the 11th inning. The Red Sox went ahead by one on a Tim Naehring solo home run, but Aguilera gave up a blast to Albert Belle that tied the score at 4.

Mike Maddux replaced Aguilera when he suffered an injury. That was the end of Aguilera's brief career in Boston. Zane Smith then replaced Maddux. Smith gave up a walk-off homer to Indians catcher Tony Peña to end the five-hour game and Cleveland led the series 1–0.

The next day, Cleveland shut out the Red Sox 4–0. We all flew back to Boston. The Red Sox's backs were up against the wall in Game 3. It was win or go home for Boston.

They lost that third game and were swept. Amazingly, the team batted only .184 for the three-game series. I was pretty surprised that the Red Sox had been swept in the ALDS because they had led the division virtually the entire season.

Even though the season was over, our broadcast was not. As usual, after the final game of the season I read a passage from Bart Giamatti's "The Green Fields of the Mind" on the air. The station ran some highlights from the season's broadcasts, and we left. We went to a restaurant called Artu's in the North End to commiserate.

1996

The '96 season did not start well for Boston. The Red Sox were swept in Texas in three games, then lost two more in Kansas City. José Canseco, Mo Vaughn, and John Valentin were the Red Sox power hitters, but the team seemed to be going nowhere, with only an outside chance to be the wild-card team. By September, even Roger Clemens had a losing record.

On September 18, on a chilly night in Detroit, before a "crowd" of fewer than 9,000 at Tiger Stadium, a ballpark that seated 52,000, Clemens tied his own record by striking out 20 batters with no walks in a 4–0 complete-game win. The broadcast booth at Tiger Stadium was nearer home plate than was the pitcher's mound, so I could hear the ball popping catcher Bill Haselman's mitt. I could also hear the hiss of a swing and a miss. There were many. What a performance!

That incredible game helped lead to Clemens' departure from the Red Sox after 13 years following the '96 season. It gave him a stronger hand and much more bargaining power in contract negotiations with the team, but management didn't want to meet his demands. So he left for a better offer from the Toronto Blue Jays.

By late September, the Sox still had a shot at the wild-card. But Boston won only six of their last 10 games and finished third in the AL East behind New York. Baltimore was the wild-card team.

The end of the '96 season brought a lot of changes to the Red Sox. Manager Kevin Kennedy was gone after just two years. He never managed again. Gone too were Roger Clemens, Mike Greenwell, and José Canseco.

The Red Sox wanted to sign Jim Leyland as their new manager. When that didn't work out they made what turned out to be a very good move, naming Jimy Williams as the new skipper.

1997

The Red Sox had the '97 AL Rookie of the Year in Anthony "Nomar" Garciaparra, one of the best players I've ever seen, certainly in a Red Sox uniform. As a leadoff hitter, he set a rookie record with 209 hits. But not much else worked.

1998

Something was missing. The Red Sox needed a new starting pitcher to be the ace of the staff. They got one: Pedro Martinez. Because he had pitched for the Montreal Expos, I had never seen him pitch before he came to Boston. Martinez, though, was one of the greatest pitchers in the game.

Boston's home opener that year was against the Seattle Mariners. The Red Sox were behind until the ninth inning when they loaded the bases. Mo Vaughn homered past the Pesky Pole in right field for a walk-off grand slam. It doesn't get more dramatic than that! The team stayed in contention for much of the season but finished 22 games behind the Yankees. Tom Gordon set the Red Sox record for saves in a single season with 46. Pedro Martinez also had a very good year in '98 (19–7). With a 92–70 record, the Red Sox were the AL wild-card team.

In the ALDS, the Red Sox faced the Cleveland Indians. Mo Vaughn was incredible in the first game: seven RBIs. Martinez won the game 11–3, but Boston lost the second game 9–5. In the third game of the best-of-five series, even though Boston scored twice in the bottom of the ninth inning, Cleveland won 4–3. Manager Jimy Williams opted to start Pete Schourek in Game 4, instead of Martinez on short rest. In my view, Williams made the right choice. But David Justice's eighth-inning double for Cleveland off Tom Gordon won the game and the series for the Indians. Another devastating loss and another disappointing end to the season.

In December, after eight years in Boston, Mo Vaughn signed with the Angels, which was the only team that made him an offer.

1999

Nomar Garciaparra won the batting title with a .357 average, but the highlight of the '99 season was not really part of the season. The All-Star Game was held at Fenway Park for the first time since 1961. After I emceed the mascots game (featuring Wally the Green Monster, the Phillie Phanatic, and Fredbird the Redbird), and the Baseball Chapel breakfast featuring Hall of Famer Bobby Doerr and Frank Wren (now the general manager of the Atlanta Braves), Jan and I sat behind home plate to watch the All-Star Game. This was the first time since 1975 I had sat and watched a game at Fenway without broadcasting it.

The All-Century team, which included Willie Mays, Stan Musial, Hank Aaron, Carl Yastrzemski, Carlton Fisk, and Tony Gwynn, was introduced by Kevin Costner and walked dramatically out onto the field from the gate in center field to join the current All-Stars. Then, something magical happened. Out came Ted Williams in a golf-cart driven by Al Forester, who had worked at Fenway for more than 50 years. Williams was mobbed by the All-Stars, past and present. Williams asked, "Where's my kid?" (Nomar) It was a five-blimp event. Williams threw out the first pitch.

Pedro Martinez struck out five of the six NL All-Stars he faced and was voted the game's MVP. After the game, he went up to the owner's suite to meet Ted Williams and talk pitching. I wish I had heard that conversation.

In his first game with the Angels, Mo Vaughn, at first base, chased a foul ball into the dugout, tripped on the stairs, and was hurt all season. The Red Sox missed his output and his leadership. Brian Daubach, who would become a very good friend of mine, came up and hit 21 home runs as a rookie. Mike Stanley also had a good year (19 home runs, .281, 120 hits in only 136 games). John Valentin and Tim Wakefield had good seasons, as did Lou Merloni, Nomar Garciaparra, Tom Gordon, and Jason Varitek, who was turning into a very good catcher.

Thanks in great part to Pedro Martinez, the Red Sox had the lowest ERA in the AL (4.00) for the first time since 1914. Martinez went 23–4, set a Boston record with 313 strikeouts, had an ERA of 2.07, and won the Cy Young Award.

Despite all that, the Yankees won the AL East title. Again. But the Red Sox were the wild-card team in the AL and were in the postseason for the second consecutive year for the first time since 1915–16, when they won the World Series.

The '99 ALDS was very exciting and it went down to the wire. In Game 1, Pedro Martinez pulled a muscle in his upper back and left with a 2–0 lead in the fifth inning. Boston lost that game and the next in Cleveland. We were all glad to be going back to Boston, but realized that the Red Sox were in a must-win situation. Boston won Game 3 9–3 and set a record with 24 hits in Game 4, which they won 23–7.

We had to fly back to Cleveland for the deciding Game 5—our third "win or go home" game in a row.

The final game of the '99 ALDS was one of the most dramatic I've ever seen. Pedro Martinez came out of the bullpen to pitch six no-hit innings of relief, even though his fastball was clocked at only about 91 miles per hour. In fact, when Pedro got up to loosen in the bullpen, a hush came over the crowd in Cleveland due to the fear of the great Martinez.

In the seventh inning, Cleveland walked Nomar intentionally for the second time in the game in order to pitch to Troy O'Leary. Troy had hit a grand slam on the first pitch in the third inning. This time it was a three-run homer as Boston went on to win the game 12–8 and win the series 3–2. A very exhilarating game to end an exciting series.

But there was the other ALDS going on. There, the Yankees swept the Texas Rangers in three games. That meant that, unlike the Red Sox players who had just completed an exhausting five-game series, the Yankees were well-rested. The Red Sox and the Yankees met in the best-of-seven game ALCS which started in New York.

The first two games were depressing one-run losses. Bernie Williams hit a walk-off homer off Rod Beck to end the first, and the second ended in the ninth when, with two runners on base, Damon Buford struck out on a pitch from Mariano Rivera. I thought that some of the umpire's calls could have gone the other way.

Game 3 in Boston pitted two of the best pitchers in the game against each other: Pedro Martinez for Boston versus Roger Clemens for the Yankees. Clemens lasted only two innings but he gave up five runs and took the loss as Martinez went seven scoreless innings and Boston won 13–1.

Game 4 was different. The Red Sox committed four errors and lost 9–2.

The '99 season ended as it almost always did, with a loss to the Yankees in the deciding game. New York went on to sweep the Atlanta Braves in the World Series.

2000

Although he got lost on his way to Fenway Park for the Red Sox's home opener on April 11, 2000, Carl Everett still managed two home runs.

On May 28, Pedro Martinez was matched again with Roger Clemens at Yankee Stadium. Trot Nixon, who always hit Clemens well, tripled in the seventh inning. In the ninth inning, Nixon hit a two-run homer into the bleachers in right-center field. This was the most exciting moment of the entire season. In the bottom of the inning, the Yankees had the bases loaded, but Pedro shut the door. Red Sox 2, Yankees 0.

On July 15, in an interleague game against the Mets, Carl Everett had a "discussion" with home plate umpire Ron Kulpa about whether he was standing in the batter's box. Carl had had a good first half of the season, and I got along well with him. He did many postgame interviews with me and was always accommodating.

Mets manager Bobby Valentine, however, had managed Everett with the Mets a few years before and knew how to push his buttons. The previous day he'd argued about where Everett was standing to bat. Home-plate umpire Kulpa went so far as to draw a line on the ground to keep Everett in the box, but Everett argued and bumped Kulpa with the bill of his batting helmet. Apparently, that was not enough. Everett threw down his helmet and butted Kulpa with his head. Coaches ran onto the field to separate them. Everett was ejected and then suspended for 10 games. Boston won that game 6–4, but it was pretty much all downhill after that.

The trouble continued. Everett and manager Jimy Williams had a confrontation in the clubhouse in August that had been overheard by teammates and reporters. Not good. The Red Sox had a tough time with two home day-night doubleheaders against Cleveland in late September. The team was pretty much out of the pennant race by then. Supposedly, Carl was injured. But since he didn't come to the ballpark in time for treatment, Williams thought he was okay and put him in the lineup. Everett said he couldn't play and his replacement, Darren Lewis, had a major argument with Everett.

The Yankees won the AL East pennant again. The Red Sox came in second (two and a half games back) for the third year in a row. But the Seattle Mariners were the '00 AL wild-card team. Boston's season was over.

2001

The Jimy Williams–Carl Everett antagonism continued. Management backed Everett—at Williams' expense. Everett was said to be making more than $7 million in '01. The Red Sox had a lot invested in him.

In May, there was a testy meeting in the clubhouse in Oakland after Tomo Ohka kicked a water cooler after being yanked from a game. Everett spoke out during the meeting and supported Ohka.

In one way—the most important way, really—the '01 season was all too similar to the '00 season: the Red Sox did not make it to the postseason. One reason might have been an injury to Nomar Garciaparra's right wrist on the second day of spring training. His wrist operation was done on Opening Day as Boston lost to Baltimore in 11 innings. Many thought he was back to stay when he returned to the team in late July and hit a home run against the White Sox, but wrist problems returned and he was used sparingly until he was just shut down. It was a real disappointment, leading many to wonder what might have been.

Pedro Martinez got off to a good start in '01, but ended up spending at lot of time on the disabled list. On the brighter side, newly acquired Manny Ramirez hit a home run in his first Red Sox at-bat at Fenway. Jimy Williams kept the team in contention, even without Nomar, who was still recovering from wrist surgery. Mike Lansing and Dante Bichette were both in the last year of their contracts, and they both wanted more playing time.

Things came to a head on August 16, when general manager Dan Duquette said that he'd been hoping for more "Morgan Magic." He fired Jimy Williams and announced that pitching coach Joe Kerrigan would be the new manager.

Unlike Williams, Kerrigan announced that under his leadership, the lineup would be the same every day, to provide some stability to the team. But that didn't happen. Kerrigan used 24 different lineups in his first 24 games. The Red Sox slipped to 17–26 under Kerrigan as the team was beset by nagging injuries. Pedro Martinez tried to come back, but couldn't sustain it. He went home. Bichette had a sore elbow. Carl Everett had issues with his knee. Manny Ramirez was hit in the hand by a pitch and couldn't play during the final week of the season.

The Red Sox were visiting New York on September 10. I took the subway, as I frequently do in New York, from midtown Manhattan to Yankee Stadium in the Bronx. But the game was rained out. We flew from LaGuardia Airport to Tampa. I didn't get to bed at the Renaissance Vinoy hotel until about 4:30 AM. I was still sleeping on the morning of September 11 when the phone rang. Jerry Trupiano told me to turn on the TV: the World Trade Center in New York had been attacked. I saw the second plane hit.

I was worried because my son Duke and my daughter-in-law Kiki lived in midtown Manhattan. Nobody really knew what was happening. Even though the phone lines into New York were clogged, I got through and spoke to Duke. He and Kiki were fine. Jan was in school with her second-grade class, Tommy was at medical school in Worcester, and Kate was working for an advertising firm in Boston.

Ballgames were postponed for a week. Flights were grounded. Although the Renaissance Vinoy is a beautiful luxury hotel, we felt we were stuck there for three days. Finally, on September 13, the Red Sox chartered a bus to Sanford Florida, where we boarded the Auto Train to Lorton, Virginia, accompanied by all our equipment. From there, we got on a chartered bus to Baltimore–Washington International Airport, and got on a charter flight—the first out of Baltimore in three days—to Providence, Rhode Island. There, we boarded our third bus of the day for the surreal trip through the streets of Boston to Fenway Park, which took about two hours.

The Red Sox spent the weekend working out at Fenway, but there was enough time for Kerrigan to have separate heated arguments with Pedro Martinez and Carl Everett. It didn't matter. The rest of the '01 season was pretty much downhill. Boston faced Baltimore in what turned out to be Cal Ripken Jr.'s final game. Everett left after the season ended. In 14 seasons, he played for eight franchises. Yes, Carl had an unpredictable personality, but he was always fine with me.

Usually, I'm sad to see the baseball season come to an end. But not in '01. The Red Sox finished the year 82–79, 13½ games behind the first-place Yankees.

We had to wait until December 20 for some good news: the Boston Red Sox had been sold by the Yawkey Trust to a group headed by John Henry, Tom Werner, and Larry Lucchino for $660 million, double the previous record price for a ballclub.

2002

Clearly, the highlight of the '02 Red Sox season was the 10–0 no-hitter that Derek Lowe pitched on April 27 against the Tampa Bay Devil Rays at Fenway Park.

One other highlight: Manny Ramirez hit .349 and won the AL batting title. Nomar Garciaparra returned from his wrist surgery. And even though he told me that he never felt right, he hit 24 home runs, drove in 120 runs, and scored 101.

Lowlights? There were plenty in '02. The Red Sox finished with 93 wins and 69 losses. Good enough for second in the AL East, but 10½ games behind the Yankees.

CHAPTER 5

"A Rush of Blood to the Head"

2003

IT WAS AN EXCITING AND FUN SEASON THAT ENDED IN HEARTBREAK. The Red Sox and the Yankees contended all year long, and including their memorable seven-game ALCS, they played each other a record 26 times. Each game seemed like an epic battle. The teams split six games in their first meetings in May, including a Boston win over Roger Clemens, who was trying to record his 300th win. Two days later, the Sox lost on a walk-off walk by Jorge Posada.

On June 27, Boston had a memorable victory over the Florida Marlins at home. Boston scored 10 runs in the bottom of the first inning before an out was recorded and 14 in the frame. Johnny Damon tied Gene Stephens' 50-year-old record by getting three hits in one inning. Boston 25, Florida 8. The next night, Boston lost a crusher on a ninth-inning home run by Mike Lowell (then with the Marlins), a big moment in Florida's run to the world championship.

The Red Sox set a team record with 238 home runs that season. On July 4, they hit a team-best seven against the Yankees, plus another three on July 5, for a team record of 10 against New York in two days. David Ortiz became the first visiting player to hit two home runs in consecutive games at Yankee Stadium.

The '03 Red Sox were a very resilient team. Nearly a quarter of their wins came in their final at-bat. On the other hand, the bullpen was unreliable, at least in the regular season. Newcomers Kevin Millar, David Ortiz, and Bill Mueller with their big bats (Mueller won the batting title) and clubhouse presence, helped spark the team all season, The team's catchphrase, introduced by Kevin Millar, was "Cowboy Up." If you're thrown from your horse, get right back on.

David Ortiz hit his first home run for Boston as a pinch hitter in the 14th inning to beat Anaheim on April 27. The Red Sox had only one losing month all season: May, when they went 13–14.

At the All-Star break, New York was ahead of Boston by two games.

On July 27, I brought Ken Coleman to the booth in what turned out to be his final visit. He had a great time renewing acquaintances with old friends like Hall of Famer Joe Morgan and his ESPN broadcast partner Jon Miller.

But Ken fell ill a month later and passed away on August 21. I was honored to do a reading from scripture at Ken's funeral.

Bill Mueller had a memorable night on July 29 in Texas. He hit grand slams in consecutive innings, becoming the first major leaguer to do so *from both sides of the plate.* He had a third homer in that game, too.

In my opinion, the most important meeting of the season was a late-August four-game series with Seattle. At the time, the Red Sox and Mariners were battling for the wild-card. The Red Sox swept the Mariners, outscoring them by 15 runs in the four games. As September started, Boston was still 5½ games behind the Yankees, but only 1½ games behind Seattle in the wild-card race.

September 23 proved critical. Todd Walker came to bat with the Red Sox behind Baltimore 5–2 at home. Jason Varitek and Nomar Garciaparra were on base. On a 3–2 pitch, Walker sent a Jorge Julio pitch into the visitor's bullpen at Fenway, tying the game at 5. On the air I said, "Can you believe it?" Then in the bottom of the 10th, David Ortiz hit a walk-off home run into the Monster seats. Red Sox win 6–5. They clinched the wild-card two nights later.

John Henry, the principal owner of the Red Sox, came into the broadcast booth during the eighth inning of the clinching game. He thanked us and everyone behind the scenes for our efforts. The celebrations, both by the team and by the fans, lasted for hours. The players genuinely liked each other and were proud of their achievements. They had finished the season 95–67.

The ALDS pitted Boston against Oakland. 2003 was the fourth time Boston had faced Oakland in the postseason. Boston swept Oakland in the ALCS in 1975, and in 1988 and 1990, the A's swept the Red Sox.

Game 1 of the Red Sox–A's series was a matchup of the two best right-handers in the AL: Pedro Martinez and Tim Hudson, but neither one figured in the decision. The game was exciting, and Boston had its chances. But Alan Embree gave up a game-tying hit in the ninth inning, and in bottom of the 12th the game ended on a Ramon Hernandez bunt. Oakland won 5–4 in an emotionally draining, four-and-a-half-hour game.

Game 2 was not much better. Oakland scored five runs in the second inning, and that was all they needed. They won 5–1. We flew back to Boston for Game 3, knowing it was do or die. Derek Lowe faced Theodore Roosevelt "Ted" Lilly of the A's, but as in Game 1, neither figured in the decision. Unlike Game 1, Boston won.

One of the key plays in the game had Eric Byrnes trying to score in the top of the sixth. But he missed the plate, and Jason Varitek tagged him out back by the screen. Later in the same inning, in one of the strangest plays I have ever seen, Varitek made another heads-up play when he tagged Miguel Tejada between third and home when Tejada stopped running after an obstruction call at third.

Just like Game 1, Game 3 went into extra innings. It ended on Trot Nixon's walk-off home run. Red Sox 3, A's 1. There would be a Game 4.

Tim Hudson started Game 4 for Oakland on just three days' rest against Boston's 38-year-old John Burkett. The A's led 4–2 in the sixth inning when Todd Walker homered to narrow Oakland's lead to 4–3. Two more runs scored on David Ortiz's clutch double in the eighth and Boston held on to win 5–4. Scott Williamson got the win. The series was now tied at two.

We flew back to Oakland for the deciding Game 5, played before a crowd of nearly 50,000. Pedro Martinez, on four days' rest, faced Barry Zito, who had had three.

Oakland scored first in the fourth inning on a walk and a double, but Boston came back with four runs in the sixth inning.

In the seventh inning, center fielder Johnny Damon collided with second baseman Damian Jackson trying to field a pop-fly. Damon lay unconscious on the field for 10 minutes as we all held our breath. We later learned that he had suffered a concussion. An ambulance was driven onto the field—a rare sight. As Damon was lifted into the ambulance, he raised his right hand to the crowd. The ovation was tremendous. Adrian Brown replaced Damon in the field.

Then Oakland scored two more to make it 4–3 in the ninth. Scott Williamson was on the mound for Boston, and he walked Scott Hatteberg and José Guillen. Manager Grady Little sent Derek Lowe to the mound. Ramon Hernandez bunted. Oakland manager Ken Macha called upon career minor leaguer Adam Melhuse to pinch-hit for Jermaine Dye. Lowe struck him out. Boston was ahead 4–3 in the bottom of the ninth inning. Two outs, runners on second and third.

By this time, Trup had gone down to the clubhouse for postgame interviews and celebrations, if the Red Sox won. But there were only two outs.

With me in the broadcast booth for that game were former Giants broadcaster Hank Greenwald and his son, Doug. I felt as close to being what ballplayers call "in the zone" as I have ever felt: I was bearing down, concentrating, intent on every pitch. The tension was palpable. Boston was in the field, trying to protect a one-run lead. After Chris Singleton walked to load the bases, Lowe ran the count to 1–2 on Terrence Long and then came through with the best sinker he ever threw. Strike three called. Ballgame over. Red Sox win. My call: "Bring on the Yankees!"

Everyone on the Red Sox was extremely excited and confident during the long flight from Oakland to New York. Boston had finally beaten Oakland in the postseason, and they had done so in very dramatic style, going down to the bottom of the ninth inning of the final game. Now, the only thing standing between the Red Sox and the World Series was their longtime rival, the New York Yankees.

In Game 1, Grady Little sent knuckleballer Tim Wakefield to the mound to face the Yankees' 17-game winner, Mike Mussina. David Ortiz came to bat in the fourth inning. He had never gotten a hit off Mussina, but with Manny Ramirez on base, Big Papi hit a monster blast into the third deck at old Yankee Stadium. 2–0 Boston.

In the fifth inning, second baseman Todd Walker hit a ball by the right-field foul pole. Right-field umpire Angel Hernandez originally called it a foul ball, but he was overruled by home plate umpire Tim McClelland. Home run. Boston 3, New York 0. Manny Ramirez also homered in that inning, making the score 4–0 Boston. That was the final score.

The Yankees started Andy Pettitte in Game 2. He was 11–7 in postseason play. Although the Red Sox had their chances, they were outplayed and lost 6–2 to tie the series at one.

Game 3 saw a pitching matchup for the ages: Pedro Martinez (14–4) for the Red Sox against Roger Clemens (17–9) for the Yankees. The game was tied 2–2 in the fourth, but Yankee rookie Hideki Matsui—whose nickname in Japan was "Godzilla"—doubled to give New York the lead.

The next Yankee batter was Karim Garcia. Pedro's first pitch hit him in the back. Heated words were exchanged. Jorge Posada, Clemens, and Yankee bench coach Don Zimmer joined in screaming at Martinez. Martinez screamed back and pointed to his head. The shouting escalated and players rushed the field. Home-plate umpire Alfonso Marquez ran out to nip the argument in the bud, but the benches had already cleared. There was some pushing and shoving. This had turned into a real grudge match with very high stakes between two evenly matched teams who genuinely didn't like each other.

Both teams were warned by the umpires.

Then 72-year-old Don Zimmer, the Yankee bench coach who had been in uniform as a player, coach, and manager since 1954, left the dugout and ran right at Pedro Martinez. Pedro did not swing at Zimmer, but he pushed him aside in a defensive gesture. Zimmer went down and was helped off the field.

Afterward, Pedro said that he regretted the incident. He was embarrassed. Zimmer broke down while apologizing for his behavior.

The game was delayed for a few minutes when a member of the grounds crew in the Yankee bullpen got into a fight with 6'8" Yankee reliever Jeff Nelson. Karim Garcia, the right fielder, jumped over the bullpen fence to protect Nelson. The groundskeeper went to the hospital with cleat marks on his back and arm.

As happened so often, Mariano Rivera came on in the eighth and was perfect for two innings. The final score was New York 4, Boston 3, and Rivera got the save.

Game 4 was rained out on Sunday. That turned out to be lucky for the Red Sox because now they could give Tim Wakefield another day of rest before starting on Monday against Mike Mussina. The game featured home runs by Todd Walker and Trot Nixon, but one of the biggest plays was the hustle of Jason Varitek, who beat out a potential inning-ending double play for the decisive RBI in the seventh inning. Final score: Boston 3, New York 2. The series was now even at two.

Derek Lowe was the Red Sox starter in Game 5 at Fenway Park. He pitched well—except for the second inning, when he gave up three runs. Those runs proved crucial as the Yankees came out on top again 4–2. Mariano Rivera got the save again, and the Yankees took a 3–2 lead. The Red Sox felt determined as we flew back to New York for Game 6, and a possible Game 7.

Game 6 seemed like a mismatch. Boston sent John Burkett to the mound to face Andy Pettitte. Burkett only lasted into the fourth inning. Pettitte was knocked out after five, but he left with a 6–4 lead. José Contreras came on in relief for New York, but allowed three runs. There was some poetic justice in this because the Yankees and the Red Sox had battled during the off-season to see who would sign the Cuban right-hander. The Yankees won that battle and signed him for a reported $5.5 million.

Trot Nixon added a two-run home run in the ninth off Gabe White to give Boston a 9–6 win. The series would go to a dramatic Game 7.

I taped my pregame show with Theo Epstein in the parking lot because we had done so before Game 6, which the Red Sox won. Players aren't the only ones who are superstitious.

I knew that Game 7 of the '03 ALCS was going to be a memorable, historic game. Of course, the Red Sox and the Yankees could never play each other in the World Series, so this was as close as they could get. They'd been East Coast rivals for a century, and had battled for the league championship. One team would go to the World Series. The other team would just go home.

Game 7 featured a dream pitching matchup of two future Hall of Famers: Pedro Martinez against Roger Clemens—probably the two best pitchers in the league, and two of the best pitchers of all time. A crowd of 56,000 were jammed into Yankee Stadium to see one of the most anticipated games of the year, or of any year.

But by the second inning, it did not look like Clemens' night. Trot Nixon smashed a two-run home run. In the fourth, he gave way to Mike Mussina making the first relief appearance of his 13-year career (at that point). Mussina inherited runners at first and third with nobody out and prevented further scoring. This proved to be pivotal.

In the top of the seventh inning, after Hideki Matsui grounded out and Jorge Posada lined out, Martinez gave up a home run to Jason Giambi (his second of the night) and singles to Enrique Wilson and Karim Garcia. Then Pedro struck out Alfonso Soriano to end the inning. Pedro left the mound, pointed to the sky, and hugged his teammates. The Red Sox led 4–2. Many thought that he was through for the night.

In the top of the eighth inning, David Ortiz homered off David Wells to make the score 5–2 Boston. In the bottom of the inning, I was just as surprised as anyone when Pedro went out to the pitcher's mound. Grady Little had decided to keep him in the game. He was the ace of the staff, it was the eighth inning, and the Red Sox led 5–2.

After Nick Johnson was retired on one pitch, Derek Jeter doubled on an 0–2 pitch. Bernie Williams brought Jeter home when he singled. 5–3.

Grady Little jogged out to the mound to talk with Martinez. Everyone looked into the Red Sox bullpen to see who was warming up: left-hander Alan Embree and right-hander Mike Timlin. They were both ready.

Usually, when Little jogged out to the mound, he did not pull the pitcher. And he didn't do so this time. Martinez stayed in the game—a decision that probably cost Little his job.

The next batter was left-handed-hitting Hideki Matsui, who had doubled off Martinez in Game 3 and earlier in Game 7. Strike one. Strike two. Then Matsui doubled down the right-field line, a shot that was fair by a few inches. Now Williams was on third, and Matsui, the tying run, on second. The next batter was switch-hitting Jorge Posada, who had exchanged nasty words with Martinez in Game 3.

As with Matsui, Martinez got ahead 1–2. Then Posada hit a blooper over second. I thought that second baseman Todd Walker might be able to catch it, but it landed in shallow center field for a double. Two runs scored and the game was tied.

I called the play, and anyone listening to my voice could tell that I was stunned. The Red Sox had been so close to going to the World Series—ahead by two runs in the eighth inning! Now the game was tied.

I felt awful. '03 had been such a wonderful year, for me and for the Red Sox. Was it all going to end in disaster at Yankee Stadium?

Grady Little walked back to the mound to take out Pedro Martinez, though perhaps a few batters too late. He brought in Embree and then Timlin. The Red Sox's nemesis Mariano Rivera was on the mound for New York. He was brilliant, pitching three scoreless innings. The game remained tied through the top of the 11th inning.

Then Aaron Boone hit a home run on the first pitch off Tim Wakefield. I tried to wish it foul but to no avail. My call: "Home run and the Yankees win the pennant." Those were the toughest words I ever had to say on the radio. I was crushed. Instead of going to the World Series for the first time in 17 years, we were all going home.

Pedro was gracious in defeat. He tried to take the blame for the loss, but the fans weren't having it. Their venom was directed at manager Grady Little. The vitriol was even worse than what had been directed at Bill Buckner, Calvin Schiraldi, and John McNamara after Game 6 of the 1986 World Series.

Although it was said that his decisions in Game 7 had nothing to do with it, Red Sox management decided not to bring Grady Little back in '04.

I was sad for a lot of reasons. I had grown to like and respect Grady. Now he was gone. I thought the Red Sox had the better team in '03—except for Mariano Rivera. But they lost. I thought the Red Sox deserved a better ending for their great season. I was also sad that the Red Sox have always been beaten by the Yankees.

During the flight back to Boston I tried to think which was worse, which hurt more: losing in '86 when the Red Sox were one strike away from winning the World Series, or losing a game and the AL pennant when Boston was so close to beating their archrivals? I still don't know.

A few days later, I got a call from my friend Pat Hughes, the Cubs' broadcaster. He said "Can you believe, we both had three-run leads in the eighth inning with one out and nobody on, and both of us lost the pennant?"

On November 28, 2003, my father, Dr. Frank Castiglione, passed away after a long series of illnesses. He died peacefully and at home. Dad had a long, meaningful life. He practiced medicine until he was 85. My mother did a great job of taking care of him. She made it possible for Dad to spend his final days surrounded by his family in the home he loved. He left eight children and 22 grandchildren.

CHAPTER 6

"Don't Stop Believin'"
2004

DURING THE OFF-SEASON, THE RED SOX ACQUIRED CURT SCHILLING FROM ARIZONA AND CLOSER KEITH FOULKE. But the biggest addition was manager Terry Francona. What a signing that turned out to be. In his very first year at the helm he guided Boston to its first world championship since 1918.

I had an inkling that the Foulke move was in the works because when I was in St. Louis in December for Brian Daubach's wedding I went to the hotel gym to ride the exercise bike, and there, riding the bike next to me was Foulke's agent, who was on his cell phone trying to negotiate a deal either with Oakland or Boston.

Keith Foulke's signing by the Red Sox turned out to be a key move not only for the regular season, but for the postseason.

No other team expressed any interest in Manny Ramirez after the Red Sox put him on waivers (because nobody wanted to pay his giant, $20-million-per-year salary). Ramirez's salary was said to be the second highest in baseball, behind Alex Rodriguez. A-Rod, in fact, was involved in trade negotiations that would have put him a Red Sox uniform for less money than he was making in Texas. But the Players' Association vetoed a deal that would have allowed A-Rod to sign for a lower salary.

Then Aaron Boone, whose walk-off home run in Game 7 of the ALCS had closed the door on Boston's 2003 season, injured his leg playing a pickup game of basketball. The Yankees needed a first-string third baseman, and they surprised everyone by trading Alfonso Soriano and cash to the Texas Rangers for Alex Rodriguez, who moved over from shortstop to play third. It seemed like another

Yankee victory when A-Rod went to New York instead of Boston, but it worked out very well for the Sox.

The Red Sox's '03 pitching rotation, including Pedro Martinez and Derek Lowe, was returning. Lowe, Martinez, and Nomar Garciaparra were in the last years of their contracts. The addition of Curt Schilling seemed to cement the air of enthusiasm and portent in New England. *This is the year!*

But it didn't look that way when the season started. Trot Nixon, coming off a season in which he had hit .306 with 28 home runs, had driven to Ft. Myers from his home in North Carolina and wound up with an injured back. Nobody knew it at the time, but between his back injury and a later quadriceps injury, Nixon would play only 48 games for Boston all season.

Nomar was also injured. Luckily, the Red Sox had signed former Pittsburgh Pirate and Cincinnati Red Calvin "Pokey" Reese. He turned into a terrific shortstop.

Things that had looked so good for the Red Sox at the start of spring training looked rather different once the season started, especially with the injuries to Nixon and Garciaparra.

Boston's pitching, which had looked so good on paper at the start of the season, didn't look so good. During the Red Sox home opener, their fifth game of the young season, the pitching staff had been so depleted by a six-pitcher, 13-inning game in Baltimore that they called on first baseman Dave McCarty to pitch. Boston needed more pitching. So, to make room on the roster, Brian Daubach—with whom Jan and I had become close—was sent down. He stayed with Pawtucket for most of the season, rejoining the team later that year.

On Easter Sunday, DH David Ortiz hit a walk-off home run against the Blue Jays; a portent of things to come. The team was 15–6 in April. In May and June, the Red Sox and Yankees seemed to alternate between first and second place in the AL East. Schilling, Martinez, and Lowe—the core of the starting pitching staff—didn't miss a single start all season because of injury. When Byung-Hyun Kim struggled as a starter, Bronson Arroyo took his place.

But the Red Sox were still eight and a half games back. Then in early July, Boston played the Yankees in a three-game series. On July 1, in a game in New York, Yankee shortstop Derek Jeter made an unforgettable play, diving into the stands to catch a foul pop-up. Nomar Garciaparra told manager Terry Francona that his Achilles tendon hurt, but that he'd be available if needed, despite his pain. The TV cameras showed Nomar sitting on the bench while Jeter dived into the stands to make a spectacular play. It was not really fair to show the two shortstops that way when one was clearly injured, but the image of Nomar just sitting on the bench made a strong negative impression.

Things were not looking good for the Red Sox going into the All-Star break in July.

The Red Sox were struggling as the Yankees came to Boston for a three-game series in late July. After losing the first game, Boston came back to take the second game on July 24. The game was delayed by a heavy rain, and the front office thought seriously about canceling the game. But after Jason Varitek and some other players met with team executives and insisted that they wanted to play, the game was not canceled. When the game finally started, nearly an hour late, New York took a 3–0 lead. In the third inning, Boston pitcher Bronson Arroyo hit Alex Rodriguez. A-Rod shouted at Arroyo and started toward the mound. Then Varitek intervened, shoving his catcher's mitt in A-Rod's face. Photos of that incident were printed in every newspaper in the country the next day. That was the Red Sox's season in microcosm at that point.

Boston had been behind the entire game. In the ninth inning, with New York up 10–8, Mariano Rivera was on the mound with one out and Nomar Garciaparra on third. The tying run came to the plate in the person of Kevin Millar. He singled, scoring Nomar. Up stepped Bill Mueller. He hit the most dramatic, most important home run of the Red Sox's season: a walk-off-two run homer. Red Sox win 11–10.

As the ball left the park, I said, "Can you believe it?" I may have used that phrase before, but that's the first time I remember using it. Since then I have used it only when something truly amazing happened, such as winning the World Series in '04 and '07.

4:00 PM on July 31 was the deadline for trades without waivers.

I was in the clubhouse with the team at the Metrodome in Minneapolis that afternoon. I saw Nomar Garciaparra, and a number of reporters were milling around him. A moment later, somebody from the Red Sox's front office asked everybody except the players to leave the room. Something was up. We learned shortly thereafter that the Red Sox had made a three-way trade. The big news was that Boston had traded Nomar to the Chicago Cubs. Boston got Orlando Cabrera from the Expos, Doug Mientkiewicz from the Twins, and Dave Roberts from the Dodgers.

The dozen or so reporters and broadcasters who had been asked to leave the clubhouse were standing in the hallway discussing the trade when Nomar walked out in his street clothes. I had broadcast every game Nomar played for eight and a half years, and we had become good friends. He gave me a hug. It was very emotional for both of us. Then he went back to the hotel to pack and catch a flight to join the Cubs.

By August 15, the Red Sox had dropped to 10½ games behind the Yankees. But on August 16 they went on a tear. They swept three at home against Toronto, swept another three in Chicago, then won two out of three against the Blue Jays in Toronto. Starting on August 24, Boston won 10 games in a row. By September 11 they had won 22 of 25 games. Considering where they had been and what they had been through, it was an amazing accomplishment. In fact, they came within two and a half games of the first place Yankees, but that was as close as they got.

Cabrera hit a walk-off home run for Boston on September 22 at home against the Orioles. He always seemed to have a smile and played with great enthusiasm. But the major factor that propelled the Red Sox, particularly in the later part of the '04 season, was pitching. Curt Shilling won 21 games. Pedro Martinez pitched well until the last month of the season. He'd won 16 games, but lost his last four starts and finished 16–9. And Derek Lowe was struggling. In fact, he was not in the rotation for the first round in the postseason. Mike Timlin and Alan Embree were strong as set-up guys.

Despite the late-season winning streak and the strong pitching, Boston finished second in the AL East, three games behind the Yankees. But on September 27, Boston beat the Rays in Tampa and won the AL wild-card. They were going to the postseason.

The ALDS started on Thursday, October 5 in Anaheim. Curt Schilling started Game 1 for Boston and faced Jarrod Washburn in a day game at Angel Stadium that took more than three hours. Kevin Millar hit a two-run homer and Manny Ramirez hit a three-run shot as Boston scored seven runs in the fourth.

Schilling was still pitching in the seventh with the score Boston 8, Anaheim 3, when he chased a Garret Anderson two-out dribbler down the first base line. Two things happened: Schilling made a throwing error, and he aggravated a previous injury to his right ankle. He'd had an ankle tendon problem, and had taken shots to numb the pain and stabilize the ankle. (Schilling was a real gamer.) Eventually, he stopped taking the shots because he said he had no feeling on his follow-through.

Curt pitched 6⅔ innings and got the 9–3 win.

Game 2 was a very similar story. On the night of October 6, Pedro Martinez faced Bartolo Colon. Pedro pitched seven innings and won. Highlights of the game included Jason Varitek's sixth-inning home run to tie the game at 3, and Manny's sacrifice fly in the seventh. Boston scored four more runs in the ninth to seal the 8–3 victory.

We were back at Fenway for Game 3. Games 1 and 2 were long enough, but Game 3 turned into a four-hour–11-minute affair before a packed house of 35,500.

Boston led early, but Angels slugger Vladimir Guerrero hit a grand slam in the seventh inning and soon the game was tied at 6. It stayed that way until the 10th, when Anaheim put men on first and third. Derek Lowe came into the game to shut the door and strand the runners. In the bottom of the 10th inning, the Angels brought in Jarrod Washburn, who had lost Game 1, to face David Ortiz with a runner on first. Ortiz then planted a pitch in the Green Monster seats to win the marathon game 8–6. The Red Sox swept the series.

In the other ALDS, the New York Yankees beat the Minnesota Twins 3 games to 1. The ALCS would pit Boston against New York yet again.

Game 1 was a night game played at Yankee Stadium on October 12 before a sellout crowd. Schilling—facing Mike Mussina—gave up two runs in the first and four more in the third. He was not himself. The tendon in his ankle was causing him great pain. Mussina, on the other hand, was perfect through six and a third. Boston rallied in the seventh: A double by Mark Bellhorn ignited a five-run inning. New York led 8–5. In the top of the eighth inning, Ortiz tripled off Hideki Matsui's glove in left center, scoring two runs, but he was stranded at third with the Yankees still ahead 8–7. New York scored two more in the eighth. 10–7. In the ninth, Yankee closer Mariano Rivera gave up singles to Varitek and Cabrera, but Bill Mueller grounded into a game-ending double play. The Yankees won 10–7.

What a disappointment. Boston scored seven runs, enough to win on most nights, but not on this night.

Game 2 was also a night game at Yankee Stadium. Pedro Martinez started for Boston to chants of "Who's your daddy?" (During a series in September, Martinez observed that he could not seem to beat the Yankees, so he referred to them as his "daddy.")

Daddy or not, Pedro pitched well. He gave up a run on a walk, a stolen base, a hit batsman, and a single, but New York didn't score again until the sixth. Unfortunately, Boston didn't score at all!

In the sixth, John Olerud hit a two-run home run. (Which would be his last hit for the Yankees. In the next game, he stepped on a bat and injured his foot.) The Yankees were leading 3–0. Their pitcher, Jon Lieber, was throwing a cutter down and in to the Boston lefties, resulting in ground ball after ground ball. He allowed just three hits through seven, then gave way to Tom Gordon. Boston scored a run. Then Mariano Rivera relieved Gordon and struck out Johnny Damon to end the inning. 3–1 Yankees. Manny Ramirez doubled in the ninth, but once again, Rivera shut the door, striking out Kevin Millar to end the game. The Yankees led two games to none.

Game 3 was scheduled for Friday, October 15. We did the pregame show, but the game was rained out. Nobody knew it at the time, but that turned out to be a good thing for the Red Sox.

Game 3 was played in Boston on October 16. The Red Sox starter, Bronson Arroyo, didn't make it out of the third inning. He was replaced by Ramiro Mendoza after allowing a game-tying homer to Alex Rodriguez followed by a walk and a double. By the end of the third, the score was even at 6. New York scored five more runs in the fourth inning, two in the fifth, four in the seventh, and two in the ninth. To add insult to injury, the game took more than four hours and didn't end until after midnight with a 19–8 Yankee win.

Gary Sheffield and Hideki Matsui were having a very strong series: together they had 24 hits and 15 RBIs. Tim Wakefield went to Terry Francona and offered to pitch in the Game 3 blowout to save the bullpen. He'd give up his Game 4 start. Wakefield came into the game in the fourth inning and pitched three and a third innings. This was a turning point of the series. It gave the bullpen some needed rest. Once the game ended, I remember saying on the air, "This one, mercifully, is over."

Boston had lost the first three games to the Yankees—the last one in a depressing blow out—but I remember thinking that the Red Sox were better than this, better than getting swept. There had to be more to the Red Sox than this. I didn't know just how much more.

Game 4 could be the final game of the season for Boston, so I brought the Bart Giamatti quote from "The Green Fields of the Mind" just as I always do. For years I've been reading it after the final game of the season, just as my predecessor Ken Coleman did. It's a beautiful piece of writing that goes:

"It breaks your heart. It is designed to break your heart. The game begins in the spring, when everything else begins again, and it blossoms in the summer, filling the afternoons and evenings, and then as soon as the chill rains come, it stops and leaves you to face the fall alone. You count on it, rely on it to buffer the passage of time, to keep the memory of sunshine and high skies alive, and then just when the days are all twilight, when you need it most, it stops."

The paper stayed in my pocket. I wouldn't read that quote on the air until the final game of the World Series, eight games later.

Game 4 was one of the most dramatic games in baseball history.

By the sixth inning, the Yankees led 4–3 and it looked like I might have to pull out the Giamatti quote. The score stayed 4–3 until the bottom of the ninth inning.

With the great Mariano Rivera on the mound hoping to wrap up the game and the series, Kevin Millar led things off with a five-pitch walk. Manager Terry Francona had recently-acquired Dave Roberts pinch-run for Millar in what turned out to be one of the key managerial decisions of the entire season.

Boston was desperate for a run. Roberts had been caught stealing only three times all season. He had been successful 38 times. Everybody knew what was coming next: the players, the coaches, the fans at Fenway or watching on TV or listening to the radio. Everyone knew that Roberts was going to run; including Mariano Rivera. He threw over to first three times before delivering a pitch to Bill Mueller. His first pitch was almost a pitchout: up and away. Roberts was off with the pitch and slid head-first into second. There was a play at the bag, but second-base umpire Joe West called him safe on a very close play. You could almost hear Red Sox Nation breathe a collective sigh of relief. Boston was still alive in the ninth inning, and the tying run was in scoring position.

Mueller hit one to the right of the pitcher's mound which Rivera just missed. Mueller had a single and Roberts scored to tie the game at 4.

Keith Foulke was key. He pitched the eighth through the 10th innings without allowing a run. The score remained tied at 4 until the bottom of the 12th inning. By this time, the Yankee pitcher was Paul Quantrill, a former Red Sox player and a good friend of mine. Manny Ramirez singled and David Ortiz brought him home with a walk-off blast into the right-field bullpen to end the five-hour game.

The Red Sox had staved off elimination. There would be a Game 5. The Giamatti quote stayed in my pocket.

Game 5 also wound up going more than five hours. In fact, at five hours and 49 minutes, it was even longer than Game 4.

The starting pitchers were Pedro Martinez for Boston against Mike Mussina for New York. Martinez pitched into the sixth inning with a 2–1 lead. Then the Yankees scored three runs—but they might have scored more. Hideki Matsui, who had hit very well in the postseason, came to bat with the bases loaded. He hit one to right field but Trot Nixon came in to make a diving catch for the third out. Three Yankees were stranded on base. The score was New York 4, Boston 2.

Mike Timlin relieved Pedro Martinez in the top of the seventh. Except for Mariano Rivera, the Yankee bullpen was suspect. In the bottom of the inning, Tanyon Sturtze (from Worcester, Massachusetts) came on in relief of Mussina. He faced Johnny Damon, who popped out to Jeter at shortstop, and Orlando Cabrera, who walked. Then Tom Gordon relieved Sturtze and got Manny Ramirez to hit into an inning-ending double play.

But in the eighth inning, David Ortiz got hold of one of Gordon's pitches and sent it into the Monster seats. Boston was rallying. Once again, Terry Francona tapped Dave Roberts to pinch-run for Kevin Millar and he scored the tying run when Jason Varitek hit a sacrifice fly off Mariano Rivera. Rivera had blown two saves in two nights. When was the last time that happened in the postseason?

In the top of the eighth, the Yankees had a runner on third, one out, and Alex Rodriguez at the plate. He had hit 36 homers during the regular seasons, but Mike Timlin struck him out, another key play in the game.

If the Yankee bullpen was suspect, the Boston relievers were not. In Game 5, Mike Timlin, Keith Foulke, Bronson Arroyo, Mike Myers, Alan Embree, and Tim Wakefield provided eight shut-out innings. By the end of nine, the score was tied at 4.

Ruben Sierra walked with two outs in the ninth. Then Tony Clark bounced a ball down the right-field line. Luckily for the Red Sox, the ball bounced into the stands for a ground-rule double. Had the ball stayed in the park, Sierra would have scored. But he had to retreat to third. Then Foulke got Miguel Cairo to pop to first for the third out, stranding both Sierra and Clark. Still 4–4. And that's where it stayed until the 12th inning. Tim Wakefield took the ball for Boston and pitched three scoreless innings, redemption for the man who had given up the walk-off home run to Aaron Boone in the ALCS in '03.

In the bottom of the 14th, Johnny Damon was on base when David Ortiz blooped a single in front of Bernie Williams in center field. Damon scored, and the Red Sox won again, 5–4. Boston had left 12 runners on base, while New York had stranded 18.

I was not alone in thinking that the momentum had swung in the Red Sox's favor. They'd come back from 3–0 to reach 3–2. We flew to New York after the game. Because of the rainout, there was no travel day. We arrived at our hotel in Manhattan at about 4:00 AM.

Curt Schilling was on the mound for Boston in Game 6 to face New York's Jon Lieber. Schilling was pitching with a dislocated ankle tendon. Bill Morgan, the Red Sox team doctor, had gone to the University of Massachusetts to work on a cadaver to see if he could create a temporary fix for Schilling's ankle. The day before Game 6, Dr. Morgan put three sutures in Schilling's tendon. It worked. Schilling pitched seven innings with four strikeouts and no walks.

In the fourth inning, Mark Bellhorn hit one to deep left field. It looked like a home run, but Jim Joyce, the left field umpire, ruled the ball in play. Francona came out to dispute the call. Clearly, the ball had hit a fan in the seats. Then the six umpires conferred and finally got the call right: a three-run home run to give Boston a 4–0 lead.

In the 1999 ALCS, the Red Sox had been victimized by two bad calls by the umpires. But things had changed. By '04, umpires had come to believe that getting the call right was the most important thing, rather than the umpires' authority. Getting the call right commands respect.

In the seventh inning, Bernie Williams homered for New York and Derek Jeter had an RBI single, making the score 4–2 Boston. Then Alex Rodriguez hit a slow roller up the first-base line. Boston pitcher Bronson Arroyo fielded the ball and was tagging him out when Rodriguez slapped the ball out of Arroyo's glove, one of the strangest and most unprofessional moves I have ever seen. The ball rolled foul, Jeter scored from first, and Rodriguez ended up on third. First-base umpire Randy Marsh, who is usually a good umpire, was screened on the play and didn't see it. I remember thinking that the Red Sox were going to lose again, because of an ill-timed disaster that the umpire closest to the play didn't see! Images of Bill Buckner and Aaron Boone ran through my mind.

Umpire Joe West called a conference of the six umpires (the second such conference in Game 6) and they made the right call. Rodriguez was called for interference and he was out. Jeter had to go back to first. Arroyo then got Gary Sheffield to pop out to the catcher and the inning was over.

Joe Torre was angry. The umpires had just taken a Yankee run off the scoreboard. Fans threw debris—including baseballs—onto the field. New York City police in riot gear were dispatched to stand along both sides of the field until the bottom of the ninth inning.

Boston still led 4–2. Keith Foulke pitched the ninth. He walked Matsui, then struck out Bernie Williams. Jorge Posada popped to third. Then Ruben Sierra walked and Matsui moved to second. The go-ahead run, in the person of 6'7" Tony Clark came to the plate with the game (and the Red Sox season) on the line. Foulke struck him out to preserve the Red Sox victory. The series was tied at three games.

Boston had become the first team to come back to play a Game 7 after being down 3–0. Once again, the Giamatti quote would have to wait.

On the morning of Game 7, October 20, I got a call from my friend Andre Thornton wishing us well. Duke and I had take-out food from Yolanda's in the Bronx. I went to the Stadium at about 3:00 PM, five hours before game time.

The Boston starter was Derek Lowe, pitching on two days' rest. I didn't know what to expect. Facing him was the angry Kevin Brown. On September 26, the last time he faced the Red Sox, Brown was bombed 11–4. That turned out to be prophetic.

In the first inning, David Ortiz hit a two-run homer. Then Boston loaded the bases in the second inning. That was it for Brown. Joe Torre brought in the shaky Javier Vasquez to face Johnny Damon. He parked Vasquez's first pitch in the right-field stands for a grand slam. 6–0 Boston.

The Yankees scored a run in the third. Then Boston scored two more in the fourth on another Johnny Damon home run. 8–1 Boston.

Derek Lowe was pitching very effectively over six innings. His pitch count was low and he was inducing lots of ground balls. In the seventh inning, Francona made an unusual move. He brought in Pedro Martinez in relief. Pedro had not flown to New York with the team before Game 6. He had stayed in Boston to work out with the Red Sox trainers. New York scored two in the seventh off Martinez as the Yankee Stadium crowd shouted, "Who's your daddy? Who's your daddy?"

In the eighth inning, Mark Bellhorn homered off the screen on the right-field foul pole. In the Yankees' eighth, Mike Timlin relieved Martinez and had a 1–2–3 inning. In the Red Sox ninth, Trot Nixon scored on two singles and two fly outs. Boston led New York 10–3 in the bottom of the ninth.

Hideki Matsui singled but was erased on a fielder's choice when Bernie Williams grounded to second. One out. Then Jorge Posada popped up. Two outs. Williams advanced to second base. After Kenny Lofton walked, Alan Embree replaced Timlin on the mound. Ruben Sierra grounded to Pokey Reese at second base, who threw to Doug Mientkiewicz at first for the third out. I remember my call: "The Red Sox have just pulled the greatest victory in team history!" and "Move over Babe!" They had beaten the Yankees when it really mattered, winning four elimination games in a row, something which had never been done before.

The Red Sox had won the ALCS and were going to the World Series for the first time since '86. Just as important, particularly for Red Sox fans, Boston had defeated the New York Yankees for the first time in a winner-take-all series since 1904, ending a century of frustration.

After the last out of the game I went down to the Boston clubhouse. As I was leaving the broadcast booth to go down to the clubhouse, Yankees broadcaster John Sterling graciously said, "Congratulations. You guys deserved it."

In the clubhouse, Trup was already drenched in champagne. The players went back on the field, where I did some interviews. I got soaked too. On the field, as it does at the end of every game, the PA system played "New York, New York." But it was the Frank Sinatra version, not the Liza Minnelli version. Then the entire Red Sox team went onto the field. So did their families and the team owners.

Two hours after the final out we went to LaGuardia for our flight back to Boston. I remembered similar flights: flying back to Boston after losing Game 7 of the '86 World Series to the New York Mets. And '03, after losing Game 7 of the ALCS to the Yankees on Aaron Boone's home run. Those flights were deadly silent. Not this one. This was quite a joyous affair. We didn't need wings. I got home at about 5:00 AM.

The next day, Thursday, was an off-day. I watched as the St. Louis Cardinals beat Roger Clemens and the Houston Astros in the deciding game of the National League Championship Series. Frankly, I was glad that the Cardinals won. I had never broadcast a game from St. Louis, but it has a great baseball tradition and I was very excited by the matchup. The Cardinals had won more World Series (They had won nine at that time. They won their 11th in 2011.) than any team except the Yankees.

I also bought a plane ticket to St. Louis for Jan. The principal and superintendent at her school were kind enough to give her a week off so she could share this rare experience with me.

After Jan's last class, I picked her up and we drove to the JFK Library in Boston for the Red Sox World Series party. What a great experience. Jan and I visited with many old friends and Red Sox staffers including scouts and minor league executives. The Red Sox logo was on the wall in bright lights.

The Red Sox had come so far, overcome so many obstacles. I felt that they *had* to win because of their history. This was the year.

October 23 was cold and wet for Game 1 at Fenway Park. Tim Wakefield started for Boston, facing the Cardinals' Woody Williams. Johnny Damon led off the Boston first with a double. The next batter, Orlando Cabrera, was hit by a pitch. Manny Ramirez flied out to right field. Then Big Papi came to the plate for his first World Series at-bat. He had been named the MVP in the ALCS, and the Boston sportswriters had given him a new nickname: *Señor Octobre*. Ortiz homered. 3–0 Boston. The Red Sox scored again and it was 4–0 in the first. But Wakefield only lasted through three and two-thirds innings. The Cardinals battled back from 7–2 and 9–7. St. Louis tied the game in the sixth. Then Boston scored two more in the seventh. David Ortiz's screamer that scored Cabrera bounced up and hit Tony Womack in the collarbone. He was hurt, but the X-rays were negative. 9–7 Boston.

St. Louis tied the game in the eighth. In the eighth, facing Julian Tavarez, Mark Bellhorn hit one deep to right. I knew the ball was going deep, but I couldn't tell if would stay fair or go foul. The ball hit the "Pesky Pole" (the right-field foul pole named for former Red Sox Johnny Pesky) with Jason Varitek aboard to make the score 11–9 Boston. How fitting! Johnny Pesky, who was at the game, had played for the Red Sox against the Cardinals in the 1946 World Series.

In the bottom of the ninth, Foulke struck out Roger Cedeño with Marlon Anderson on second to end the game.

Game 1 was a high-scoring game which used 11 total pitchers and lasted exactly four hours. Boston had won despite four errors, including two by Manny Ramirez in left field on consecutive plays in the eighth inning. I took that as a good omen.

That victory meant that the Red Sox had won five games in a row in the postseason.

Game 2 was very similar to Game 1. Boston survived four errors, including three by Bill Mueller. Curt Schilling was the scheduled starter, but he woke up with a lot of pain in his ankle. He drove to Fenway and said that there was no way he could pitch that night. Then he saw the fans and the signs. His adrenaline pumping, Schilling thought about playing. But he and his family didn't think he should even try.

Dr. Morgan, the team doctor, examined Schilling's right ankle. He determined that one of the sutures he had put in was pressing against a nerve, so he clipped it. Schilling was able to warm up. Meanwhile, rumors were circulating that the Red Sox would have to use an emergency starter. The rumblings about another starter lasted until Schilling went to the pitcher's mound to warm up just before the game.

Jason Varitek tripled in the first inning into the triangle in right-center field. Boston went ahead. The blow which broke things open for Boston was a two-run double by Mark Bellhorn in the fourth. Cabrera drove in two runs in the sixth. Schilling went six innings, giving way to Alan Embree, Mike Timlin, and Keith Foulke. Despite their four errors, the Red Sox hung on to win 6–2 and go up two games to none.

I remembered '86, when Boston won the first two games of the World Series, only to lose in seven to the Mets.

Game 2 used only nine pitchers and was another long one: three hours and 20 minutes. So it wasn't until early Monday morning that we arrived at the Adams-Mark Hotel in St. Louis. I went to the team workout at Busch Stadium on Monday, then I waited for Jan to arrive on a commercial flight in the afternoon. We went to a World Series party at a downtown museum. It was a very nice party, but there were lots of people there who had nothing to do with the World Series or with either team. I saw many old friends, such as John Schuerholtz and Frank Wren from the Braves.

Tuesday, October 26: Game 3. That morning, Jan and I went for a riverboat cruise on the Mississippi, which was a first for both of us. The only time I'd ever been in St. Louis before was for Brian Daubach's wedding. But I had read all of Mark Twain's books about the Mississippi, and I felt like we were riding on the Proud Mary. The boat went down the river about a mile and then turned back. Jan and I had lunch with Brian and Chrissie Daubach. He had finished the season with the Red Sox's AAA team in Pawtucket, Rhode Island. Chrissy was very pregnant. (Caden Daubach arrived on November 27, our 33rd wedding anniversary.) The Daubachs lived in O'Farrell, Illinois, very close to St. Louis. Although Brian had not been with the team at the end of the season, he had been a big part of the club in previous years, and I was glad that he could join in the Red Sox's postseason success.

It rained later that day. I thought the game would be postponed, but the skies cleared and Game 3 started. The Red Sox pitcher was Pedro Martinez. He faced Jeff Suppan. Manny Ramirez homered in the top of the first, but the keys to the game were two defensive plays. With one out in the bottom of the first inning, the Cards got a walk, a single, and another walk to load the bases. Jim Edmonds, who hit 42 home runs and batted .301 that season, hit a fly ball to left field. Manny Ramirez, who had made two errors in Game 1, made a good play to catch the ball. Larry Walker, who had been on third, tagged up and tried to score, but Ramirez's throw was excellent and nailed him at the plate as Jason Varitek applied the tag for an inning-ending double play. The Cardinals left two men on base.

In the bottom of the third inning, the Red Sox caught a crucial break on a base-running error by Jeff Suppan. He was on third with Edgar Renteria on second. Larry Walker grounded to Bellhorn at second, who threw to Ortiz at first for one out. Big Papi was playing first to keep his bat in the lineup, as no DH was used in the NL park.

An aside here about Boston baserunners. Trup and I had kidded during the season about how poorly the Red Sox had run the bases all season. They were slow and made bad decisions on the base paths. Trup said that the Red Sox uniforms must have been very heavy.

Once the throw was made to Ortiz at first, Suppan, who came up through the Red Sox farm system, stopped and tried to get back to third base, even though Cardinals third base coach José Oquendo was shouting at him to score. Ortiz threw to third and Bill Mueller tagged him out for a 4–3–5 double play. Then Albert Pujols grounded out to end the inning.

My reaction was to think that this play was the opposite of what had happened to the Red Sox during the 1975 World Series against the Cincinnati Reds. In that game, Denny Doyle had tried to tag up on a shallow fly ball to left field with nobody out. Doyle said later that when George Foster caught the ball, he thought he heard his third-base coach Don Zimmer shouting, "Go, go, go!" so he went and was tagged out at the plate. Zimmer had actually shouted "No, no, no!"

I wondered on the air whether Suppan had heard Oquendo shouting "No, no, no!" when he might actually have been shouting, "Go, go, go!" The Cardinals' failure to score on that play was a pivotal play in the game and in the series. Boston still led 1–0. St. Louis scored a run in the bottom of the ninth, but it was not enough. Final score: Boston 4, St. Louis 1. The Red Sox led the World Series three games to none.

The next day, Jan and I had lunch with my former intern Jeff Idelson (now president of the Hall of Fame) and sportswriter Bill Madden of the *New York Daily News*. We ate at Mike Shannon's restaurant.

I hoped that the Red Sox could wrap things up in Game 4. Jan and I didn't pack, and we didn't get ready to leave. We wanted to win it in St. Louis. I really hoped that the Red Sox would not blow a 3–0 lead.

Johnny Damon led off Game 4 with a home run off Jason Marquis. Then the Red Sox loaded the bases in the third inning. On a 3–0 pitch, Trot Nixon doubled for two more. (He may have missed a sign and thought he had the green light.) Derek Lowe delivered a brilliant pitching performance. He went seven innings and gave up three hits and a walk, while striking out four. No runs.

By the bottom of the seventh I was very excited. I thought Boston was going to win, so I went into the bathroom to put on my "get wet" champagne clothes. I ran into Bruce Manno, the Cardinals' farm director. He was an old friend from my days with the Milwaukee Brewers. As soon as I told him what I was doing, I regretted it. I should not have said that to somebody who worked for the Cardinals. I'm sure Bruce was crushed that his team was about to get swept.

After the eighth inning, with the score still 3–0 Boston, Trup went down to the clubhouse for postgame interviews. The Red Sox had just one hit in the top of the ninth, and it was on to the bottom of the ninth.

I thought it was fitting that during Game 4, when the Red Sox won their first World Series since 1918, there was a full lunar eclipse; the first ever during a World Series.

I was very anxious. I had thought for years about what I'd say if I were on the air when the Red Sox won the World Series. I started to make some notes. Then I stopped. I told myself, *Don't do that. You might blow it. Just do it naturally as it comes to you.* But I had anticipated this moment for 22 seasons with the Red Sox and I wanted to get it right. I did not want to be trite or to mention the curse, and I did not want to overstate it. I wanted to say something simple that would stand the test of time.

Keith Foulke pitched the top of the ninth inning for the save. After Albert Pujols singled, Scott Rolen flied out and Jim Edmonds struck out. The next batter was Edgar Renteria.

Jason Wolfe, our program director, and Doug Lane, our broadcast engineer, were behind me in the broadcast booth. But I was zoned in on the action on the field in front of me. This was surely the highlight of my career as a broadcaster and I wanted to get it right. I tried to be relaxed, not to anticipate. I hoped that the game would have a definitive ending on a batted ball, not a checked swing or a fly ball where the umpire has to decide whether it's a catch or a trap. I wanted something decisive.

With a 1–0 count, Renteria swung. He hit a grounder right back to Foulke. Here's my call: "Here's the 1–0 pitch. A ground ball stabbed by Foulke. He underhands to first, and the Red Sox are world champions. For the first time in 86 years, the Boston Red Sox are the champions of baseball. Can you believe it?"

As the Red Sox were celebrating on the field, I wanted to pay tribute to Ned Martin, who had broadcast more Red Sox games than anybody else: 32 years on radio and television. Ned never got to announce a Red Sox world championship. I said, "Ned would have said, 'Pandemonium on the field.'"

Later, I paid tribute to Ken Coleman. As he had done so many times, I finally pulled the Bart Giamatti quote out of my pocket and read: "It breaks your heart. It's designed to break your heart." That's how we ended the broadcast.

Trup was on the field. Red Sox fans and family were on the field, too, but the players were already in the clubhouse. Trup interviewed the team owners and the players when they emerged onto the field. I anchored our coverage from the broadcast booth. Finally, I went down to the clubhouse. I noticed two things. First, Tim Wakefield had tears in his eyes. He'd been with the Red Sox for 10 years and was the senior member of the ballclub. I also saw that Johnny Pesky had tears in his eyes. He'd been branded the goat of the '46 World Series, but that was wrong. "Mr. Red Sox" had been a player, coach, manager, broadcaster, and special assistant to the club. He epitomized what it meant to be a member of the Red Sox. Johnny certainly deserved to be there.

I was moved when my old friend Bud Selig (who had owned the Milwaukee Brewers when I worked there) presented the world championship trophy to team owners John Henry, Tom Werner, and Larry Lucchino.

After that, we did some more player interviews and I got doused with champagne, but not as much as Trup, who had been in the clubhouse longer.

I went back up to the broadcast booth to sign off the broadcast. I couldn't wait to get back to the hotel to celebrate with Jan. Jan had watched the game with two friends who were great Red Sox fans: Bill Gould and Joe Hall. Both had been Red Sox fans since the '40s. These two men had never met before. They met for the first time just when the Red Sox won their first World Series in 86 years.

I was very glad that Jan had been able to share the Red Sox victory with me in St. Louis. She'd been with me for 22 years of Red Sox games: the heartbreaks and disappointments, the letdowns, and the unfulfilling endings.

Jan and I celebrated at the hotel with Joe and Bill, Tito Francona, Brian Daubach's parents, and, surprisingly, Dan Duquette. Then we went back to our hotel to pack for the flight back to Boston.

I checked with Red Sox traveling secretary Jack McCormick to make sure there was room for Jan on the plane back to Boston. Luckily, there was.

On the flight, which left shortly after 3:00 AM, the world championship trophy was strapped into the seat next to Pedro Martinez. Jan and I sat near Dr. Morgan, who had helped make this all possible.

There was a lot of security as we landed at Logan Airport near Boston. People's faces lit up when our buses drove by at 6:30 or 7:00 AM. These buses were carrying the world champion Boston Red Sox! They clapped and honked horns. The enthusiasm was incredible. Boston fans had waited a long time for this moment, and now, here we were!

On the bus, Jan and I sat in front of Doug Mientkiewicz and his wife. I asked, "Where's the ball?" He replied, "I've got it and I'm keeping it! I gave the ball from Game 7 of the Yankee series to Alan Embree. I'm keeping this one!" Later, when Dan Shaughnessy of the *Boston Globe* asked Mientkiewicz about it and was told that Mientkiewicz was keeping it, he printed it. Mientkiewicz and the team later compromised on the ownership of the ball, but the Red Sox were allowed to display it.

Our buses reached Fenway Park at about 7:30. The mood among the players and the front office people was still ecstatic. We stayed at Fenway for a while, found our bags and our car, and then drove home. When we got home, Jan and I went right to bed. We were exhausted. We didn't get up until about 1:00 PM.

The rest of that day, we stayed home, relaxed, and watched the celebrations on TV. At about 1:30 that afternoon, our radio station woke me up to congratulate me on the Red Sox great victory, and to remind me that now that the season was over I no longer needed the car which the station had provided for me. Welcome back to reality!

Boston's plans for a victory party or parade were still a little up in the air. We did know that there was a breakfast party at Fenway Park the next day at 7:00 AM. After that, there would be a parade on Duck Tour boats (amphibious vehicles that give tours of Boston, including water tours of Boston harbor). We certainly wanted to be part of that. Tommy's wife, Rachel, and Kate's fiancé, Mike, spent the night at our house so we could all leave together early for the Duck boat parade. Boston mayor Thomas Menino didn't call it a parade. He called it a "rolling rally"—no speeches. The plans for the "rolling rally" were cleverly drawn up by Dr. Charles Steinberg, the team's VP of public affairs, along with the team owners.

We all got up and were ready to leave at 5:00 AM, but Jan was not feeling well. She didn't think we'd be invited on the actual Duck boats for the "rolling rally," and so she stayed home and watched on TV.

We drove into Fenway for the breakfast. We were interviewed on NESN, the Red Sox's cable station, and Channel 4 with Bob Lobel and Trup. I don't think I'd ever been interviewed at 6:30 AM.

I found out that I had indeed been assigned a spot on one of the Duck Tour boats. I wanted to have my family ride with me. So we walked out to left field with Pedro Martinez. He was always fond of Kate, who spoke Spanish. Pedro hugged us and posed for photos with Kate, Mike, Rachel, and me.

When I asked team executives about getting my family on the Duck Tour boat, I was told yes if there's room. Despite some reluctance from the security people, I got them all on. We were on a boat with Kevin Youkilis and Dr. Morgan. Also on board was Ellis Burks and his family. Kate was thrilled, because Ellis had been one of her favorite players. Ellis was particularly excited by the Red Sox victory because he was retiring. During the four hours on the Duck boat, nobody shouted more or enjoyed himself more than Ellis.

The Duck boat tour was unforgettable. We went down Boylston Street near City Hall and out onto the Charles River.

My son Tom, was not able to ride with us, because he was working the night shift at the Leahy Clinic, where he was a resident. But he was standing on the Massachusetts Avenue Bridge with hundreds of other fans, waving to us.

As we traveled on the "rolling rally," the streets were packed 10 to 15 deep. People wanted to see the new world champion Boston Red Sox. Many of the signs were quite moving: THANKS FOR WINNING IT FOR MY LATE FATHER...THANK YOU GUYS FOR DOING THIS...GRANDPA WOULD HAVE LOVED IT...MY UNCLE CAN REST IN PEACE. Manny Ramirez held up a sign that read: JETER IS PLAYING GOLF TODAY. THIS IS BETTER.

The crowd that witnessed the parade was estimated at 3.5 million enthusiastic, happy fans.

We got off the Duck boats in Cambridge. There we boarded buses back to Fenway. My friend Bill Pusari, the owner of Modern Pizza in New Haven, met us at Fenway with 10 pies. I walked him (and the pies) through security and we went to the .406 club, where the pizza could be kept warm. I took Bill's seven-year-old son into the clubhouse to get some autographs. By about 2:30, I called the .406 room to ask that the pies be brought down to the Crown Royal Room where the players had gathered.

But we were told that the pizzas had been sent to the Red Sox executive offices. Theo Epstein, Tom Werner, and Larry Lucchino loved Modern Pizza from their days at Yale. The staff in the executive offices ate nine and a half pizzas. We brought down the remaining half a pizza. Everybody seemed pleased, including Bill. He even had his photograph taken with the World Series trophy.

I had my picture taken with the trophy, too. Team owner John Henry insisted that my kids have their photos taken with him and with the trophy.

We got home around 5:00 PM. Jan told us that she was disappointed that she had not gone on the tour with us. (She did go on the Duck boat tour three years later, in '07.)

The celebrations continued. On Sunday morning, the front page of the *Boston Globe's* sports section had a photo of Keith Foulke getting the final out of the Series. My words were printed on the bottom of the page: "The 1–0 pitch. Foulke stabs at it, underhands it to first, and the Red Sox are the world champions for the first time in 86 years. Can you believe it?" I was thrilled.

The following Thursday, the Clift-Rodgers Library in Marshfield, Massachusetts, had a book signing for my first book, *Broadcast Rites and Sites: I Saw it on the Radio with the Boston Red Sox.* We sold almost 100 copies.

The World Series trophy went on a tour of New England. I was invited to accompany it to New Haven, Connecticut, where I was born. I stayed at my mother's house and went to Yale Law School. Larry Lucchino is an alumnus. I took my nephew Sam Potolocchio.

The dean of the law school at the time was Harold Koh, a longtime Red Sox fan. He went to prep school with my brother Frank. At the ceremony, Yale's athletic director, Tom Beckett, spoke. He was a high school teammate of Larry Lucchino and they remain close friends. Larry and I both spoke. Then we took the trophy to the New Haven Green, the center of town. Kevin Youkilis, Mike Timlin, and the mayor, John DeStefano Jr., were there. So were 2,000 people. What a thrill! Larry spoke and I spoke. Theo Epstein was there, and he spoke too. I introduced George Grande, one of my oldest friends.

I got a special thrill in introducing John Smith, my father's best friend during the last years of his life. John was the New Haven fire chief. He'd been listening to Red Sox games on the radio long before I came along, though he became a more avid fan when I started doing the games. John often came to Fenway with my father. I was to glad to have this special moment with the '04 Red Sox World Series trophy with John, who passed away in '05.

We went to Modern Pizza after the ceremony to celebrate. Then it was off to another ceremony in Hartford. Radio station WTIC in Hartford has our most powerful affiliate outside of Boston.

I made a number of trips with the trophy. We went to Springfield and Worcester, Massachusetts, and Manchester, New Hampshire. My son Tom had gone to college at Holy Cross and medical school in Worcester, and Duke had worked in Springfield. I felt that I had a real connection with so many towns and cities on the trophy's tour.

When I got home that evening I went to the premiere of the World Series video at the Wang Center in Boston. I was thrilled that my call was on the video.

Eventually, the trophy went to all 351 townships in Massachusetts and many more throughout New England. I was thrilled and honored to have been a part of the tour.

I had told Kate not to plan her wedding for October 2004, because I thought the Red Sox would be in the World Series. She didn't and they were. The wedding was set for January 15, 2005. We had a rehearsal dinner in Dedham, Massachusetts at a restaurant owned by a relative of Mike Romano, my soon-to-be son-in-law.

Chuck Steedman, the Red Sox broadcast director was nice enough to send the Red Sox World Series Trophy to the reception on the Friday night before the Saturday wedding. We thought that was the best time because if we had it at Kate and Mike's wedding reception, it might detract from the bride.

We did not tell anyone that it was coming, because we didn't want the whole town of Dedham there to see the trophy. As we started the rehearsal dinner, Dave Brady, a security guard for the Red Sox, brought the trophy in. We made sure Dave was well fed. The trophy stayed for about an hour, and everyone in the bridal party had their picture taken with the World Series Trophy.

We were fortunate to have very nice weather the next day, the day of Kate's wedding at St. Mary's, a church in Dedham. St. Mary's was built around 1890 by the great-great-grandfather of my good friend William Gould, a former chairman of the National Labor Relations Board and since 1972 a professor at Stanford Law School. Bill is also the No. 1 Red Sox fan on the West Coast. William Gould I was a runaway slave from Wilmington, North Carolina, who went north on the Underground Railroad. He became an officer in the Union Navy during the Civil War and later became a mason.

The wedding was beautiful. We held the reception at Luciano's in Wrentham. Had we scheduled the wedding for the following week, it would have been a disaster. There was a blizzard so bad that Masses as well as weddings were canceled.

But everything went well for Kate and Mike, whose wedding had an Italian theme. Mike's family is from the island of Ponza. I was just sorry that my dad, who passed away in 2003, wasn't there to share our happiness for Kate.

The Red Sox were not interested in signing Derek Lowe for '05, even though he had won games in the Division Series, the Championship Series, and Game 4 of the World Series. I also hoped that Pedro Martinez would be back in '05. Things went back and forth until he finally signed with the Mets. They offered him one year more than Boston had, guaranteed. Pedro probably thought that it was time to go. Although the move worked out well for Pedro professionally (In his first year with the Mets, he went 15–8, struck out 208, and had an ERA of 2.82), I missed him. I went to see Pedro on an off-day when the Red Sox played in Philadelphia in June '05. We had a wonderful reunion. He told people that he was honored because I had come to see him.

Nomar had been traded and the Red Sox decided to pursue Edgar Renteria at shortstop instead of Orlando Cabrera. That was the big free-agent signing of the off-season. Personally, it was an exhilarating off-season. I did a lot of book signings for *Broadcast Rites and Sites,* including one at Colgate, my alma mater, where we sold nearly 100 books. One man bought 26 copies. I learned that his name was Lee Woltman, captain of the 1964 football team when I was a freshman. I had broadcast his games.

I also did a book signing at the National Baseball Hall of Fame in Cooperstown with Doug Lyons. We had dinner with my old intern, Jeff Idelson. Jeff invited me to cut the ribbon at the Hall's new World Series exhibit in November, but I had to drive Jan back in time for school. Jeff then offered to have a car service drive Jan back home to Massachusetts on Sunday night, in time for school on Monday. That was great. I was honored to cut the ribbon to open the exhibit that included Curt Schilling's bloody sock.

But even with all of the changes, the Red Sox still thought that they had a very strong club and had a good chance to repeat as world champions. It's become very rare, particularly in baseball, for a team to repeat as world champions because of competitive balance and injuries. In '04, no Red Sox starting pitcher missed a start because of an injury. That's not the case in most years, and it wasn't the case in '05.

Some players had tremendous years in '05. Manny Ramirez, for example, had 45 homers and knocked in 144 runs. David Ortiz had 47 homers and drove in 148 runs. They formed one of the deadliest one-two punches in baseball history. But the Red Sox did not have the pitching depth they had had in '04. 42-year-old David Wells won 15 games. Tim Wakefield, 38, had a good year, leading the pitching staff with 16 wins, and Bronson Arroyo won 14.

But the team was beset by injuries. Matt Clement went 13–6, with most of his success early in the season. Keith Foulke struggled as a closer. He had 15 saves, but his ERA was 5.91—a real point of uncertainty for the team. Nevertheless, the Red Sox remained in the race just about all season, finishing second in the East with a record of 95–67. However, they were swept in the first round of the playoffs by the eventual World Series champion White Sox.

In the fall of '05, general manager Theo Epstein temporarily left the Red Sox. Nonetheless, the Red Sox made a very big trade with the Florida Marlins. The key was getting right-handed pitcher Josh Beckett to be the ace of the staff. The Sox also acquired Mike Lowell, primarily because he had a big contract that the Marlins were trying to dump. To get them, the Red Sox gave up some top prospects, including Hanley Ramirez, who has gone on to star for the Marlins at shortstop, and Anibal Sanchez, who has become a very good pitcher. The trade helped both clubs.

2006 was a very tough season, but there were some highs. In his first year with the Red Sox, Mike Lowell hit 20 homers and 47 doubles. Manny Ramirez knocked in 102 runs and hit 35 home runs. But the key highlight was David Ortiz leading the AL by hitting 54 home runs, shattering the previous Red Sox record of 50 set by Jimmie Foxx in 1938.

As I said, injuries took their toll in '06. Jason Varitek needed knee surgery and was able to play in only 103 games. The low point was a crushing five-game sweep by the Yankees at Fenway Park in mid-August. Manny Ramirez pulled himself out of one of those games with some sort of an ailment and played sparingly the rest of the way.

The pitching was not as strong as it had been, and the Red Sox finished third in the East with an 86–76 record, missing the playoffs. No one was sure what to expect for the '07 season.

CHAPTER 7

"You Belong With Me"
2007

2004 HAD BEEN ALL ABOUT MIRACLES, MAKING HISTORY, AND THE GREATEST COMEBACK OF ALL TIME. It was about ending curses for dead relatives and friends, and it was a chance to celebrate for all of New England.

2007 was about having the best team in all baseball. And the Boston Red Sox did have the best team in baseball. It got off to a tremendous start despite a loss in Kansas City on Opening Day. In April, the Red Sox were 16–8. Then 20–8 in May, and they were in first place with a 36–16 record. The lead remained fairly comfortable, although the pennant race tightened up somewhat when Boston lost three straight in Detroit just before the All-Star break. But with the ebb and flow of the season, they came back to go 16–11 in September and won the AL East Division title outright for the first time since 1995.

David Ortiz had another big year: 35 home runs, 52 doubles, 117 RBIs, and a career-best .332 batting average. He also led the AL with 111 walks and an on-base percentage of .445. Manny Ramirez, who had some injuries, still managed to hit .296, with 20 home runs and 88 RBIs. Mike Lowell had a big year too, batting a career-high .324, with 21 homers, 37 doubles, and 120 RBIs. Kevin Youkilis emerged as the team's first baseman with 35 doubles and a .288 batting average.

A big key was Dustin Pedroia, who was named the AL Rookie of the Year. After a slow start, the 5'9" 23-year-old second baseman bounced back to hit .317 (a major league rookie record for second basemen), with 39 doubles and 86 runs scored in just 139 games. His play at second base was sensational, and he gave the Red Sox a tremendous spark.

J.D. Drew, signed as a free agent, had a disappointing regular season but had one big hit in October that would be critical to the Red Sox's success. Jacoby Ellsbury (the first Navajo to play in the majors) came up in June and had an immediate impact. He's the fastest Red Sox player I've ever seen. (He went on to lead the AL in stolen bases in '08 and '09. In '09, he also led the league in triples, with 10.)

The ace of the pitching staff, without question, was Josh Beckett. He had a big year, including a league-leading 20 wins with only 7 losses and an ERA of 3.27. He came in second for the Cy Young.

The big story out of spring training was the signing of 26-year-old Daisuke Matsuzaka. The Red Sox had to put up a "posting fee" of $50 million for the right to sign him from the Seibu Lions in Japan's Pacific League. Then they paid another $50 million or so to sign him to a six-year contract. He had some ups and downs, but won 15 games for the Red Sox while losing 12.

Curt Schilling was hurt part of the year, but still won 9 games. Jonathan Papelbon had a great year as the Red Sox closer with 37 saves. Rookie Japanese import was left-handed reliever Hideki Okajima, who gave the Red Sox many key performances while going 3–2 with five saves. I'll never forget a game against the Giants at Fenway Park. He had fallen behind 2–0 to Barry Bonds. Then he threw three straight strikes. Bonds couldn't pull the trigger and was a strikeout victim.

2007 had many other key performances: Javier Lopez pitched very well out of the bullpen. A very good August call-up was Clay Buchholz. On September 1, he pitched a 10–0 no-hitter in which he struck out nine Baltimore Orioles. This was the sixth no-hitter I have broadcast. I'll never forget that during the game I leaned over to Hall of Famer Jim Palmer, who was broadcasting the game in the next booth for the Orioles on TV, and asking, "Jim, does this pitcher remind you of anybody?" Palmer said "Yes, He reminds me of me, because he comes right over the top, and has an outstanding curveball, a great fastball, and an excellent changeup." I reported that conversation on the air as Buchholz struck out Nick Markakis on a curveball to complete the no-hitter.

After his cancer treatments, Jon Lester came back and went 4–0 in 12 games. All in all, the Red Sox had the best team in baseball.

They began the ALDS against the Los Angeles Angels of Anaheim. David Ortiz and Kevin Youkilis both homered in Game 1 in Boston on October 3, but the big story was the pitching of Josh Beckett: a four-hit shutout as Boston beat John Lackey (who came to the Red Sox in '10).

In Game 2 on October 5, the game went to the sixth inning tied at 3 and stayed that way until the ninth. With two men on, the Angels had their closer Francisco Rodriguez (K-Rod) on the mound. Manny Ramirez came to the plate with Julio Lugo and David Ortiz on base. Manny swung and hit one high over the monster seats and out of the park, and as I said on the air, "deep into the night" for a three-run home run. The ball landed across Lansdowne Street! The Red Sox won 6–3 on Manny Ramirez's walk-off home run, his 21ˢᵗ round-tripper in postseason play—probably the biggest of his eight-year Red Sox career. The Red Sox led the best-of-five series 2–0. The game lasted more than four hours because there were seven pitching changes.

Then it was off to Anaheim for what we hoped would be just one game. Game 3 was a Red Sox romp, with Big Papi and Manny hitting home runs, and Curt Schilling pitching a strong ballgame. Boston beat Anaheim 9–1 to sweep the series with relative ease. Manny and Ortiz each had two home runs in the three-game series and Boston moved on to face the Cleveland Indians, who had defeated the New York Yankees 3–1 in the other ALDS.

The pivotal game in that series was the second game in Cleveland when Yankee pitcher Joba Chamberlain was attacked by a swarm of Canadian Soldier gnats, which fly across Lake Erie from Canada. As soon as they bump into something, they die, but they were all over Chamberlain. The trainer came out to the mound to spray him with some kind of bug repellant, but all that did was make it worse. He gave up the tying run, and the Indians went on to beat New York 3 games to 1.

Josh Beckett continued his outstanding postseason, winning Game 1 of the ALCS in Boston. The Red Sox romped, beating Cleveland's 6'7" pitcher CC Sabathia 10–3.

Game 2 was a different story. Manny Ramirez's home run in the fifth inning was his 23ʳᵈ in postseason play, surpassing the record previously held by Bernie Williams of the Yankees. But by the sixth, the game was tied at 6. The score remained the same until the 11ᵗʰ inning, when the Indians scored seven runs, including a three-run home run by Franklin Gutierrez. A great pitching performance was turned in by Rafael Betancourt of the Indians. He had been a shortstop in the Red Sox farm system. Then my good friend Bob Schafer, who was director of minor league operations for the Red Sox and later coached for the Oakland A's and the Los Angeles Dodgers, converted him to a pitcher in the minor league camp.

I called Bob the next morning at his home in Ft. Myers, Florida, and told him that he was ruining our season by turning Betancourt into a reliever. He came into the game in the seventh inning and pitched through the ninth, shutting the Red Sox down. Betancourt's performance was a key factor in the Indians' 13–6 win.

On Monday, October 15, we were in Cleveland for Game 3. I saw my old friend Andre Thornton.

Daisuke was the starting pitcher for the Red Sox. The Indians built a four-run lead. The Red Sox scored two runs in the seventh inning when Jason Varitek homered with J.D. Drew on base, but that was it. The Indians won 4–2.

The next day, in Game 4 at Cleveland's Jacobs Field, the Red Sox started knuckleballer Tim Wakefield. The Indians starter was Paul Byrd, who later pitched for Boston. The game was scoreless through the top of the fifth. But in the bottom of the inning Cleveland scored seven runs. Then, in the top of the sixth, Youkilis, Ortiz, and Ramirez hit consecutive home runs—a first for the League Championship Series—but Cleveland won the game 7–3 to take a 3–1 series lead. Then came a much-needed day off between Games 4 and 5.

Game 5 was a critical game, because the Red Sox faced elimination. As in Game 1, the pitchers were Josh Beckett and CC Sabathia. The tone for the game was set by the second batter of the game: Kevin Youkilis. He hit a bomb off Sabathia onto the left-field pavilion. The Indians tied the game in the bottom of the inning, but the Red Sox moved ahead in the third and scored two in the seventh inning and three in the eighth and went on to a 7–1 victory. Cleveland now led the series 3–2.

Both teams had the next day off as the series returned to Boston. This was pivotal because it allowed the Red Sox to set up the pitching the way they wanted it. Curt Schilling started Game 6 on October 20. The Red Sox loaded the bases in the first inning with two outs and Fausto Carmona on the mound. J.D. Drew had the biggest hit of his Red Sox career. While he hadn't done a lot during the regular season (.270, 11 homers), Drew lined one to deep center field, just left of dead center. I thought for sure it was going to hit the wall, but the ball kept rising. It just made it over the 18' wall into the center-field seats for a grand slam. They got six more in the third. Schilling went seven innings and pitched well. The Red Sox won 12–2, to tie the series at 3.

Doing what I love. Calling a 2011 game at Fenway. (Courtesy of Boston Red Sox)

Here's me as a young man, interviewing the great Ted Williams, who managed the Washington Senators from 1969 to 1971.

The kids at my first spring training in Winter Haven, Florida, 1983. From left, there's Duke, Me, Tom, and Kate.

One of my all-time favorites, and my broadcast partner from 1983 to '89, it was Ken who started the tradition of reading A. Bartlett Giamatti's "The Green Fields of the Mind" at the end of each season. (Courtesy of Boston Red Sox)

Interviewing Roger Clemens. (Courtesy of Jack Maley)

Here I am with Andre and Gail Thorton and Jan at a party celebrating my new job with the Red Sox in 1983.

Carl Yastrzemski visiting the booth on Yaz Day, August 6, 1989, the day his number was retired.

"Burly Bob" Starr, my partner in the booth from 1990 to '92. (Courtesy of Boston Red Sox)

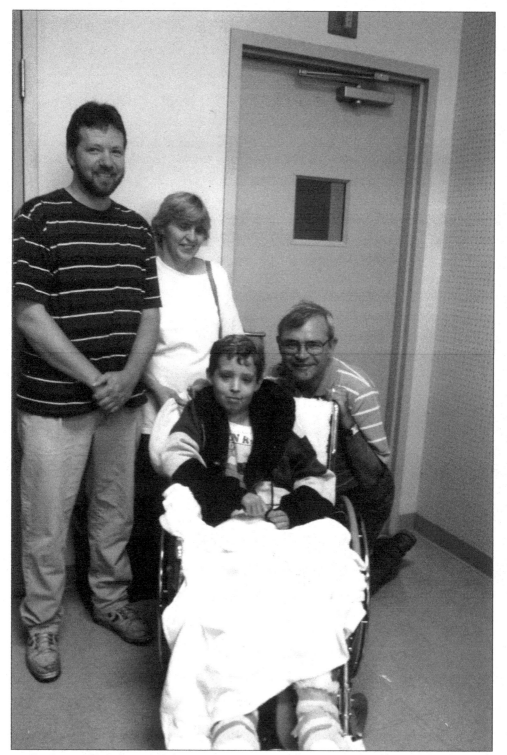

Here I am in 1994 with Jimmy Fund patient Jason Leader and his parents, Phil and Sue Leader.

Game 7. Rookie Dustin Pedroia led off the bottom of the first with a single against starter Jake Westbrook and scored the first run on an RBI single by Ramirez. Daisuke was pitching for the Red Sox. Boston had a 3–2 lead. The Indians had some questionable baserunning and coaching in the seventh inning when they left the tying run on base. This was a big play. Cleveland third base coach Joel Skinner held Kenny Lofton, who should have scored the tying run for Cleveland.

Boston scored two runs in the bottom of the seventh on Pedroia's home run and then wrapped it up with six runs in the eighth. The game ended on a great play by Coco Crisp in the top of the ninth. He ran deep into the triangle in right center, jumped, hit the wall, and made a spectacular catch to end the game and win the pennant. Dustin Pedroia drove in a total of five runs that game and the Sox won decisively, 11–2. Josh Beckett was the MVP of the series. J.D. Drew knocked in six runs and hit .360 (9-for-25), with a critical grand slam. Manny Ramirez hit .409 with two homers. He knocked in 10 runs. Kevin Youkilis hit three homers and hit .500. David Ortiz hit .292. Mike Lowell had a home run and eight RBIs and hit .333. Boston was going to the World Series to face the Colorado Rockies. They had beaten the Philadelphia Phillies 3–0 in the NLDS and then swept the Arizona Diamondbacks 4–0 in the NLCS to advance.

I'd been with the team in June '04 when the Red Sox played three games in Colorado. I liked Coors Field. On a clear day, you can see all the way to the Rocky Mountains.

Jan was able to make the trip to Cleveland with me as she usually does and got to see some of her family in Youngstown. I remember getting tickets for her brother Billy and his family. Of course, they rooted for the Indians. In Game 5, Jan sat with our good friend Ted Lux, a longtime Cleveland disk jockey, who had been our friend since we first got to Cleveland in 1972. Ted was also rooting for the Indians. During this series, I actually felt sorry for the losing team. Cleveland's manager, Eric Wedge, had been a good friend of mine when he played for the Red Sox in the early '90s. Also, of course, I'd spent so much time in Cleveland. It was great to win, but it wasn't quite like beating the Yankees, because of my strong feelings for Cleveland.

The Rockies won two out of three games at Fenway in June when they outscored Boston 20–5. So their pitchers weren't complete strangers. Likewise, they knew a little about our pitchers, and about Fenway Park.

The Red Sox opened the 2007 World Series (my third and their second in four years) at home. I thought it was so typical that Dustin Pedroia, the first batter in the first inning, homered in his first World Series at-bat. The Red Sox scored three runs off Jeff Francis. Josh Beckett, the Boston pitcher, spun a beauty and went seven strong innings as the Red Sox won 13–1.

The pivotal game of the Series was Game 2. The Rockies sent Ubaldo Jimenez to the mound to face Curt Schilling. The Red Sox led going into the eighth. The Rockies had Matt Holliday on base, with Jonathan Papelbon on the mound. I don't believe Pap threw over to first base at all during the regular season to hold the runner. But Brad Mills, the Red Sox bench coach, smelled it out. He called for a pickoff throw. Holliday, ready to steal second on the first pitch, tried to get back to the base but Papelbon picked him off. It was a huge out, as Boston went on to win 2–1. That was the single biggest play of the '07 World Series. Curt Schilling won the game which turned out to be his final game in the major leagues. He certainly lived up to his big-game billing. With a 216–146 career win-loss record, plus going 11–2 in the postseason, and 3,116 strikeouts, Curt will certainly get some consideration for the Hall of Fame.

We flew to Denver up two games to none. Jan joined me there on her first visit to Denver. The Rockies had a very nice party at the convention center. I got to renew acquaintances with Jack Corrigan, radio voice of the Rockies. Jack is a Cleveland native I got to know in Youngstown. When I left Youngstown, Jack was still a student, an All-Ivy wide receiver at Cornell. Jack then got a job offer to go to WFMJ-TV 21 in Youngstown. He called me for advice, and I gave it to him: they're cheap, and you'll be frustrated, but you'll learn; probably worth the sacrifices you will make financially. He did it, and did well. He moved on to Richmond to anchor TV sports. We had hired Jack at our fledgling cable TV network in Cleveland.

Jack replaced me doing games for the Cleveland Indians on TV. After that he went to the Rockies, and he's been there ever since. What are the odds that two broadcasters who worked in Youngstown, Ohio, would both be calling the 2007 World Series on radio?

Jan and I went out to Red Rock, a beautiful setting in the Rocky Mountains about 45 minutes from Denver. This was different from anything she had seen before and we really enjoyed it.

The weather in Denver was great: clear and in the 60s and 70s. Game 3 on Saturday night was a blowout, with Boston scoring six runs in the third inning. One of the big hits was a single to left by Red Sox starting pitcher Daisuke

Matsuzaka. It was his first major league hit and RBI. He pitched into the sixth inning, long enough to get the win. The Red Sox only had a 6–5 lead going into the eighth inning, but they scored three in the eighth and another in the ninth. The final score was 10–5. Papelbon got his second World Series save.

During Game 3, Jan sat in the stands with former Massachusetts governor and 1988 Democratic presidential nominee Michael Dukakis, who was with his grandson and son-in-law. Jan found him to be extremely charming and knowledgeable about baseball. Gov. Dukakis has taught a course at Northeastern, and I would often see him on campus followed by many of his students as though he were the Pied Piper. He also came to our book signing at the Fenway authors' series in '04.

The next day, Sunday, Jan and I went to the Cathedral Basilica of the Immaculate Conception in Denver for an 11:00 AM Mass. On the road I usually went to Mass with Mike Lowell, but his family was in town with him. He went with his father, his brother, and other relatives. We saw him in the cathedral. Up to this point, Mike had had a great series. I looked over at Jan and I said to her, "If Mike hits a home run and a double tonight, he will be the World Series MVP." That's just what happened. He had a big home run and an RBI double. The Red Sox won the game 4–3. Jon Lester got the win.

On September 2, 2006, it was revealed that 22-year-old Jon Lester was suffering anaplastic large cell lymphoma, a form of non-Hodgkin's lymphoma. He had been pitching so brilliantly even with cancer. He had treatments both in Boston and at the Fred Hutchinson Cancer Center in Seattle.

Jon has made a remarkable recovery, highlighted in the '07 season when he was 4–0. Jon beat the Rockies in Game 4, the final game of the World Series.

Papelbon got the save, his third of the Series. Jacoby Ellsbury had a sensational series. Manny was replaced for defensive purposes in late innings, with Jacoby Ellsbury moving from center field to left, and Coco Crisp to center. With one out in the ninth in a one-run game, Jacoby banged into the wall to make a great catch and hung on for the out. Then Papelbon closed out the Series. The batter was Seth Smith, a left-handed hitter. Again, I was hoping for a definitive end, as in '04. My call: "Papelbon sets. The pitch. Swing and a miss. Strike three. And the Red Sox have swept the Colorado Rockies. The Red Sox are the world champions for 2007, and the Boston Red Sox become the first team in the 21st century to win two world championships. Can you believe it?"

After the game, Dave O'Brien, Glen Geffner, Jon Rish, and I did a long wrap-up. Mike Lowell hit .400 (6-for-15) with a home run, three doubles, and four

RBIs in the four-game series. We were so thrilled when Mike was named MVP of the World Series as I had predicted that morning in the Denver cathedral.

After the last out, I tried to go down to the visitors' clubhouse at Coors Field. Even though I had the right pass, I had some trouble with a guard. Luckily, I had scouted this out before the game. I took the roundabout way onto the field and through the dugout to the clubhouse, where I interviewed several of the world champions. I got pretty well doused with champagne, but I was there for the awarding of the World Series trophy by commissioner Bud Selig.

After that I interviewed some more players on the field. I wrapped up the broadcast, as I always do following the final game of the season, by reading from Bart Giamatti's "The Green Fields of the Mind."

Jan and I stayed for the media party afterward. We spent the night at the hotel in Denver, and the next morning we were on the plane to Boston which the Red Sox had chartered for front-office people.

Two days after we returned triumphantly to Boston, the city of Boston gave us another parade on the amphibious Duck boats. But unlike the parade in '04, this time we did not go into the Charles River. We boarded the Duck boats at Fenway. Jan did not ride in the parade with me in '04 and she regretted it. This time, she was there with me, riding the Duck boat through the city of Boston. The response from the fans was tremendous. Many fans held up signs saying "SIGN MIKE LOWELL." As of the end of the '07 season he was a free agent. The Red Sox did sign him. He took a three-year contract, instead of the four-year offer he had from the Phillies. We were very glad about that, because we were so close to Mike. Most of the other signs were for Jacoby Ellsbury, who had become a Red Sox hero and a matinee idol with the "Pink Hats" (female Red Sox fans). After the Duck boat tour ended in Cambridge, we went back to the ballpark for a little more celebration.

We had another tour with the World Series trophy in '07, but not quite as elaborate as it had been in '04, because there was a difference. 2004 was about ending curses, miracles, and great comebacks. In contrast, '07 was simply all about being the best team in baseball!

CHAPTER 8

"Missed Opportunity"
2008

The Red Sox opened the 2008 season against the Oakland A's in Japan. We also played two exhibition games against Japanese teams. Through the courtesy of Mike Dee, then the Red Sox chief operating officer, Jan was invited along on the trip. We left on March 19, 2008—St. Joseph's Day—so we could spend a day or two in Japan to become acclimated to the time difference before playing. The trip started in Ft. Myers. We flew on a big Airbus to Chicago, where we changed planes, then over the North Pole to Tokyo. Jan and I sat in the upper part of the plane. We stayed at the New Otani, a very nice hotel in Tokyo. The rooms were small, but the hotel was huge, with a great buffet of American food if you wanted it, including a Tully's coffee shop which was very popular with our group. The Japanese people were very courteous. Major League Baseball had a wonderful party for us the first night with MLB officials breaking bottles of sake with baseball bats.

We toured the Imperial Gardens and most of the sights. Tokyo was amazing, like another world. There were about five downtowns. We learned the subway system, which is incredibly clean and safe.

We took the subway to see the big Buddha statue in Kamakura. It's more than 36 feet high and weighs 125 tons. This impressive statue, built in the late 1200s, was so big we were able to go inside of it.

I was not crazy about the food. Jan and I ate three times at Sabatini's, an Italian restaurant on the 13th floor of the Ibis Hotel in the Roppongi district. We toured most of the sights.

The Tokyo Dome, where we played our exhibition games and our games against the A's, had plenty of security and our broadcast booth was fine. The fans at the Tokyo Dome were great. Some had fishing poles, dangling magazines and other items for the players to sign. Concession stand foods are served in plastic bags, which fans take to their seats. Jan ordered what she thought was a large lemonade. It turned out to be a huge cup of a lemon-based alcoholic mix. The ushers are dressed in skirts and the vendors are teenaged girls in shorts, knee socks, and baseball caps with the brims bent backward. Fans are very loyal.

On Easter Sunday, we had breakfast at the hotel then went to Mass at St. Ignatius Church. The Mass was celebrated in Japanese.

The Red Sox split the two games with Oakland before crowds of more than 44,000.

In Japan, we connected with my good friend and great Red Sox fan Bill Gould. He is well versed in Japanese baseball and culture. Jan and I enjoyed the abbreviated trip to Japan.

On the way back, rather than fly back directly to Ft. Myers (even though the games with Oakland in Tokyo counted as regular season games, we still had some more spring training to go), we stopped in Los Angeles, where the Red Sox played two exhibition games with the Dodgers. The first game was at Dodger Stadium. The second was played at the Los Angeles Coliseum. The idea was to have the biggest crowd in history during the celebration for the Dodgers' 50th year in Los Angeles. The game was played inside the Coliseum Complex before more than 115,000 fans. It was very hard for me to see the game from a very high press box designed for football. Pop-ups all looked like home runs, and it was tough to see through the screen. Vin Scully, who has broadcast Dodgers games since 1950, was honored that night. He got a tremendous ovation. His first line, after acknowledging the applause, was vintage Scully: "It's only me." That brought down the house.

It was great to broadcast a game from the Coliseum, even though it was difficult.

We stayed in Pasadena. We drove over to see the Rose Bowl. Lots of cultural things to see and do in Pasadena: wonderful gardens, a great bookstore, some fine theaters, and it's pretty close to Dodger Stadium.

Then we went up to Oakland to play the A's before returning home. I recovered pretty quickly from the long trip (about 26 hours in the air in three different time zones), but it does take something out of athletes. I think it took the players a little while to recover from time-zone fatigue and to get back on track.

After winning the world championship in 2007, expectations again were very high for the 2008 season. Once again, the Red Sox got some strong pitching. Jon Lester showed that he had completed his recovery from his cancer treatment. Jon was getting stronger. He won 16 while losing just 6. Daisuke Matsuzaka led the staff with 18 wins and only 3 losses in '08. But the credit should go to manager Terry Francona. He really managed him to that record. Matsuzaka really didn't pitch as well as his numbers indicate, although he had a good ERA of 2.90. Terry handled him extremely well.

And the bullpen did an excellent job relieving Matsuzaka. Jonathan Papelbon had another great year, saving 41 games. Hideki Okajima also had a strong season.

There was controversy involving Manny Ramirez. He had two years left on his contract. The question was whether the Red Sox would pick it up. Manny behaved badly. In effect, he quit on the Red Sox. He had been the MVP in the '04 World Series, and he had lots of big hits, including a walk-off home run against the Angels in the '07 ALDS. He'd been a big contributor and had helped the Red Sox win two world championships. But "Manny being Manny"—including some questionable injuries—led him to leave the ballclub. I'll never forget being in Anaheim shortly after the All-Star break, Manny shouted to me across the clubhouse, in front of many reporters, "Hey Joe, can I buy my way out of my contract?" Obviously, he was looking for attention. I asked him why he'd want to do that. He didn't answer.

The team was getting on our plane to fly to Seattle to play the Mariners. Manny did not want to get on the flight. He wanted to leave the ballclub, but he was talked into going. That pretty much sealed his fate. With his comments and his desire to be traded, his behavior eventually led to a three-way trade involving the Pirates and the Dodgers. Manny Ramirez went to the Dodgers. The Red Sox got Jason Bay who was quite a find. Jason—in many ways the antithesis of Manny—was a wonderful guy, very calm, very low-key. Jason was very much a gentleman. I asked him once what made him so nice, and he told me, "I'm Canadian." He's from Trail, British Columbia. In 49 games he hit .293 and smacked nine homers for the Red Sox.

2008 also saw the emergence of some terrific infielders. Kevin Youkilis had 115 RBIs, 43 doubles, and 29 homers. He hit .312. But the year belonged to Dustin Pedroia. Pedie was the MVP in the AL and won a Gold Glove at second base. He hit .326, had 54 doubles, two triples, stole 20 bases, and hit 17 home runs, and all of that while standing only 5'6". (The Red Sox media guide lists

Pedroia at 5'9" but he's not.) Pedroia had an absolutely sensational season and deserved the MVP. So much for the sophomore jinx!

After Manny left, the Red Sox played very well. Sean Casey was a nice addition to the team. He hit .322 in limited duty with 14 doubles. It was so much fun to have "The Mayor" around. Alex Cora performed very well filling in at short. Alex became a good friend of mine. We used Alex on the pregame show during the postseason for the ALCS. He was an excellent student of the game, and spoke English very well, although Spanish is his first language. Alex Cora will probably be a manager someday.

It was an interesting race because the Yankees fell out of it with injuries and other problems. The Tampa Bay Rays emerged. Manager Joe Maddon is one of my favorite opposing managers ever, and one of the smartest guys in baseball. Joe and I share the Patriot League bond; he went to Lafayette, and I went to Colgate. I always kid him about the football games when Colgate dominated Lafayette most of the time. Joe spent more than 30 years playing and managing in the minors, primarily as a catcher in the Angels' system. Then he became a coach with Mike Scioscia of the Angels, and got the Tampa Bay job. He took a team with a low payroll but a lot of high draft picks and molded them into a championship team. The AL East became a battle between the Red Sox and the Rays down the stretch. There was a big game in September in which the Red Sox looked like they would perhaps establish a big lead. Dan Johnson was a journeyman hitter who had established good power numbers in the minors. He had just been brought up from AAA Durham. He was supposed to start but his plane was late, and he was scratched from the starting lineup. He arrived during the game, pinch-hit in the ninth inning, and hit a game-tying home run off Jonathan Papelbon. (This is the same Dan Johnson who homered for Tampa in the 9th inning on the last day of the 2011 season to tie game against the Yankees, which they went on to win in extra innings to knock the Red Sox out of the playoffs.)

Dioner Navarro doubled later than inning and Tampa Bay had the win. Had the Red Sox won that game they would have been in first place in the AL East.

The next night, Carlos Pena hit a three-run homer in extra innings. Tampa Bay pulled away and won the division, two games ahead of the Red Sox.

In Joe Girardi's first year as the manager, New York had all kinds of problems. For the first time since 1993, the postseason did not include the Yankees. The Red Sox settled for the AL wild-card.

In the ALDS, Boston faced the Anaheim Angels. The Red Sox had beaten the Angels in the memorable 1986 postseason and in the remarkable '04 ALDS.

Jason Bay had a great ALDS against the Angels. He hit .412 with two homers and five RBIs. He hit a big homer to help Jon Lester beat John Lackey in Game 1 in Anaheim.

Bay and J.D. Drew both homered in Game 2 as Boston won again. Back home at Fenway, Boston lost Game 3, a game that used 12 pitchers and lasted a whopping five hours and 19 minutes.

But in Game 4, the Red Sox scored in the bottom of the ninth on an RBI hit by Jed Lowrie to beat the Angels 3–2 and win the ALDS. Once again, with a walk, a single, and a double, Jason Bay was the hitting star.

Boston moved on to the ALCS against the Tampa Bay Rays, who had beaten the White Sox in the other ALDS. Things looked good for the Red Sox. Daisuke Matsuzaka pitched seven innings before giving way to Okajima, Masterson, and finally Jonathan Papelbon. Papelbon got his sixth postseason save in a 2–0 win in Game 1 at Tropicana Field in St. Petersburg.

Game 2 was really pivotal. Josh Beckett was pitching hurt. Boston was up 6–5 and had many opportunities to take a substantial lead, but Tampa Bay pulled ahead in the fifth. Boston eventually tied the game in the eighth inning, but after five and a half hours, the Rays won it 9–8 in the 11th. Evan Longoria and B.J. Upton homered for the Rays. That would set a tone for the rest of the series. Each hit four home runs in the series to really hurt the Red Sox. Dustin Pedroia had two home runs and Kevin Youkilis and Jason Bay also homered in a losing cause.

The series then moved to Boston for Game 3. Matt Garza, who would prove to be a real Red Sox nemesis both during the regular season and during the postseason, pitched six innings and got the win. Jon Lester had a rough outing.

Tampa Bay had 13 hits in the game, including home runs by Upton, Longoria, Rocco Baldelli, and Carlos Peña, as the Rays rolled to a 9–1 victory. The three and a half hour game, while long, was still about two hours shorter than Game 2!

The next day, in Game 4, Tim Wakefield was knocked out in the third inning. Peña and Longoria homered again as Tampa Bay rolled to a 13–4 win. Tampa Bay now led three games to one.

In Game 5, it looked like Tampa Bay would pull ahead and win the series in five games. They actually had a 7–0 lead going into the bottom half of the seventh inning. But the Red Sox scored four runs in the bottom of the seventh, including a three-run homer by David Ortiz. In the eighth, Drew homered in a three-run inning that tied the game at 7.

In the top of the ninth, Justin Masterson gave up just one hit and kept the Rays from scoring. The game went to the bottom of the ninth, still tied at 7. Pedroia grounded out and David Ortiz struck out. Two outs. Then Kevin Youkilis singled and moved to second on an error by Evan Longoria, who had done so much damage to the Red Sox with his bat. After Jason Bay was intentionally walked, J.D. Drew singled and Youkilis scored the winning run. Boston had overcome a seven-run deficit, the largest in League Championship game history. It was also Boston's eighth consecutive win-or-go-home game victory in the ALCS, going back to '04. The 8–7 Red Sox victory kept the series alive. After five games, Tampa Bay was up three games to two.

Then the series went back to Tampa Bay for Game 6. In that game, Josh Beckett pitched again, although he was not 100 percent healthy. He gutted it out through five innings. The Red Sox got home runs from Youkilis and Varitek to beat the Rays 4–2, tying the series at three.

I thought that the Red Sox were in good shape for Game 7.

Jon Lester started against Matt Garza, a fidgety, nervous sort, who was always spitting and twitching. He looked like he was about ready to explode emotionally.

When Dustin Pedroia, the second batter of the game, hit a home run to put the Red Sox ahead 1–0, I thought Garza would implode. I thought Boston would get Garza out of the game in a hurry and run up a big lead. But that's not what happened. He just kept getting better and better. The Rays tied the game in the fourth and went ahead in the fifth when Wily Aybar doubled and scored on a single by Baldelli. Aybar homered in the seventh inning to increase Tampa Bay's lead to 3–1.

The Red Sox had a great opportunity. In the eighth inning, they loaded the bases with two outs. David Price, who had been the Rays No. 1 pick the '07 draft, came out of the bullpen and struck out J.D. Drew to leave the bases loaded. The ninth inning was uneventful and Tampa Bay went on to a 3–1 win.

Not going to the World Series when we were so close really hurt. We thought it would be a Philadelphia-Boston World Series. But it was not meant to be.

I didn't feel as bad as I had in '03 when the Red Sox lost to the Yankees in the ALCS because it wasn't the Yankees this time. I respected Joe Maddon and the Rays, especially Carlos Peña.

In fact, before the game I spoke to Peña behind the batting cage and told him, "If you guys win, we'll be rooting for you in the World Series." He said, "Thank you, sir. I know you really mean that." Carlos went to Northeastern. He's a very gentlemanly guy from a great family. He came over from the Dominican Republic to Haverhill, Massachusetts, at the age of 14. His dad, Felipé, had obtained his engineering degree at the age of 58. Felipé worked at Northeastern. Carlos went there and was the best player they ever had. The baseball coach, Neil McPhee, said that Carlos was also the most charismatic player he'd ever had at Northeastern.

Carlos was drafted in the first round by the Rangers in 1998 and bounced around a little. He was with the Red Sox briefly in '06, which is where I got to know him, before finding a home in Tampa Bay. His younger brother Omar was signed by the Cardinals, and spent eight years in the minors and independent leagues, but never made it to the majors. Another brother, Pedro, has a dual Ph.D.

The Rays went on to lose the World Series in five games to the Philadelphia Phillies.

CHAPTER 9

"Hello, Goodbye"
2009–11

2009

DURING THE WINTER OF 2008 THERE WAS BIDDING BETWEEN THE
YANKEES AND RED SOX FOR THE SERVICES OF SWITCH-HITTING FREE-
AGENT FIRST BASEMAN MARK TEIXEIRA. It was not really a case of Boston
being outbid. He wanted to play for the Yankees, and he said later that his wife
wanted him to play for the Yankees, too. So he signed with New York, as did
pitcher CC Sabathia. After the signings, the Yankees were much more formidable
than they had been in '08 when they failed to make the playoffs.

In '09, the Yankees won the AL East and won the world championship by
beating the Phillies 4–2 in the World Series.

The Red Sox played well but finished the season 95–67. That would have
been good enough to win the division title in four of the six divisions, but in the
AL East, they were eight games behind the Yankees, who ended the '09 season
103–59. Boston won the wild-card.

Then it was on Anaheim for the ALDS against the Angels—a team the Red
Sox had always beaten in the playoffs. In Game 1, Jon Lester (who had won 15
games in the regular season) started against John Lackey. Torii Hunter, a good
friend of mine who reminded me very much of the late Kirby Puckett, who had
been his mentor on the Twins, had a big three-run home run in the fifth inning.
Lackey, who would join the Red Sox in 2010, pitched scoreless ball through seven
innings. The Angels won 5–0.

Josh Becket started Game 2 against Jered Weaver. Anaheim broke a tie with three runs in the seventh and went on to win 4–1. So in the first two games, the Red Sox had scored just one run. Then the series switched back to Fenway Park. In Game 3, Boston had a 5–2 lead after seven innings. But the Angels scored two in the eighth. Then in the bottom of the eighth, the Red Sox scored to make it 6–4 Boston. With two down and nobody on base in the ninth inning, Jonathan Papelbon, who had never given up a run in 26 innings of postseason play, struggled. Erick Aybar started with a hit. Eventually, Bobby Abreu had an RBI double off the left-field wall. Still with two down, Vladimir Guerrero then blooped a two-run single to center, giving the Angels a 7–6 lead. Papelbon was relieved by Okajima but it was too late. The damage had been done. The Red Sox went down 1–2–3 in the bottom of the ninth and the Angels had a 7–6 win and a three-game sweep of the Red Sox. The '09 season was over.

2010

The 2010 season was one of the most disappointing Red Sox seasons in recent years because it started with such high expectations. But I thought the Red Sox had a pretty good excuse for their struggles in '10: injuries. They got off to a tough start (a sub-.500 record in April) and the injuries hit them hard. Josh Beckett hurt his back early and wound up going 6–6. Mike Lowell had hip surgery, but after he came back, he was not the same player, especially in his ability to run.

Things started to look up in June when the Red Sox went to Denver and San Francisco during the interleague period, and even though they lost two games in Colorado, the series ended on a very high note: second baseman Dustin Pedroia hit three home runs in a game on a Thursday night to give the Red Sox a victory. The Red Sox went into San Francisco with high hopes. Who knew that the Giants would be the eventual World Series winner? Of course, it was a full house at AT&T Ballpark. The Red Sox won two and lost only one to the Giants, but for all intents and purposes, the season really was ruined right there. In the Friday night game, Dustin Pedroia fouled a ball off his left foot, something he does quite frequently. We didn't think a whole lot of it, even when he eventually left the game. But the next day, June 25, the night after his three home runs, it was announced that he had broken a bone in his foot.

This was absolutely crushing. Dustin Pedroia is the heart and soul of the Red Sox team. He gets hits when they matter the most. He makes great defensive plays when they matter the most. He's a very smart baserunner. Pedroia is a treasure to watch day in and day out. For all practical purposes, the Red Sox lost Pedroia for the rest of the season. He had a metal pin inserted in his foot, and tried to come back, even fielding ground balls on his knees in practice and playing a couple of games, but he just couldn't do it. He appeared in only 75 games in '10.

In that same series, Clay Buchholz, a right-handed pitcher who bats left, who was having a great year, came to the plate in the Saturday game, and got a base hit to right field. He's an outstanding athlete. Once, in AA ball with the Portland Sea Dogs, he had a race with Jacoby Ellsbury, the fastest runner I've ever seen in a Red Sox uniform. Clay says Ellsbury nosed him at the wire.

Buchholz was running to second base on a ground ball when he strained a hamstring. He went on the disabled list. Another tough break. Buchholz went on to win 17 games, but without the injury, he might have been the AL Cy Young winner, rather than Felix Hernandez of the Seattle Mariners.

Those weren't the only injuries. Victor Martinez had fouled a ball off his toe and had been out the previous few weeks. He left the Sunday game. At the time, I wasn't sure what the problem was. A little while later the media relations department announced it: he'd been hit with a foul tip a few innings before and Martinez had a broken finger. It was hard to believe: three major injuries in one weekend series in San Francisco.

And that pretty much ruined the season. A number of other injuries also contributed: Mike Lowell's hip, Josh Beckett's back, and catcher Jason Varitek later getting hit by a foul tip and breaking a bone in his foot. The Red Sox were pretty much out of the pennant race by September. It was a rather unusual position to be in. This was the first time that the Red Sox had missed the postseason entirely since 2006.

2011

There was a drop in the TV ratings and a little bit in the radio ratings, but in the off-season the Red Sox created the biggest off-season media splash in their history. In one week in December, the Red Sox made a trade for Adrian Gonzalez, the much-coveted first baseman, a power-hitting left-handed batter. He had been the No. 1 pick in the country out of high school by the Florida Marlins in 2000. He was traded to the Texas Rangers and then the San Diego Padres. Gonzalez drove in more than 100 runs in three seasons for the Padres. The Red Sox had tried to get him for a long time, but to finally get him they had to trade three of their best prospects.

Just a few days later, the Red Sox created another big media splash when they signed speedy outfielder Carl Crawford, who had been making the Red Sox's lives miserable with stolen bases and big hits during his nine years with the Tampa Bay Rays. He led the AL in triples and in stolen bases four times each. He hit a three-run walk-off home run to beat the Red Sox on Opening Night '03.

The assumption throughout baseball was that Crawford would sign with the Angels, because Tampa Bay simply could not afford him. But the Red Sox swooped in and made the deal, signing Crawford on December 10, 2010, to a seven-year free-agent contract said to be worth $142 million.

This created a tremendous buzz for the rest of the off-season that lasted until spring training—more anticipation than I've ever seen since '05 and '08, the years after the Red Sox world championships. There was tremendous excitement about this team. But the Red Sox got off to a slow start, going 0–6 and then 2–10 at the beginning of the season.

But over the next four months, from May through August, the Red Sox may have been the best team in baseball. They were back to .500 by mid-May after sweeping a three-game series at Yankee Stadium. And they continued to dominate the Bombers, sweeping another three-game set in the Bronx the first week of June, capped by a win over CC Sabathia in the finale of the series, which started at 10:30 PM after a three-and-a-half-hour rain delay.

The season was marked by long games, late-night travel, and early morning arrivals. Back on May 4, an excruciating 13-inning loss to the Angels at Fenway ended at 2:45 AM. That marathon lasted five hours, not including a two-hour-35-minute rain delay, and was followed by a 1:00 PM game later that day. Then after the All-Star Game came a 16-inning, 1–0 win at Tampa Bay on a Sunday night played in five hours and 44 minutes, which was followed by a flight to Baltimore. Still, the Red Sox spent most of July and August in first place. Heading into September they were 83–52, a season-high 31 games over .500, and even after losing the rubber game of the series to the Yankees on September 1, they still led the AL East by half a game. For most of those four months, and because they won 11 of their first 14 meetings with the Yanks, the Red Sox looked like the superior team and seemed on their way to winning the division title. They would lead the AL in runs scored and several categories, perhaps masking the pitching woes and other shortcomings that were there all season but really came to a head in September. For much of the year, Adrian Gonzalez, Dustin Pedroia, Jacoby Ellsbury, and David Ortiz had MVP qualifications. Ellsbury went on to emerge as the leading candidate, becoming the Red Sox's first 30/30 man: 32 home runs and 39 stolen bases, along with 119 runs scored, 212 hits, a .321 batting average, and Gold Glove–caliber defense. He also provided the most exciting moments with a walk-off home run, an inside-the-park home run, and another key blast late in September.

However, the pitching staff was ninth or 10th in team ERA most of the season and would prove to be the Achilles' heel. Clay Buchholz did not pitch after mid-June because of a stress fracture in his back and was sorely missed. Dice-K Matsuzaka had Tommy John surgery in June, as did Rich Hill, who was the only really effective left-handed reliever the club had all year. The bullpen was inconsistent, except for Daniel Bard, who was outstanding until September, and Jonathan Papelbon, who was totally dominant except for two games against the Orioles the final week. The back end of the starting rotation was inconsistent as well.

After the games of September 3, the Red Sox fell behind the Yankees but still led Tampa by nine and a half games in the wild-card race. Most of us never saw the collapse coming, but in retrospect, the symptoms were there.

Things really started to slide away when the Red Sox lost three of four in Toronto, starting with a 1–0 11-inning loss, followed two nights later by a bullpen implosion in the eighth inning of an 11–10 loss. Then it was on to Tampa Bay where the Sox were swept in a three-game series. Next came the worst homestand of the season with the Red Sox losing seven of 10 to the Jays, Rays, and lowly Orioles. The month of September was marred not only by poor pitching but a suddenly leaky defense and bad base running. It all seemed to be coming unglued. The Red Sox never did post consecutive wins after August 27. And after losing two straight in New York to the AL East champs, who had already clinched the division title, the Red Sox lead was down to half a game over the Rays. Then, in a makeup game on Sunday night September 25, the Red Sox got another key hit from Ellsbury in the 14th inning, a three-run game-winning home run in the Bronx that made it a one-game lead with three to play. It seemed like that home run may have wrapped up both the MVP for Ellsbury and the wild-card for the Red Sox. But the Red Sox couldn't sustain it. When they lost in Baltimore the next night, the Rays beat the Yanks to tie for the wild-card lead. Boston needed eight runs to win the next night, 8–7, to stay tied with the Rays going into the final game.

The Red Sox had a 3–2 lead in the finale behind Jon Lester over the Orioles, a team that had lost 93 games, when the rains came in the middle of the seventh inning. It looked certain there would be a tomorrow when the Rays fell behind the Yankees 7–0. We were watching the Rays game during the rain delay as it moved along and then I remember getting a sinking feeling when the Rays put a rally together in the bottom of the eighth, scoring six times. Somehow I had a premonition that if the Rays caught up and moved ahead, so might the Orioles, as illogical as that sounds.

With two out in the ninth and the bases empty, Joe Maddon sent up Dan Johnson to pinch-hit—the same Dan Johnson who had pinch-hit that home run in September 2008 against Papelbon to knock the Red Sox from the division lead. And Johnson did it again, going deep on a 2–2 pitch to tie it. Then our game resumed after a rain delay of one hour and 26 minutes and the Red Sox wasted two scoring chances to break the game open with a baserunning blunder in the eighth and a first and third nobody out squander in the ninth. The Rays game moved into extra innings and the Red Sox were one out away from insuring at least a play-in game when Papelbon struck out the first two hitters in the ninth. Then came doubles by Chris Davis and Nolan Reimold to tie it, and a line drive to left by Red Sox nemesis Robert Andino that Carl Crawford failed to catch with a sliding effort that drove home the season-ending run. My call: "The Red Sox season hangs in the balance of the Tampa Bay Rays and Yankees." We broke for commercial and exactly three and a half minutes after the Red Sox game ended, Jon Rish reported on our postgame show that Evan Longoria had hit a walk-off home run to make the Rays the wild-card winners, ending the Red Sox season.

As I have done for 30 years, I closed the broadcast of the final Red Sox game of the season by reading a passage from "The Green Fields of the Mind." Giamatti's words had more meaning in '11 than in most previous seasons. It was never more appropriate.

It was stunning. It was painful. The Red Sox had gone 7–20 in September and lost a nine-and-a-half-game lead—an epic collapse. The charter flight home was exceptionally quiet. After landing I remember walking through the airport terminal with Terry Francona and DeMarlo Hale feeling and sharing their pain.

Less than 40 hours later, Terry Francona's eight-year tenure—which included two world championships, four postseason appearances, and the second-best winning percentage of any Red Sox manager—came to an end. Tito will be remembered for his grace under fire, his selflessness, and his character, as well as for the championships he helped Red Sox Nation achieve. I will always appreciate the cooperation and consideration he showed for those of us who worked with him every day.

It was a brutal ending to a season, certainly the toughest since the Aaron Boone walk-off in '03, but thankfully Red Sox Nation can take consolation in those world championships of '04 and '07, which in the long run may ease some of the pain.

A few weeks after Francona's departure, Theo Epstein, who grew up in the shadows of Fenway and then presided over two world championship teams in his nine years as Red Sox General Manager, moved on to the Cubs.

His assistant, New Hampshire–native Ben Cherington, who had already proven himself very capable in his previous scouting and development duties, was quickly named general manager. Then, after a long search, Bobby Valentine, a brilliant baseball mind and an engaging and sometimes true personality, was named the 45th manager of the Boston Red Sox. Bobby, who was doing a terrific job as an insightful and sometimes provocative ESPN analyst, will bring a certain cachet to the manager's office. I have liked and respected Bobby V. for many years. To me, he's the greatest athlete my native state of Connecticut has ever produced. A legendary high school baseball player and a spectacular running back who scored 34 touchdowns in one season at Rippowam High School in Stamford, Bobby could have gone to USC and been part of their great tradition of tailbacks, but signed with the Dodgers instead. A broken leg curtailed what could have been a terrific playing career, but it didn't stop him from becoming one of the dominant personalities in the game on both sides of the Pacific. He is revered in Japan, where he managed for several seasons. In '05, he managed the Chiba Lotte Marines to their first Japan Series title in 30 years.

Despite the epic collapse that ended the '11 season, the Red Sox return a good nucleus of players for '12. They have strong leadership, starting with president and CEO Larry Lucchino, whose track record in sports includes a Final 4 appearance with Princeton as a player on Bill Bradley's great teams; a Super Bowl ring from his days as an executive with the Washington Redskins; and three world championships rings, one with the 1983 Baltimore Orioles, and of course two with the Red Sox. And when you add in his vision for ballparks, creating the concept of the retro parks as he did with Camden Yards in Baltimore, building beautiful Petco Park in San Diego to fit the culture of that area, and rebuilding Fenway Park, Lucchino has established strong Hall of Fame credentials.

CHAPTER 10

"Midnight Confessions"
Me and the Yankees

I USED TO BE A YANKEES FAN. Now I root against them. It's often been said that the only thing that makes a Red Sox fan happier than a Red Sox victory is a Yankee defeat. Naturally, we root against the Yankees because they are our archrivals and we are usually very close to each other in the standings. At least that's the way it's been during most of my Red Sox career. There were times, such as in the late '80s to the mid-'90s, when the Yankees weren't very good. And there were times when the Red Sox struggled—also in the early '90s. But for the most part they compete for division supremacy.

For 100 years, the Yankees always won the most important game, the game that decided the pennant. In 1904, the Red Sox beat the Yankees and won the pennant, beating Jack Chesbro, who'd won 41 games for the New York Highlanders, the predecessors of the Yankees. How did they win? Chesbro threw a wild pitch. That was the year in which New York Giants manager John McGraw refused to play a "World Series" against the upstart AL.

Since then, particularly after selling Babe Ruth to the Yankees in 1920, the Red Sox could not get by the Yankees. In 1949, they had a one-game lead, but they lost their last two games to the Yankees. They lost the AL East pennant in 1978 on the Bucky Dent home run that gave Dent a new middle name, at least in New England. They lost to the Bombers in the 1999 ALCS. In 2003, they lost the ALCS on Aaron Boone's 11th-inning walk-off home run.

Finally, in '04, for the first time in 100 years, the Red Sox came from three games down to beat the Yankees 10–3 when it mattered most: in a deciding Game 7 of the ALCS.

I was conflicted because I grew up a Yankees fan. I grew up a Mel Allen fan and a Mickey Mantle fan. My home near New Haven, Connecticut, was closer to New York (75 miles) than to Boston (150 miles). I was a Yankees fan because my family members were Yankees fans. My *nonno*—my grandfather—came over from Sicily and didn't know much about baseball. But he did know that Joe DiMaggio came from a Sicilian fishing family, so he was his hero. And DiMaggio played for the Yankees. My dad followed suit. He was a Yankees fan. He went to New York Medical School, then Flower Fifth Avenue Hospital.

When I was growing up in the New Haven area, we had Yankees fans, Brooklyn Dodgers fans, some New York Giants fans, and later Mets fans. But I did not know a single Red Sox fan. This was in the mid- to late '50s and early '60s, when the Red Sox were terrible. There weren't many Red Sox fans at all in southern Connecticut. Now a Quinnipiac University poll shows that fans in Connecticut are divided almost 50–50 between Yankees fans and Red Sox fans. Female Red Sox fans outnumber female Yankees fans.

As a kid, there was no greater Yankees fan than me. I lived for the games. I wished that the games started earlier than the 8:30 starts they had so I could stay up to watch the end of the games. My dad used to let me stay up a little later if Mickey Mantle was coming to the plate because I wanted to see him hit one 500 feet. He was my hero—at least until I met him. I still have good feelings about Mantle.

Mel Allen, the "Voice of the Yankees" was my hero on the air. I listened to him constantly. Mel is the reason I became a broadcaster. Mel was the model. He had the gift of gab plus a great set of pipes. Mel was also a great storyteller. His Alabama twang helped make him very easy to listen to. Allen brought the game to life, both on radio and on television. I used to imitate Allen. What he would do with Ballantine Beer—pouring a bottle into a tall glass right on the air, then making the "three ring sign and asking the man for Ballantine. You'll be so glad you did"—I would do it with a bottle of Pepsi. Mel also called Yankee home runs "White Owl wallops."

Yes, Mickey and Mel were my heroes, but I loved all the Yankees. The first major league ballgame I ever went to was at Yankee Stadium on Jerry Coleman Day in September 1953. Jerry was a hero. So was Gil McDougald.

I went to two or three games a season, and I remained a Yankees fan. Once, I went with my little league team. Occasionally, my dad took me. I also went with friends on the train. Annie and Tony Iacobacci, my cousins, who were great Yankee fans, took me. In fact, they met talking about the Yankees when Tony was the cashier at the Villanova Restaurant on 46th Street in Manhattan. They spoke one day about Joe DiMaggio and fell in love. My brother Frank and I would take the train to 125th Street in Manhattan, where Annie and Tony would meet us and take us to the game. Frequently, we went to the first game of a double-header—which were quite common in those days—and after the first game they'd take us out to dinner. I would have preferred to stay for the second game.

I was a Yankee fan until the mid-'60s when I went to college. Perhaps I was a "fair-weather" fan. The Yankees of those days—what came to be known as the "Horace Clarke era"—were terrible. After losing the last game of the '64 World Series, the Yankees faded into mediocrity, finishing under .500. In '66, they finished last, half a game behind the ninth-place Red Sox.

When I went to Youngstown, Ohio, to work, I became a Pirates fan because I covered the great Pirates teams of the early '70s. But this Yankee thing always existed. My goal, frankly, was to be the voice of the Yankees. I think I would have given up that dream at a younger age to broadcast for the Pirates, who were so good at the time. I also had so much fun covering them when I was with a TV station in Youngstown.

I was a Cleveland Indians fan when I broadcast their games. When I broadcast for Milwaukee I became a Brewers fan. By this time, in '81, I had gotten away from the Yankees. Then, in '83, I came to Boston to broadcast Red Sox games. By then it was very easy to root against the Yankees. As a member of Red Sox Nation I hoped that the Yankees lost every game.

But I have so many connections with the Yankees. I tell the stories elsewhere of how good Phil Rizzuto and Bill White, his broadcast partner, were to me.

It was always a thrill to go to Yankee Stadium. I'll never forget the first time I went there as a broadcaster. I was with the Cleveland Indians in '79. We broadcast a Friday night game on June 22, and the Indians were in the middle of a 10-game losing streak. Cleveland was losing 3–0 in the ninth inning. They scored two runs and loaded the bases with one out, before hitting into a double play and losing 3–2.

The fact that I root against the Yankees and for anybody who beats the Yankees doesn't mean that I don't have a lot of respect for them. Certainly I respect Derek

Jeter, a truly great player and a class individual. Jeter is now a member of the 3,000 hit club, and has the most hits in Yankee history. Joe Torre was very kind to my son Duke when he covered the Yankees first for NY1, then WCBSTV Channel 2, and now for Fox. I had a lot of respect for Torre, who used to work with my old partner, Bob Starr, with the Angels. Torre and the Yankees PR people have always been great to work with, especially former media relations director, Rick Cerrone. The current media relations director, Jason Zillo, grew up on Coronada Avenue in Youngstown, the same street as Jan. Their families knew each other.

New York is still one of my favorite stops as the Red Sox travel around the country. It's always a great thrill to go to Yankee Stadium. But I continue to root against them. I rooted against their late owner George Steinbrenner. He had the perception of being a bully, but he was nice to my son Duke. Steinbrenner was also very giving to the Jimmy Fund. I spoke with him shortly after Ken Coleman died, and he made a generous contribution to the Fund in Ken's name.

Of course, my other connection to the Yankees is my son Duke, who covers the Yankees now for Fox Sports, New York's channel 5. When the Yankees won the World Series in 2000, Duke was able to host the victory parade on NY1. When the Yankee games are broadcast on WOR-TV, channel 9, Duke hosts the postgame show. Duke has his own Yankee connections.

Another Yankees connection for me: Yankees radio broadcaster Suzyn Waldman grew up as a Red Sox fan in Boston. I grew up as a Yankees fan in Connecticut.

Mickey Mantle

The Red Sox opened the 1999 season in Kansas City. We were off the next day, so I did something I had always wanted to do. I rented a car and drove to Commerce, Oklahoma, to see Mickey Mantle's home. He had always been my favorite player. Mantle was born in Spavinaw, but grew up in Commerce.

Except to change planes, I had never before been to Oklahoma. On the way, I went to Baxter Springs, Kansas, where young Mantle played for the Whiz Kids. I also visited Joplin, Missouri, where Mickey played his minor league ball. The ballpark in Joplin is only 45 minutes down Route 66 from Commerce. Some of the highway has been renamed Mickey Mantle Boulevard.

There's a small home in Commerce where Mickey grew up. Although it was under renovation the day I visited, there was some Mantle memorabilia on display.

I saw the high school ballfield where Mickey played (now known as Mickey Mantle Field). I also saw the softball field named for Mickey's father, "Mutt" Mantle.

Mel Allen

When I think of broadcasting, I think of the reason I got into broadcasting and my hero when I was a kid, Mel Allen, the Voice of the New York Yankees. I hate to say it now, but watching the Yankees and rooting for the Yankees, Mickey Mantle and Mel Allen were 1 and 1A, and I'm not sure which was on top. Mel made the game so exciting with his booming voice, his Alabama drawl, his gift of gab. "How about that?" "That ball is going, GOING, GONE!," "A Ballantine blast!" "A White Owl wallop!" "I have to wait until after the game to have my Ballantine." (Ballantine beer and White Owl cigars sponsored the broadcasts.)

Mel was a great broadcaster. After 25 years behind the mikes for the Yankees (1939–1964, broadcasting on radio and TV in some years), the team fired him after the '64 season without explanation. To this day, although there is widespread speculation, nobody knows the real reason.

Mel's resume as a broadcaster includes: 24 All-Star Games, five Orange Bowls, two Sugar Bowls, 14 Rose Bowls, and 20 World Series.

In '68, Mel went to Cleveland to do games for the Indians. He also did Milwaukee Braves games the year before the Braves moved to Atlanta. In '69 he returned to Yankee Stadium for Mickey Mantle Day. He did Yankees games on cable in later years.

Starting in 1977 and through his death in 1996, Mel enjoyed a second career as the voice of the syndicated *This Week in Baseball,* which is still on the air.

This show introduced his great voice, his love, and his command of the game to new generations of baseball fans too young to remember him as the Voice of the Yankees, or, as he was sometimes called, just "The Voice."

I met Allen a number of times. I remember July 4, 1983, in my first season with the Red Sox, Dave Righetti pitched a no-hitter for the Yankees against the Red Sox. Mel broadcast that game on TV. It was the first no-hitter at Yankee Stadium since Don Larsen's perfect game in the 1956 World Series.

I got to know Mel and did an interview with him. When I found out that he was undergoing open-heart surgery I wrote him a long letter to tell him how much he had meant to me as a broadcaster and as a role model. He didn't respond, but when he recovered I saw him at Yankee Stadium, and he said, "I owe you a letter." He was very complimentary about my work, which gave me a tremendous feeling. To hear that from the man I consider the greatest baseball broadcaster ever meant a great deal to me. When the Hall of Fame instituted the Ford C. Frick Award for excellence in baseball broadcasting in '78, the first two given the award were Red Barber and Mel Allen.

Gene Michael

Gene "Stick" Michael, a good friend of mine, has done just about everything for the Yankees. He was their shortstop, manager, general manager, super scout, and director of scouting. Gene's also a good friend of my son Duke. Gene has been a great source of information for me. We often speak by phone and of course when the Red Sox play their archrival Yankees. Because we play against the Yankees so often, I get to see Stick quite a lot. I love to hear about his exploits on the basketball court when he was a high school star in Akron and then at Kent State. In fact, the baseball field at Kent State was named for Stick. But when they built a new field, a donor gave more money, so the new field was named for him.

As the Yankees general manager (1990–95) he signed and developed Derek Jeter, Bernie Williams, Jorge Posada, Andy Pettitte, and Mariano Rivera. He also refused to trade them.

Bobby Murcer

Bobby came up to the Yankees in 1965, heralded as the "next" Mickey Mantle because, like Mickey, he was from Oklahoma. He was switched from shortstop to centerfield. Bobby was one of the most wonderful people I ever met. He never had a negative word to say about anybody. He did, however, have negative things to say about Candlestick Park, where he played for the Giants in 1975 and '76. The Yankees broke his heart when they traded him after the '74 season.

Bobby returned to the Yankees in '79, and was there until he retired in mid-1983.

Bobby was a former player who really did his homework as a broadcaster for the Yankees. He lasted a long time in the Yankees' broadcast booth.

When he was a broadcaster, Bobby used to call me before a Yankees–Red Sox series to get updates on some of the new players whom he hadn't seen. I relied on Bobby for information about new Yankees, and for updates on the team dynamics.

He was a real inspiration. Bobby was very active in Baseball Chapel, and showed his great faith during his final battle with brain cancer.

He appeared with me on the radio during a Jimmy Fund Radio/Telethon. After his death in 2008, his widow, Kay, and son, Todd, both appeared on the Radio/Telethon and still do to this day.

Bobby Murcer was chairman of B.A.T. (the Baseball Assistance Team) and was very concerned about the plight of members of the baseball family who were down on their luck.

I got to know Bobby socially at Pino's, a restaurant on East 34th Street in New York owned by former Red Sox, Angels, and Tigers pitcher Jerry Casale. Every time we played a day game in New York against the Yankees, we'd go to Pino's. Bobby and Kay stayed in a hotel in that neighborhood during the season but lived in Oklahoma City the rest of the year.

I still love to visit with old Yankees from my childhood, like Jerry Coleman. It's always a thrill to see Moose Skowron when we visit U.S. Cellular Field in Chicago where Moose works for the White Sox. I get him to tell stories about Mantle and others and the long home runs he hit over the 457-foot mark in left-center field at the old Yankee Stadium before it was remodeled.

Another favorite from that era is Tony Kubek. In later years, when Tony broadcast for the Yankees, we would take the subway to mid-town Manhattan together after games, always exchanging scouting reports. I always loved Tony's enthusiasm and called him when he was honored with the Ford Frick Award in '09. It was most deserved.

Chapter 11

"With a Little Help From My Friends"
Partners and Engineers

Ken Coleman

KEN WAS MY FIRST BROADCAST PARTNER WITH THE RED SOX. He was also my mentor and my friend. Ken was instrumental in my being hired for this job, which has turned into a 30-year career. We worked together for seven terrific years. I looked forward to coming to the ballpark every day to see Ken, to talk with Ken, and to work with Ken. Stories about Ken Coleman are throughout this book.

Fred MacLeod

My first Indians partner was Fred MacLeod. Fred and I were hired to do Indians broadcast in 1979.

Fred worked at TV8 as the weekend news anchor. Fred worked all the time. Fred was hired to be the No. 1 broadcaster for Indians games, and I was the No. 2 guy in '79. Fred was only 26. I was 32. He was very innovative. He used a pitch counter. This is a hand-held device frequently used to count laps. Fred had pitched at Point Park University, a small school in Pittsburgh, which also produced John Stuper, a hero for the Cardinals of the 1982 World Series who is now the baseball coach at Yale. Fred was 13–0 in college as a relief pitcher. He was from Pittsburgh and always wanted to get into broadcasting. He moved to Cleveland where he became a sports anchor on a local TV station. Then we landed the job broadcasting Indians games.

We didn't have a very good team (81–80) in '79, but Fred and I had a lot of fun together.

We only did 40 Indians games. At the time, we were on WJKW-TV, a CBS affiliate owned by Storer Broadcasting. They did not want to preempt the regular CBS programing for a bad Indians team. Fred continued to anchor weekend sports and report sports for the TV station. At the end of the season, we lost the contract, so Fred and I stayed at the station to report on sports.

Fred eventually left for a TV anchor job in San Francisco and then to do games for the Detroit Pistons. Fred stayed in Detroit for many years, including the Pistons' NBA championships.

Fred returned to do the Cleveland Cavaliers games during the LeBron James era. Fred was (and is) a very hard worker. He was also a good partner.

Tom Collins

In Milwaukee I worked with a wonderful broadcaster named Tom Collins, from Neenah, Wisconsin. His father had been a minor league ballplayer. Tom was a red-headed Irishman with a wonderful personality and a great voice. He had done basketball games for Marquette University when they won the NCAA championship with Al McGuire.

Tom did Milwaukee Braves baseball in the mid-'60s, just before they left Milwaukee for Atlanta. And he was a morning DJ on WEMP in Milwaukee. In fact, he was the city's top on-air personality. Somehow, he did the morning show, then went to the ballpark to broadcast the Braves' games. He traveled with the Braves, too.

Tom was with the Braves in '64 and '65, their lame-duck years, because they had already announced that they were moving the franchise for a second time after the first move from Boston to Milwaukee in 1953. They were going to the growing city of Atlanta in '66. The courts made the Braves stay in Milwaukee for the '65 season.

Tom did not want to leave Milwaukee. He had lived there for years, so he became the media director for Schlitz Brewing Company. In that position, he bought the advertising rights for the Brewers, the Kansas City Royals, and other teams in the Midwest.

After '69—their only season in the majors—the Seattle Pilots went to spring training in 1970 not knowing what was going to happen to them, whether they would play in '70, and if so, where. They were virtually bankrupt. Allan "Bud" Selig, who owned an auto dealership in Milwaukee, put together a group to purchase the Pilots and move the franchise to Milwaukee, which had been without Major League Baseball since the Braves left. In the interim, the Chicago White Sox played a handful of games there.

At the end of spring training, the driver of the Pilots' equipment truck was told to call when he got to Denver. He would be advised whether to turn left for Seattle or right to Milwaukee. He turned right, as the franchise was awarded to Milwaukee.

After each game we televised in Milwaukee, Tom and I and the whole staff would go out to one of the local pubs. SelecTV, our employer, had a corporate condo for me to stay at, but after our nights on the town, I would usually wind up on the couch at Tom's house on the south side of Milwaukee. Tom knew Milwaukee so well and went out of his way to help me get accepted. We had an excellent team to broadcast.

After I left, Tom continued to do the cable games and returned to Cleveland for a few years and also returned to his disc jockey roots. He remains a great friend.

I used to go back to Milwaukee each year when the Brewers were in the AL. When I did, I got together with Tom and Bill Haig, the Brewers' director of broadcasting, who had recommended me for the job in Milwaukee, and later for the Red Sox job.

In 1998, the Brewers switched to become the 16th team in the NL, leaving the AL with 14.

Bob Starr

When Ken Coleman retired after the 1989 season, a new station took over Red Sox broadcasts. Atlantic Ventures, later known as American Radio, WRKO. They were looking for a heavyweight broadcaster to succeed Ken as the Red Sox lead broadcaster. Steve Dodge, the station owner, asked me whom I recommended. I told him that, after seven years with the Red Sox, *I'd* like to be the lead broadcaster. But I knew that wasn't going to happen, at least not then.

I'll never forget a story that Joe Angel—who broadcast for many teams, including the Orioles, where he now works—told me. Joe had just been interviewed for the Red Sox job and as he got off the elevator in the lobby of the station's office building, Bob Starr was going up for his interview. Joe said he knew it was over when he saw Burly Bob.

They interviewed a number of people, including Bob, the self-proclaimed "Burly Broadcaster." Bob sometimes referred to himself in the third person as "his burliness." Bob was about 5'9" and built like a left guard. Bob had tremendous pipes, a huge booming voice with a commanding presence. He was born in Kansas City but grew up in tiny Oklahoma towns like Sapulpa, where his father, Harry, was a pipe-fitter in the oil business. He was a good baseball player in high school and was good enough at football to be recruited by Kansas University.

Bob was always an individualist. During one practice, the football coach told him to go catch the extra points which the placekicker was practicing. Said Bob, "I don't catch extra points; I kick them!" He was also a long-snapper on punts.

That pretty much ended his career at Kansas. He later went to Coffeyville Junior College, also in Kansas, where he played football. Football was something he shared with my son Tom (now Thomas Castiglione, M.D.) For some reason, Tom was in awe of Bob. I think it was Bob's voice more than anything. Bob said that Tom was like a sponge around him. But Tom was also the center on the Marshfield High School football team and Bob, having been a center, wanted to work with Tom on his long snapping. Tom, who occasionally worked as a vendor at Fenway Park, used to drive in to work with me. He'd bring his football up to the broadcast booth, which was adjacent to a long hallway. Bob said, "Time to work on your long snapping now," imitating the high-pitched voice of one of his old coaches. Tom snapped and Bob coached.

My older son Duke also had a great respect for Bob because of the authority he exuded, primarily because of his voice. My daughter, Kate, used to work as Bob's pitch counter in the booth. When she was about 12 she had some painful dental surgery after which Bob sent her flowers. That was the first time anybody ever sent her flowers, and she never forgot it. My wife Jan was also very fond of Bob. Why? Because he had an expression, "That's why we have other people." And she no longer had to wait for me to do a job around the house: she could hire qualified people and get the job done right.

He used this expression often. I would tell him my grass was so high after a two-week road trip. It had rained during the entire homestand, the boys were away at school, and Jan was teaching full-time. Jan was embarrassed because the grass was so high. And Bob would say, "That's why we have other people." So Jan hired a lawn service, much to my chagrin, because cutting the grass was something even I could do.

But the first time I drove down our driveway and saw that the grass was cut, and the yard was edged, I had to admit that I was relieved and thankful for "other people."

Jan was after me to get a car service for trips home from the airport after all-night flights. She could no longer take me to and from the ballpark or airport, and she thought a driver would be safer. I finally agreed, and could hear Bob in my headset saying, "other people," and Jan insisting that it was necessary.

"Other people" have made a difference in our lives and helped me continue broadcasting and traveling for lo these many years.

After his discharge from the army, where he'd played some baseball, Bob told his father that he was considering a career in broadcasting. Said Harry, "Well, you can talk, can't you? There can't be much more to it than that!"

That's pretty much the way Bob looked at his job. He got a job doing sports at a station in Peoria, Illinois, which spawned a lot of great broadcasters, including Jack Brickhouse; the Hall of Fame broadcaster for the Cubs; Jack Quinlan, also a Cubs broadcaster, and many more.

Then he went to Boston to broadcast games for the then–Boston Patriots (1966–1970, the team was renamed the New England Patriots in '71). He was also the sports anchor for Channel 4 in Boston. Gil Santos was his color man then, and is still the voice of the Patriots. Bob was very good, and had an excellent reputation.

Bob, a very principled man, had some disagreements with management, and he left after the '70 season. He went to San Francisco to anchor TV sports for one year and then he went to St. Louis, where he did Cardinals baseball and Cardinals football. Bob did the baseball Cardinals games from '72 to '79, working with Jack Buck and Mike Shannon.

In addition, Bob broadcast football and basketball games for the University of Missouri, and did morning sports for KMOX, the great flagship station of the Midwest. He was constantly working. Bob loved working with Jack Buck, who left one year to do NBC's *Grandstand*. Bob said he knew Jack would be back, and he was right.

Bob was a great football announcer. I heard Jack Buck and many other knowledgeable people say that Bob was the best radio football announcer ever. I've heard a lot of people say that about Ken Coleman regarding TV football. Ken did Cleveland Browns TV for 15 years and Ohio State and Harvard football on radio.

Bob didn't have a spotter, charts, or spotting boards. All he had was a numerical roster. He knew all the names and numbers and was never faked out. He could make you visualize where the ball was at all times. He had incredible visual skills. Of course, I knew him as a baseball announcer where I thought he was terrific.

Bob and I had three wonderful years together between 1990 and '92. He liked to mimic me because I took it so personally when things went against the Red Sox. I'll never forget one game against the White Sox at old Comiskey Park in Chicago. In the ninth inning, with two outs, Jody Reed hit a hot shot up the middle that would have tied the game. The pitcher, Bobby Thigpen (who once held the record for most saves in a season with 57), reached up and caught the ball. Game over. Red Sox lose. On the air, Bob said that even though it was a tough loss, he could not help laughing. He looked over at me and said on the air that I looked like I'd been harpooned. All the life taken out of me as a result of this loss.

I learned a lot from Bob: how to laugh at myself, how not to take the game of baseball, myself, or my own job too seriously. I learned how to relax during a game. Bob had a great saying, "It's not my life and it's not my wife." I like the statement, but I cannot put it into practice in my own life because I still take Red Sox wins and losses too much to heart. People frequently tell me that they can tell whether the Red Sox are winning or losing just by the sound of my voice. I take that as a compliment. Of course, it would be a criticism if I were doing a national network broadcast.

Bob was a wonderful guy to work with. He had a four-year deal with WRKO. The station manager wanted to save money. At the time, the Red Sox charged those of us who traveled with the team—beat reporters and broadcasters—for a first-class ticket for each road trip on the Red Sox charter. (Today, we are not charged separately. Our travel expenses are covered by the rights fee paid by the station to the team.) This station manager thought he could save a significant amount of money if the team broadcasters traveled on their own and paid only "Supersaver" coach rates. When the last game of a typical three-game series was a night game, after the game the team went from the ballpark right to the airport to get on its charter flight to the next city. Broadcasters couldn't do that for a simple reason: there were no commercial flights that late. So we'd stay over at a hotel (more expense) and fly the next day. One Sunday, we finished a night game in Texas and were going on to our next game in Detroit. We had a 10:00 AM flight the next day, but that flight was canceled and there was no other flight until midafternoon. We were very lucky to get on that flight, which got us into Detroit at about 5:30, barely in time for a 7:05 PM game. It was very hairy. Bob was very upset. He thought that the radio station's cheapness was interfering with our ability to do our jobs professionally.

I knew it was over for Bob during the last series of the season in '92. We were taking a 7:00 AM flight from Boston to Detroit. There's the Burly Broadcaster, all 200-plus pounds of him, scrunched into the middle seat on the last row of the plane, looking absolutely miserable. He looked like *he* had been harpooned. The station had actually violated his contract, which called either for first-class travel or travel with the club.

Bob had been talking to the Anaheim Angels and the NFL Rams in Los Angeles. He went back to L.A. and broadcast both for a few years. The Angels were in a tough market, trying to compete with the institution of the Dodgers, who had Vin Scully, the voice of the team since 1950, when they were still in Brooklyn. Bob didn't think he had to try to mimic Scully. He was his own man. And he was good at it in Anaheim.

Once Bob left, the radio station and I had a little battle: I thought I had earned the position of No. 1 broadcaster and I merited a raise. I had been with the Red Sox for seven years. But I had a contract, and that was that.

Then, while struggling with his health, Bob came back to Fenway with the Angels to broadcast, but was too ill to go on the air. His health continued to deteriorate and he could no longer go on. Jan and I went to visit Bob after a day game at Angel Stadium (which was then known as Edison Field) at his home in Orange, California, in August '98, where he was getting oxygen. We had a wonderful visit. Bob was in great spirits, and we exchanged some stories about our terrific three years together and all the fun we'd had. Bob said that he was hoping for a lung transplant. As we were leaving, Bob's wife, Brenda, told us that because of his deteriorating condition, he was not going to get a lung transplant. Jan and I realized that we had probably seen Bob for the last time. Just two days later in Seattle, I got a call from Mike Port, then the Red Sox assistant general manager, informing me that Bob had passed away. He was only 65. It was a very sad time for my entire family because Bob had meant so much to all of us.

Jerry Trupiano

I didn't have much of a say in the decision to pick Bob's successor. Most broadcasters don't. Luke Griffin, a very nice guy who was our producer, would make the decision. But he asked for my opinion. We listened to a number of audition tapes, but the one we kept coming back to was from Jerry Trupiano. Like Bob Starr, Trupiano had a lot of St. Louis in his background. He grew up in St. Louis as a Cardinals fan. Ken Boyer was his favorite player. Jerry used to see the Cardinals play at Sportsman's Park. He worked in his dad's grocery store, then went to St. Louis University. Jerry loved all sports. He became a producer at KMOX, the St. Louis radio station, working all kinds of hours. The station really liked him, and Jack Buck, the Hall of Fame Cardinals broadcaster, took Jerry under his wing. He became a protégé of Jack's. Trupiano then left St. Louis to broadcast hockey games in Houston for the Aeros in the new World Hockey Association (1973–78). Led by Gordie Howe and his sons Mark and Marty, the Aeros won the league championship in '74. The league went out of business but Trup wore his '74 Houston Aeros Championship ring for many years thereafter.

While in Houston, Jerry was the play-by-play broadcaster for the Houston Oilers in the NFL for several years, then moved to baseball to broadcast Houston Astros games (1985–86) with Milo Hamilton. He didn't get to do as much play-by-play as he wanted to, so he left. Shortly thereafter he broadcast games for the Montreal Expos with Dave Van Horne, now the voice of the Marlins and the 2011 winner of the Ford C. Frick Award for broadcasting from the Baseball Hall of Fame.

Troup had a good experience in Montreal from '89 to '90, but he left to return to Houston, where he did a radio talk show for many years to be closer to his family.

As we listened to the numerous audition tapes, we kept coming back to Trup's. We liked not only his knowledge of the game and his voice, but also his easy-going sense of humor. We thought it he would fit in nicely with the Red Sox and with me. So he was hired.

Working with Trup on Red Sox radio broadcasts was a new experience for me; my first time working with a contemporary. Ken Coleman and Bob Starr were both a generation older than me. I'm only seven months older than Troup.

We shared many of the same interests, rock 'n' roll and baseball, particularly. We had a lot of fun during the 14 seasons we worked together. Trup and I called the memorable and historic 2004 season when the Red Sox won the World

Series for the first time since 1918. His signature home run call ("Way back, waaay back!") became a catchphrase throughout New England. Fans loved him for it.

Jerry's family and my family are very close. His wife, Donna, and his sons Michael, a tennis instructor, and Brian, a very good baseball player for Eastern Connecticut and Rhode Island College, gets along very well with my family. Trup was very proud of Brian's achievements on the baseball diamond.

Jerry and I were honored to be inducted together into the New England Chapter of the National Italian–American Sports Hall of Fame in '03. At the time, we were the only all-Italian broadcast team in baseball.

Jerry's contract was not picked up after the '06 season. I was sorry to lose him after 14 wonderful years.

Glenn Geffner

In 2007, Glenn Geffner and Dave O'Brien were brought in do the broadcasts. They both worked with me, but never at the same time. Geffner, a good friend and a nice gentleman, grew up in Miami, then went to Northwestern University. He worked as a radio broadcaster for the Rochester Red Wings of the AAA International League. Then he was the media relations director and radio broadcaster for the San Diego Padres, working with Hall of Fame broadcaster Jerry Coleman and Ted Leitner.

Glenn came to the Red Sox when the new ownership group took over in '02. He was the team's media relations director, but still wanted to do radio. He wrote the team's media guide. After the '04 season, the Florida Marlins offered him a broadcasting job, but he didn't take it because he was told he could do radio broadcasts for the Red Sox, which he did in '07. He did about 100 games with me, plus the Sox memorable postseason, and we had a lot of fun on and off the field.

I remember taking Glenn to meet Ernie Harwell, the great Tigers Hall of Fame broadcaster when we were in Detroit for a series.

Glenn and I had a lot of discussions about broadcasting: when to fill the time between pitches, when to let it breathe, and how to always be ready to capitalize when there is action and the ball is put in play.

After the '07 season, Glenn was offered the Marlins broadcasting job again, and this time he took it. Early in the '08 season, I got an email from Dave Van Horne, telling me how much he enjoyed working with Glenn.

Dave O'Brien

In 2007, the Red Sox Radio Network hired Dave O'Brien, known as O.B., to do about 60 games. Dave was broadcasting on ESPN at the time. Dave had a wealth of broadcasting experience, a true knowledge of the game, and a great set of pipes.

Born in Quincy, Massachusetts, he has real New England roots. He moved to Marshfield in elementary school, and went to South River School, coincidentally the same school where my three children went, and where Jan taught. (Of course, Dave was there a few years before Duke, Tom, and Kate.)

Dave then moved to New Hampshire where he played high school ball in the western part of the state. He played third base on a state championship team. He worked as a board operator, getting the games on the air and playing the commercials at WKNE in Keene, New Hampshire, one of the Red Sox' oldest affiliates, when Ken Coleman and I were doing the play-by-play. Dave always wanted to do play-by-play himself.

He went to Syracuse University and broadcast there, both commercially and on the college's radio station. After college, Dave and his wife, Debbie, moved to Spartanburg, South Carolina, where he did radio and TV at a very young age. He then moved to Atlanta, where he did University of Georgia Bulldogs games, and in 1990, while still in his twenties, started doing some games for the Atlanta Braves on both radio and TV with Skip Caray and Pete Van Wieren. He also did a drive-time radio show at WSB, the Braves' flagship station in Atlanta. The Braves went from worst to first in '90. Then, in '91, they went to the World Series, though they lost 4–3 to the Minnesota Twins.

Dave broadcast Atlanta Braves games. The brand-new Florida Marlins hired Dave in '93 to work their games with Joe Angel, and he was there for their first world championship in '97.

Then he went to ESPN full-time, doing basketball and baseball. He also put in some years doing Mets games with Tom Seaver on the weekends on New York's Channel 11.

Dave has a great set of pipes, and a great sense of humor. For whatever reason, we seemed to have instant chemistry when he joined me in the broadcast booth in '07. As he did more games, our rapport grew. We have a bond similar to what Bob Starr and I had. We're compatible when we talk about baseball and whatever else we talk about: food, music, off-field activities, etc. We always seem to be on the same wavelength. Dave does about 135 games a year with me.

Dave truly has a full plate. On Wednesdays, he leaves to broadcast *Wednesday Night Baseball* for ESPN, where he worked with Rick Sutcliffe, and in 2011, with Nomar Garciaparra.

In addition to his baseball broadcasts, Dave broadcasts about 60 men's NCAA basketball games all season and then the Women's NCAA Tournament and Final Four in March, from some tough-to-reach places like Iowa City.

Altogether he does about 100 games a year for ESPN plus the 130 he does for the Red Sox, plus whatever postseason games there might be. Dave broadcast the ALCS and the World Series on ESPN International.

Jan and I get along very well with Dave and his wife, Debbie.

Jon Rish

The first time I met Jon, he was our engineer. A very bright guy, Jon went to Boston College and worked at ESPN Radio. He was hired as our pre- and postgame host, which works very well, saving Dave O'Brien and me a lot of work. Part of his show is a talkshow, and part is an interview show. Jon has also filled in with me on Wednesday nights when Dave O'Brien is away. Jon does a very good job.

Dale Arnold

In 2008 and 2011, I worked with Dale Arnold, a professional broadcaster from Maine. Dale may be the only person to broadcast games for all four of Boston's major sports franchises. Dale had a long and outstanding career in hockey, including the American Hockey League. He came to Boston to do Patriots games. His main gig was as the host of a radio talk show on WEEI. He also did Bruins hockey on NESN for several years. Now, he fills in with me on Wednesday nights when Dave O'Brien does ESPN baseball. Dale is always very professional and very well-prepared.

Bob Feller

In 1982, Ted Stepien, the owner of 10 TV, our newly formed cable network, told me that I'd be doing Indians games on cable TV with Hall of Fame pitcher Bob Feller. I had heard the stories about Bob—that he had a star complex, that he was hard to work with. I was apprehensive, but I soon found out that nothing could be further from the truth. Bob and I had a wonderful relationship. Of course, it was a thrill to work with one of the greatest pitchers of all time, and one of the greatest war heroes, certainly among athletes. Bob was awarded eight battle stars by the Navy for his service in command of a 40mm antiaircraft mount on the battleship Alabama, in both the Atlantic and the Pacific.

By '82, Bob had been retired for more than a quarter of a century, and had been a Hall of Famer for 20 years. He knew who he was, and knew his place in the history of baseball. As a 17-year-old, he struck out 17 Philadelphia Athletics in one game. At the end of the season, he returned to Van Meter to finish high school. Feller's high school graduation was broadcast on the Mutual Radio Network by someone else who went on to great success: Ronald Reagan. He pitched a no-hitter on opening day in 1940, one of his three no-hitters.

Feller enlisted in the Navy on December 9, 1941, two days after the attack on Pearl Harbor. He was always more proud of his service in the Navy than of his great baseball career. In fact, when he was asked which of his wins he was most proud of, he used to answer, "World War II!" He never resented the fact that he missed four of his prime years to serve in the Navy, but when his Hall of Fame plaque listed the years he played, he asked that it be changed: the original plaque said: 1936–1956. The revised plaque reflects the years he missed to serve in the Navy: 1936–1941, 1945–1956. Feller won 266 games, but who knows, he might have won 100 more during those four prime years.

Bob was so much fun to work with. He knew some of the Indians' pitchers because he had been a spring training instructor with the club, but he was not that current with the rest of the league. He laughed at himself, and frequently talked about his record for walks, much more than his strikeouts.

Bob became very close with my family. During spring training, we all stayed at the Sheraton Pueblo in Tucson. Bob always called it the "Pwee-eblo." We broadcast several spring training games. His room at the hotel was just down the hall from mine. He came to Tommy's seventh birthday party, and had a catch with both Duke and Tommy. Bob was especially fond of Katie, who was nearly three at the time.

Bob's wife, Anne, was a wonderful lady. She was from Ansonia, Connecticut, and went to the University of Connecticut. She loved the Red Sox. Her favorite was Ted Williams. Anne was great for Bob and great for us.

Bob was sometimes not politically correct. He was blunt and straightforward. He said exactly what he thought, and didn't try to pretty it up. In a *Sports Illustrated* story, Anne was asked how she handled some of Bob's politically incorrect comments. "Can you die of embarrassment?" she asked.

I shared many pleasant memories with Bob. In '83, the year I started with the Red Sox, he stayed at our house outside of Boston, and we went to a Colgate-UConn football game so that Anne could root for her alma mater. Bob and I stayed in touch over the years. When the Red Sox played in Cleveland I'd see Bob in the press box, working as a special representative of the Indians. Our reunions were always very warm. We'd have him on our pregame shows, and he used to tell great stories.

I introduced Bob Feller to Roger Clemens, each perhaps the greatest pitcher of his era, although Feller was not very high on modern pitchers. They spoke briefly in the lobby of the Pfister Hotel and it was like oil and water. Very terse. Their meeting only lasted for a few minutes. But he did like Pedro Martinez. Feller thought that Pedro was something special. He was.

Feller was a very strong man physically. He's the only man I ever met who collected antique tractors. He built the Bob Feller Museum in Van Meter, Iowa. Once, when we had an off-day between games in Kansas City and Minnesota, I rented a car and drove to Van Meter. I had never before been to Iowa. On the way I stopped at the house in Winterset where John Wayne was born. I called my friend, film critic Jeffrey Lyons, on my cellphone to tell him where I was.

About 15 miles from Winterset, I saw the barn in Van Meter where Feller pitched against the wall and to his father. The baseball field his father built in a cornfield was no longer there, but the house is there. Bob's son Steve, an architect, designed the museum, which is wonderful. All of Feller's memorabilia is there. I bought a brick commemorating one of Feller's 12 one-hitters, specifically one against the Red Sox.

Bob and I remained good friends right up until his passing in December 2010 at the age of 92. He had never really been sick a day in his life. He pitched in the Hall of Fame Game in Cooperstown, now an old-timers' game, in '10 when he was 91.

Ned Martin

I never had the opportunity to do a game with Ned Martin, but I wish I had. Ned Martin broadcast Red Sox games for 32 years starting in 1961—the year Carl Yastrzemski made his Red Sox debut—longer than anybody before or since. He did it for 18 years on radio then another 14 strictly on television. From the mid-1970s to the mid-'80s, the Sox only televised about 100 games each season.

Ned was a very classy gentleman from Wayne, Pennsylvania, just outside of Philadelphia. He grew up a fan of the Philadelphia Athletics. His dad used to take him to Shibe Park (which changed its name to Connie Mack Stadium in 1953) to see Jimmie Foxx.

After his freshman year at Duke University, Ned enlisted in the Marines during World War II. He was a hero in the battle of Iwo Jima while still a teenager. We spoke about his experiences in the Marines quite often. After the War, Ned returned to Duke where he majored in English Literature. I believe that Ned was one of the most literate baseball broadcasters, if not the most literate. He often quoted Shakespeare during a game. He loved to read the great novelists like Hemingway and Steinbeck.

I enjoyed talking baseball or arguing politics with Ned. Ned was a big fan of Richard Nixon and I had a lot of fun with him on that subject.

I got to know Ned, his wife, Barbara, daughters Caroline and O'Hara, and his son, Rollie. Ned never felt at home in Boston or Wellesley where he lived. He considered himself a Philadelphia guy. Nevertheless, Ned Martin was beloved by Red Sox fans. He did not have a big ego.

In his later years, he occasionally made a mistake with a player's name, but that only endeared him even more to his many fans.

In '61, Ned was hired by Curt Gowdy ("The Cowboy," from Green River, Wyoming) to work with him on Red Sox games. Curt broadcast Red Sox games from 1951 to 1965. In those days, lead broadcasters such as Gowdy and Mel Allen of the Yankees got to hire their sidekicks.

Ned, by then in his thirties, had been doing games for the AAA Charleston Charlies. Through '72, he did both radio and television. Then when the team split the radio and television broadcasts, Ken Coleman, did TV and Ned did radio through 1978. At that time, it was the practice of many teams to have two or three broadcasters rotate between radio and television. Phil Rizzuto with the New York Yankees usually worked innings on both television and radio.

Ned Martin and Jim Woods were one of the great radio broadcast teams ever, from '74 to '78. Jim had done Yankees, Giants, Pirates, Cardinals, and A's games. Bob Prince, the Hall of Fame Pirates broadcaster with whom Woods worked through the '60s, called him "The Possum" because of his night hours. Many consider Woods the best No. 2 baseball broadcaster ever. He should be a Hall of Famer.

Of course, the Red Sox teams that they covered were power-hitting teams. During those years, the Sox finished third, first, third, second, and second in the league. But Martin and Woods always had conflicts with the station which wanted them to attend sponsor events almost every night, something they recoiled from doing. This dispute became very public. Their last game was the infamous (at least for Red Sox fans) Bucky Dent game, in which Dent's home run helped give the Yankees the AL Eastern Division title in '78.

That loss ended the Red Sox season, and also ended their stint on the radio. Woods was gone by '79, but Ned returned to do TV through 1992. He hated doing television—the openings, worrying about angles, being on camera, dressing, etc.—not that he ever wore a jacket and tie on TV. One of the explanations for his preference for radio over TV is one that I share: radio is an announcer's medium. TV is an analyst's and a director's medium. During his years on TV, he always envied my position in the Red Sox radio booth.

Ned worked until his late sixties. On the last Saturday of the '92 season he was given a letter from the TV executives saying that they were letting him go. I thought that was a very sad way to do it. But that didn't detract from his fine broadcasting career.

As I said, Ned never felt comfortable in Boston. Shortly after leaving the Red Sox, he moved to Clarksville, Virginia, not far from Duke University. Ned and Barbara bought a farmhouse. They didn't farm, but they liked the privacy. He got to read the novels that he loved.

I didn't get to see much of Ned after he left broadcasting, but he did come up to Boston in 2002 for the memorial service for Ted Williams at Fenway. Unfortunately, I didn't get to see Ned that day. We just missed each other by a few minutes. I called him the next morning and wished him well. I might have been the last person he spoke with on the phone. Ned died of a massive heart attack at Raleigh-Durham airport on the way home to Virginia. Ned Martin, a wonderful guy. He was elected to the Red Sox Hall of Fame in 2000. Ned's photograph hangs at the entrance to the Red Sox broadcast booth at Fenway Park.

Dennis Eckersley

Another guy I worked with was Hall of Fame pitcher Dennis Eckersley. He did several games with me in 2001 when Jerry Trupiano was ill. I've known Dennis since he was 20 years old, when he broke in with the Cleveland Indians as a hard-throwing right hander. The Indians manager was another Hall of Famer, Frank Robinson. (At the time, I was working on TV in Cleveland, not broadcasting the games.) Frank loved Eck because he was so confident and cocky but not arrogant. He used to "shoot" batters out with his fingers when he struck them out. Dennis is a real favorite of mine.

Then I was with him as a player. He was in the first game I ever did in the major leagues, April 5, 1979, pitching for the Boston Red Sox against the Cleveland Indians. He also pitched the first game I did for the Red Sox, April 5, 1983, when he lost 7–1 to Dave Stieb of the Toronto Blue Jays. Rance Mulliniks of the Blue Jays hit a home run off Eckersley in the second inning, leading Eckersley to say after the game, "What's a Rance Mulliniks?" That was Eck. He spoke a language all his own, and pitched effectively until he was 43 in 1998.

After three years in Cleveland, including a no-hitter on May 30, 1977, against the California Angels, seven years with the Red Sox, and an excellent career as a starter (including a 20-win season in '78 in Boston), Dennis had a brief stop with the Cubs, and then in '87 he became the premier closer in the majors, primarily with the Oakland A's. Eckersley pitched more than 1,000 games and was elected to the Hall of Fame in '04.

I interviewed Eckersley just after his no-hitter. He was largely responsible for Oakland sweeping the Red Sox in the playoffs in both '88 and '90. After a brief stint with the St. Louis Cardinals, Dennis came back to the Red Sox in '98 to finish his career.

Since then he's been a broadcaster for TBS in the studio and as a game analyst. He also did a number of games with me on the radio. One of his favorite expressions is, "That pitch had hair on it."

Dennis Eckersley is one of Jan's all-time favorites—high praise indeed. He is always honest, sometimes brutally so. Jan always found him extremely sincere. When you talk to him, he'd look you right in the eye, rather than looking around to see if there is somebody more important standing nearby. Jan has always had a special feeling for Dennis, partially because we knew him since he came to the big leagues and because he is so sincere.

One time, he was on the air with me doing a game against the Angels. They had a 5'8" infielder from Australia named Trent Durrington. Eckersley said, "This guy's a sandblower. You ought to be able to blow him away. He's a sandblower." I asked him to explain what a sandblower is. Unfortunately, he did. "That's a guy who is built so low to the ground that when he passes gas, it kicks up the sand." After the game, Dennis said to me, "Aren't you proud of me? I didn't say fart!"

Bobby "Bingo" Smith

When I broadcast Cleveland Cavaliers basketball games on television in 1980–81 my partner was Bobby "Bingo" Smith. As a player for Tulsa University, he came along too early for the three-point shot. He was a great outside shooter, and an original member of the Cavaliers in 1970–71.

We had a horrible team which finished the season with 28 wins and 54 losses, a .341 winning percentage. But Bobby made the games enjoyable.

Ron Perry

Also in basketball, I worked with Ron Perry, a great Holy Cross athlete like his dad. His father was the athletic director at Holy Cross, and was very nice to my son Tom when he went there. Ron was New England's leading scorer in basketball and was elected to Holy Cross' Hall of Fame. Ron was drafted by the Celtics, but did not make the team. Instead, he played minor league baseball in Glens Falls, New York, in the Eastern League in the White Sox's system. But his heart was in basketball. Ron was and is a great basketball analyst. He is still on TV.

Even when he had to be critical of a player, he was very gentle about it. He was doing a Northeastern game with me the night All-American Reggie Lewis, later with the Boston Celtics, broke his all-time New England scoring record.

Doris Burke

I worked with Doris Burke. She is now ESPN's top women's basketball analyst. She also does some NBA games. She did her first TV broadcast with me, a women's game at Boston University.

Doug Lane — Engineer

Doug Lane has been the engineer in the Red Sox home broadcast booth since 1996. He's done Celtics games, too. Doug is a very talented engineer/producer. Doug attended the U.S. Naval Academy at Annapolis, and knows sports very well. He claims to hate baseball, but I think he secretly likes it. He was with us during the world championship years of 2004 and '07, but he is also very supportive when the chips are down. When there is a breaking story, he responds. Doug has been a very loyal guy and a good friend over the years. Doug is multitalented. He can do anything technically. When a visitor comes into the booth, Doug uses a digital camera to take a photograph and hands a print to the guest. He has very strong opinions, likes to get people going, and enjoys a good argument.

John Mullaney and Mike Pacheco — Engineers

Doug's predecessor as our engineer was John Mullaney from 1983 to 1994, who enjoyed trying to make us laugh. In '95, we had an engineer/producer who traveled with us named Mike Pacheco. He was excellent, and we had a lot of fun with him on the road. He moved to Charlotte, North Carolina where he is on the air doing pre- and postgame shows for the Carolina Panthers as well as other sports.

On the road, we have pretty much used the same engineers in every ballpark around baseball. Carl Infantino is our engineer in New York. He's one of my favorites, very easygoing. I love to get him talking about his years working with Murray Kaufman (Murray the K), a great New York disc jockey. Carl has worked with many visiting play-by-play radio broadcasters since the late 1950s. Carl is an excellent engineer.

Another one of my favorites is Wayne Selly, our engineer in Minnesota since I started. We call him "The Captain," because he has a boat (the Radiowave) in which he has taken us out on the Mississippi and the St. Croix Rivers. He has a booming set of pipes—a better voice than most of the visiting announcers he works with. Wayne used to be a disc jockey in Minnesota who went by the name "Wayne Anthony." We always have a lot of fun with Wayne in the Twin Cities.

We've had some great engineers in Cleveland, too, including Jim Schradle who worked with greats such as Ken Coleman when Ken broadcast games for the Cleveland Browns. Dick Saterwaite was our engineer for Indians games.

Pat Maley in Baltimore worked with me when I did TV sports in Cleveland. Now he does games for the Orioles. In Oakland, John Martin is excellent. And in Anaheim, we have the always-prepared Tony Noto, who arrives six hours before the game to set up.

These guys have to be good technically, but they also have to be compatible. Having worked with so many over the years, it has really worked that way.

The Red Sox radio network hires these engineers for our road games. They bring their own equipment: soundboards, connecting wires, and headsets for the broadcasters. They connect us with the WEEI control room in Boston, make sure the circuits are clear, and that keep us in touch with our producers in Boston, who have to know when there's a break in the action so that they can the insert commercials that pay the bills.

CHAPTER 12

"Summer Breeze"
Other Broadcasters

Ernie Harwell

THE BROADCASTER OUTSIDE THE RED SOX WHOM I KNEW BEST WAS ERNIE HARWELL, THE DETROIT TIGERS HALL OF FAMER. I met Ernie when he introduced himself to me in 1979, during my first season as a broadcaster for the Cleveland Indians. We remained very close until his death 31 years later.

A native of Washington, Georgia, Ernie started his broadcasting career with the minor league Atlanta Crackers of the Southern Association, and was actually traded to the Brooklyn Dodgers for backup catcher Cliff Dapper. Ernie was a broadcaster for the Brooklyn Dodgers for three years and later the New York Giants. He played cards with, and became very friendly with, Jackie Robinson of the Dodgers. Ernie did the national TV call of the final game of the three-game Giants-Dodgers battle for the 1951 pennant in which Bobby Thomson hit what is perhaps the most dramatic home run in baseball history. That was the first major sporting event to be broadcast on coast-to-coast television. But there was no videotape at the time, and as Ernie said, "Only Mrs. Harwell remembered it." Russ Hodges' call: "The Giants win the pennant! The Giants win the pennant!" on WMCA radio got all the attention.

Then in '54, when the St. Louis Browns moved to Baltimore, Ernie became the first voice of the Baltimore Orioles. He stayed there through '59. In 1960, he went to Detroit to be the voice of the Tigers, where he stayed until he retired after the 2002 season. Though in 1992, Bo Schembechler, the Michigan football coach who had become president of the Tigers, and some faceless front-office people thought they needed a younger broadcaster and fired him—an obvious case of age discrimination. What a mistake! The public outcry was deafening. When Mike Ilitch bought the Tigers later in '92, one of the first things he did was to bring back Ernie Harwell. Ernie is the most beloved broadcaster that any city has ever had.

After Ernie announced in September '09 that he had terminal cancer, the response from the fans was tremendous. When Ernie died on May 4, 2010, thousands of fans went to Comerica Park to pay their respects.

Ernie was a wonderful role model for me, and occasionally when I had a problem, I called Ernie for advice. For example, when Wade Boggs' affair with Margo Adams became public in February 1988, I asked Ernie what we, as Red Sox broadcasters, should do: mention it on the air or ignore it? It was all over the newspapers and airwaves in Boston. Ernie's advice: If it doesn't affect the game, don't mention it. I thought that was good advice. We never mentioned it.

A few years later, on the first Red Sox wives' trip of the season, a player was accused of spousal abuse. He was not at the park that night, so we had to mention it on the air. (I think he was at the police station.)

In later years, after Ernie retired, when the Sox were in Detroit, I'd go to see him in the retirement home in Novi, Michigan, where he lived. I always took Glenn Geffner or one of our media relations people and they'd marvel at the stories he'd tell about Jackie Robinson or Willie Mays, or even interviewing Ty Cobb when Ernie was just a kid working for the *Sporting News* in Atlanta. Ernie was the most gracious, even-tempered man I have ever met.

Paul Carey

Ernie's partner, Paul Carey, was also a very good friend of mine. He worked for the Tigers from 1973 until he retired in 1991. Paul was about to announce his retirement when Harwell was fired, so it was a little overshadowed.

We called Paul "Mr. Pipes," because he had a big, booming voice. Harwell, one of the finest Christian gentlemen and spiritual leaders I ever encountered, said, "When I hear the voice of God, He's going to sound just like Paul Carey." Ernie and Paul were very close.

Herb Carneal

Herb Carneal, the Hall of Fame broadcaster for the Minnesota Twins from 1962 until his death in 2007, was a very close friend of mine, too. Herb started his broadcasting career in Syracuse, New York. Then he moved on to Springfield, Massachusetts, and the Richmond Braves. Herb got his first big league job with the Baltimore Orioles in 1957 where he worked with Ernie Harwell. Herb moved to the Twins in '62, their second year in Minnesota.

Herb was beloved by everybody—players, front office people, other broadcasters, and fans all over the upper Midwest. He had an easy voice to listen to and an even temperament. His wife, Kathy, was great. When Jan came with me to Minnesota, Kathy showed her around the Twin Cities. Kathy knew all the players and all the players' wives and families and went to every home game. She loved baseball. She made every road trip she could, too.

In his later years, when the Red Sox were in Minneapolis, I would go out to visit Herb at his home in Edina, Minnesota, about seven miles from the Twin Cities. He would take me to his famous golf club in Interlachen, and show me the spot where Bobby Jones' shot hit a lily pad on the ninth hole and bounced onto the green. Jones went on to win the U.S. Open in 1930.

Herb and Kathy became engaged during the seventh-inning stretch when he was doing games for the Springfield Cubs in Massachusetts. Stan Hack was the manager. The star of the team was Randy "Handsom Ransom" Jackson, who later played for the Cubs, the Indians, and the Dodgers. When the team was on the road, Herb would stay home and do re-creations of the games, reading the game details off the Western Union ticker tape and adding some color and a few sound effects. This was a common practice in baseball before broadcasters started to travel with the team. (A young Ronald Reagan re-created Chicago Cubs games on WHO in Des Moines, Iowa, in '37.) During the seventh-inning stretch of a September re-created game, Herb gave Kathy a ring.

In the late 1940s, Herb was broadcasting college football for WSYR radio in Syracuse. He was assigned to call a game at Colgate University, my alma mater, in tiny Hamilton, New York. Herb made the one hour trip from Syracuse the night before the game and checked into the Colgate Inn where he made up his spotting boards to help him identify the players' numbers, using India ink. The next day he did the game and on the way back to Syracuse, he realized he left his bottle of India ink in the room at the Colgate Inn. The next year, Herb was assigned to do another Colgate game and so went to stay at the Colgate Inn. He was given the same room and there on the desk he found the same bottle of India ink he left behind the year before. There is not a lot of traffic in Hamilton, New York.

John Gordon

Herb's partner in Minneapolis, John Gordon, is a contemporary of mine. I really like John. He's a very colorful broadcaster who has a style all his own. Because the Twins and the Red Sox both train in Ft. Myers, Florida, in the spring, I see John in Florida during the Grapefruit League season.

John's favorite expression—his home run call—is, "Touch 'em all!" followed by the batter's name. As in, "Touch 'em all, Kirby Puckett!" One spring training, a non-roster player was brought up by the Twins from their minor league camp. He was not listed on their numerical roster. When he hit a home run, John was not able to identify him, and when he went into his home run call he said, "Touch 'em all, Baseball Man!"

John, an excellent broadcaster, beat me out of a job once. In 1977, I was trying to interview for the Columbus Clippers radio job. They were a Pittsburgh Pirates AAA farm club at the time, with a new stadium. The general manager was George Sisler Jr., a Colgate grad like me, so I thought I had an inside track on the job. I was going to leave my Cleveland TV job to take the position in Columbus as a stepping stone to a major league broadcasting spot, which had been my dream. My competition was John Gordon, who had done Oriole baseball as a fill-in guy and other sports. John got the job. He went on to broadcast for the Yankees from 1982 to '86 and then to the Twins starting in '87. John retired after the 2011 season, his 25th in Minnesota, where he is beloved. I'll miss him, as will his many fans across the Midwest.

Herb Score

Herb Score, who had been a great pitcher for the Cleveland Indians until a comebacker off the bat of Yankee Gil McDougal hit him in the face and cost him his pitching career, was the Indians broadcaster from 1964 through 1997. During the year I traveled with Herb, he took me to Mass on the road. Byrum "By" Saam, who broadcast games for the Philadelphia Phillies from 1939 to 1949 and again from 1955 to 1975, broadcast more losing games than anyone else, but Herb Score must have been close. He had great teams in the mid-'90s, and he did the World Series in '95 and '97. It was during the '97 World Series that he leaned over and whispered to his broadcast partner Tom Hamilton, "This is it. This is my last game. I'm retiring." No one else knew about it. That was Herb. The Indians led 2–1 in the ninth inning against the Florida Marlins, but the Marlins won the game and the Series, so Herb never did get the grand prize. Herb passed away on November 11, 2008.

George Grande

George Grande and I are both from Hamden, Connecticut. George's brother Carl gave me my first job, doing public address announcing for the New Haven Wonderettes, a women's softball team, in the summer of 1966. They played at Quigley Stadium in West Haven, often against our archrival, the Raybestos Brakettes. I did the public address announcements and played music between innings. Carl was a tremendous broadcaster. He did football and basketball, but he wanted to own stations. And he did: in New Haven and in both Providence and Westerly, Rhode Island, where he had a summer home. His brother George was my contemporary. Their dad was a teacher and the truant officer at Hamden High School, where I went, though I was never called into his office. George went to prep school and was an outstanding athlete. He went to the University of Southern California where he played shortstop. He became an excellent broadcaster. He signed ESPN on the air in 1979. George broadcast baseball games for the Yankees, Cardinals, and for many years, George broadcast games for the Cincinnati Reds on television. He retired from full-time broadcasting for the Reds after the 2009 season, but George still does several games a year.

George is a guy whom everybody loves. He's kind and generous. He gave my mother some fig trees, which he helped her cultivate. For many years, George emceed the Baseball Hall of Fame induction ceremonies in Cooperstown. George's wife, Joann, taught with my sister Carolyn Peterson at an elementary school in Hamden. Our families' paths have crossed for many years. My dad knew his dad, though I didn't meet George until we were both in broadcasting.

George and I have been honored together a couple of times. On May 22, 2005, George and I were both given honorary degrees by Quinnipiac University, a beautiful school in Hamden. In the summer of 1966, when I was working as a DJ as "Joe Anthony" at WADS in Ansonia, Connecticut, and also working the all-night shift at the post office unloading trucks, I had to take a course at Quinnipiac to make up a credit at Colgate. The school is home to the Ed McMahon Mass Communications Center, which does a lot of polling. The school's radio station, WQUN, is now a Red Sox affiliate, giving us coverage in New Haven.

The guest speaker the day George and I got our honorary doctorates was Chris Matthews, host of *Hardball* on MSNBC, who was also given an honorary degree. Chris is a very big Phillies fan.

George and I also received the "Citizens of the Year Award" from the Hamden Chamber of Commerce in October '10. We remain very good friends.

Hank and Doug Greenwald

Hank was the longtime voice of the San Francisco Giants (1979–86, '89–96, with two years off to do Yankees games). He never missed a Giants game. I got to know Hank at Candlestick Park in San Francisco in '93.

Hank told me that his son Doug (named for Douglas MacArthur, one of Hank's heroes) was studying at Boston University. Doug called me when I got home, and he took my course at Northeastern although Boston University would not allow him to take it for credit. Even then, I saw Doug's potential as a broadcaster. Hank and I became great friends. His wife Carla is a lot of fun.

Another great bond is their daughter Kellie. Kellie has Down syndrome. She is an incredible source of joy to all of us who know her. Kellie has a vivacious personality. She loves baseball and she loves life. She wrote and illustrated a book. Kellie has become very close to my family. My children all love her too because she is a very special person. Hank and Carla have been wonderful parents to both Kellie and Doug.

Doug is now the voice of the AAA Fresno Grizzlies in the Pacific Coast League, and he has done some games for the San Francisco Giants, filling in when their regular broadcasters were away. Doug does some Giants games on the Internet during spring training. Doug worked his way up through independent league ball—A ball in Stockton, California, AA ball in Shreveport, Louisiana, and now the Grizzlies. Doug is an excellent broadcaster who should be doing games for a big league team very soon.

Hank came back to broadcast games on TV for the Oakland A's for two years, but he re-retired after that. He's a radio guy, and he just didn't like working on TV. Hank remains a very close friend. He and Carla split their time between homes in San Francisco, California, and Naples, Florida, and we see them during spring training and when the Red Sox visit the Bay Area.

Mark Holtz

Mark was the longtime voice of the Texas Rangers. We socialized when the Rangers came to Boston, or the Red Sox were in Arlington. Mark had a tremendous set of pipes and was a fun person to be around. We confided in each other while discussing our working conditions and salaries. He had worked for the Dallas Mavericks before going to the Rangers. His wife suffered from cancer, and had been treated for years. Mark himself had a blood condition that developed into leukemia. His death in 1997 was a real loss. He was only 51, just a little older than me. A real gentleman.

Eric Nadel

Mark's partner, Eric Nadel, has been a close confidant of mine over the years. He's been the voice of the Rangers since 1979, No. 2 in tenure in the AL to Denny Mathews (43 years on the air with the Kansas City Royals). Eric, a Brooklyn native, is a graduate of Brown University. We may have broadcast the same football games when Colgate played Brown in the late 1960s. Eric first went to Texas to do minor league hockey games. He joined the Rangers' broadcasts in '79 and has been the voice of Ranger baseball ever since.

Eric and I compare notes, working conditions, what's going on in the league, and salaries during the season and during the off-season. Eric has seen a lot of ups and downs with the Rangers—including a lot of tough years. But recently, he's seen a lot of good years. I believe he will be in the Hall of Fame one day.

When the Texas Rangers blew the 2011 World Series after being one strike away from winning it in Game 6, I got an email from Eric. It said that, considering how the Red Sox were just one strike away from winning it all in Game 6 of the 1986 World Series, of all his friends, I was the only one who could really identify with what he was feeling.

Vin Scully

Vin Scully, the voice of the Dodgers since 1950, has always been very gracious to me on the few occasions when the Dodgers played the Red Sox. Vin may be the only one of us capable of broadcasting alone, as he does on TV.

Today, Vin is the most mimicked broadcaster—the highest form of flattery and a tribute to his talent, character, and staying power.

Charley Steiner

Charley Steiner, now with the Dodgers, and I go way back together. I was in Cleveland when Charley was doing morning and afternoon drive time sports at WERE. Our careers have paralleled each other. He has a great voice and has been a friend for more than 30 years.

Tom Cheek and Jerry Howarth

I think Tom should be in the Hall of Fame. The original broadcaster for the Toronto Blue Jays, Tom was first partnered with Hall of Famer Early Wynn. An Air Force veteran from Pensacola, Tom never missed a Blue Jays game from 1977 until his dad passed away in 2004. Tom's most famous call came when Joe

Carter hit a home run in Game 6 to win the 1993 World Series: "Touch 'em all, Joe! You'll never hit a bigger home run in your life!" Tom was diagnosed with a cancerous brain tumor and passed away in '05.

Tom's broadcast partner, Jerry Howarth, has a completely different personality. Jerry is an upbeat guy who always has a great scouting report on the Blue Jays. He coaches basketball in the off-season. Jerry is a very effervescent guy whom we see for six series a season.

Pat Hughes

We don't see him very often, but I got to know Pat Hughes well when he was Bob Uecker's partner with the Milwaukee Brewers (1984–1995). We always look forward to seeing each other, and when we do, we compare notes about broadcasting booth working conditions, road trips, salaries, and families. Now the longtime voice of the Chicago Cubs, it was great to see Pat again when the Cubs visited Fenway in May 2011, their first visit since the World Series of 1918. Pat is an excellent broadcaster and a solid guy.

Bob Uecker

I got to know Bob Uecker when I worked in Milwaukee. Bob is not only a funny guy—as evidenced by his movie and sitcom appearances—but he is technically an excellent play-by-play man. His first true love has been the Milwaukee Brewers. He's been broadcasting Brewers games since 1971. That shows his dedication to baseball and to his hometown team.

Pete Van Wieren

Pete Van Wieren's career paralleled mine in many ways, although he started in the big leagues in 1976, long before I did. Pete also did games for the Atlanta Flames of the NHL, the Atlanta Hawks in the NBA, and preseason games for the NFL's Atlanta Falcons—all four Atlanta pro teams! He was the voice of the Braves from 1976 to 2008, when he retired. Pete went to Cornell, I went to Colgate, and I love to tease him about Colgate's dominance over the Big Red in football. Pete worked his way up through the minors. I think his 33 years with the Braves merit him becoming a Hall of Famer.

Skip Caray and Chip Caray

I've always had a great deal of respect for the Atlanta Braves' broadcasters. The late Skip Caray was very personable and one of the most mimicked TV broadcasters around. Skip was quite different from his dad Harry, but still a real personality and a great guy. Skip's son Chip is a good friend and a solid broadcaster. He does the Braves games on television.

Don Sutton

Don, a Hall of Fame pitcher who never spent a day on the disabled list, has been a friend of mine since my son Duke, then about 10, worked in the visiting team's clubhouse at Fenway Park. Don spent most of his playing career with the Dodgers in the NL, but he also helped the Milwaukee Brewers win the AL pennant in 1982. Don later pitched for the Oakland A's and the California Angels. Don has taken a special interest in Duke's broadcasting career. Duke worked for NY1 and WCBS-TV in New York City and did sideline reporting for ESPN baseball. He now does sports on New York's Fox-TV.

I've taken an interest in the career of Don's son Daron, an outstanding TV broadcaster for the Arizona Diamondbacks since 2007, after working Brewers and Angels baseball.

Don did Atlanta Braves games on TBS television from 1989 to 2006, and has been doing them on the radio since '09.

Jerry Coleman

Jerry was my first baseball hero. The first game I ever attended, when I was six, was "Jerry Coleman Day" at Yankee Stadium: September 13, 1953. Jerry, the only major leaguer to see combat in both World War II and Korea, was being welcomed back to the Yankees after his second tour of duty with the U.S. Marine Corps. Coleman did not have a good day on the field. He later said that he shouldn't have played that day, but that Yankee manager Casey Stengel made him play. He was underweight and not really ready to play.

Jerry later told me that the day started very emotionally. He had met that morning with the widow of one of his fellow Marine Corps fighter pilots. She knew that her husband's plane had crashed, but she clung to the hope that he might have survived and been captured. At least he might be alive. She would not believe that he was dead unless she heard it from the lips of Jerry Coleman, who had witnessed the other pilot's plane crash and burn from the air before Coleman completed his combat mission. He told her that there was no hope, her husband was dead. Then he headed for the stadium for Jerry Coleman Day before nearly 50,000 cheering fans.

I watched and listened to Jerry do Yankees baseball for many years. He broadcast games with four future Hall of Famers: Mel Allen, Red Barber, Joe Garagiola, and Phil Rizzuto.

He's been the voice of the San Diego Padres since 1972. Whenever I tell him that he was my first hero, he gets a little agitated and says that he's not that old. When Jerry Coleman, No. 42 for the Yankees, won the Ford C. Frick Award for broadcasting from the Baseball Hall of Fame in 2005, I was thrilled and I called to congratulate him. He told me that I was one of the few that he'd called back.

Hawk Harrelson, Steve Stone, Ed Farmer, and Darrin Jackson

Ken "Hawk" Harrelson and Steve Stone are the current TV broadcasters for the Chicago White Sox. Hawk actually started his broadcasting career with the Red Sox in their pennant-winning season of 1975 after being a popular player in the late 1960s. He was a big hit with Red Sox Nation. He's a very colorful guy. When Jan met him, she thought was a very charming Southern gentleman. I love his expression when a batter strikes out: "He gone!"

Ken was a pro golfer for a few years, and competed in the British Open. He is credited with "inventing" the batting glove. He started out batting with a golfer's glove.

Hawk works with Steve Stone, a very analytical guy with strong opinions. Steve, who went 25–7 in 1980 for the Orioles, on his way to a Cy Young Award, did Cubs games with Harry Caray. Harrelson and Stone make up a rare all-player broadcast crew.

Ed Farmer, the radio voice of the White Sox, has been a friend for many years. I saw him pitch for the Indians when I broadcast in Cleveland. Ed has recovered from a kidney transplant in '91 and is involved in research on Polycystic Kidney Disease. We rely on Ed for his opinions on pitching and his scouting report on all players.

Darrin Jackson, a very nice gentleman who works with Ed Farmer on the radio, is another former player. I remember he hit a grand slam against the Red Sox when he was with Minnesota. Darrin is a cancer survivor who has been very helpful to the Jimmy Fund Radio/Telethon.

Bill King

Bill, the veteran broadcaster for the Oakland A's (1981–2005), was one of the most versatile broadcasters around. He was an original broadcaster for the Giants in 1958, their first year in San Francisco. He's also been the voice of the Los Angeles and Oakland Raiders of the NFL. He used to have dinner with team owner Al Davis before every game, part of the team tradition. He was a great basketball announcer with the Golden State Warriors, which is why he moved from Illinois to the Bay Area. Bill was a true renaissance man—he painted landscapes which I've seen exhibited in a gallery—and was a true professional. Whenever the Red Sox played the Oakland A's, I always got a very thorough scouting report on the A's from Bill—who was injured, who was struggling, who was hot. In fact, Bill's scouting reports on his team were the most complete I ever got from any broadcaster or scout. Bill was a well-rounded, erudite man with many interests who belongs in the Hall of Fame. Bill passed away in October '05.

Ken Korach, who partnered with King, is a most worthy successor and one of the finest broadcasters in baseball. Ken and his partner, Vince Controneo, make an excellent broadcast team.

It's always fun to be with them. Ken Korach and Vince Cotroneo, Ray Fosse and the third Kuiper brother, Glen, on TV play-by-play do an outstanding job on Oakland A's games.

Harry Kalas and Richie Ashburn

The Philadelphia Phillies have always had great broadcasters. I got to know Harry Kalas (who announced from 1971 until his death in 2009) during interleague play and spring training. Harry was known to hang out quite a bit with the players, even the rowdy group who won the pennant in 1993. I really enjoyed talking baseball with Harry.

Phillies fans have the reputation of being tough and negative, but they sure loved Harry. Phillies fans raised enough money to erect a bronze statue of him outside of Citizens Bank Ballpark in 2011.

He was beloved in Philly, as was his partner, another Hall of Famer, Richie Ashburn, known as Whitey. Ashburn was probably the most popular Phillie ever, not only because he played there for 12 years (later, he was an original New York Met), but because he broadcast Phillies games from 1963 to 1997, nearly half a century with the Phillies.

I once had a student who wrote a paper about how much Richie Ashburn meant to him, both as a fan and student. I presented a copy of that paper to Richie. He really enjoyed reading it.

Chris Wheeler

Chris is a contemporary of mine. Chris started in the Phillies' public relations department and has broadcast Phillies games since 1977. He's a native Philadelphian and a Penn State graduate. It's always fun to play the Phillies and see Chris. The Red Sox and the Phillies have established a good interleague rivalry.

Bob Prince

When I think of the Pittsburgh Pirates, I think of Bob Prince, the Old Gunner, whom I met in 1970. He was called the "Gunner" because of his rapid fire delivery, but sometimes Bob would spend the first two innings going over birthday greetings and anniversary wishes. Bob had his own style. Bob was a homer—sometimes he referred to the Pirates as "we." Bob was a true star. He was sometimes as big as the ballclub, it seemed. His off-the-field episodes were legendary. He once dived from the third floor of the Chase Park Plaza hotel in St. Louis into a swimming pool to win a bet.

Bill Christine, a friend of mine as well as a longtime sportswriter in Pittsburgh and Los Angeles, wrote a book about Bob, tentatively titled *If I Hadn't Danced With That Stripper*. Bob's father, a career military officer, was visiting him when he was a student at Harvard Law School. He saw a photograph in a newspaper of Bob dancing with a stripper. His father thought, "If that's what I'm paying for at law school, it's a waste of money." He pulled him out of law school. Bob became a broadcaster.

Bob and his wife Betty were always very nice to me when I was doing TV sports in Youngstown, Ohio, and I went to spring training with the Pirates in Bradenton, Florida.

I asked Bob how to become a major league baseball broadcaster. He said, "Kid, all I can tell you is hit .300 or win 20 games. That's the only way I know to get to the booth these days. Otherwise, it's hit or miss." It was pretty good advice, but not what I wanted to hear.

Thanks to Bill Guilfoile, the longtime public relations director for the Pirates, Jan and I were invited to a Pirates dinner in Bradenton and were included in many Pirates activities.

The Gunner was very special. He had been with the Pirates since 1948, but he was fired after the '75 season. His firing was a terrible mistake, like the 1992 firing of Ernie Harwell in Detroit. Many of Bob's supporters and fans marched on the radio station. Bob came back to do games on cable TV for the Pirates in the mid-1980s.

Bob was given the Ford C. Frick award by the Baseball Hall of Fame in '86.

Phil Rizzuto and Bill White

Phil was great to me. We had a bond because my next-door neighbor, Joe Rossomando, was Phil's roommate in the minors in Bassett, Virginia, when they both broke in to pro ball with the Bassett Furniture Makers in the Bi-State League in 1937. Joe won the batting title that year, and went on to become the assistant baseball coach at Yale from 1945 to 1968. He was very close with President George H.W. Bush, who was his first baseman. Joe used to say that George Bush had a major league glove at first base, even though he batted ninth in the batting order.

I loved Phil's style—the cannolis, the communion breakfasts, driving home over the George Washington Bridge to New Jersey before the end of the game to beat the traffic. Phil advised me to have fun with the broadcast, loosening up especially when the club was not in the pennant race.

I also bonded with one of Phil's broadcast partners in New York, Bill White, the former first baseman for the Giants, Cardinals, and Phillies. Bill had a lot of fun with Phil on the air. Once Phil, reading a teleprompter, opened the broadcast by announcing, "I'm Bill White!" I never heard Bill laugh so hard. Bill was a real pioneer and a wonderful gentleman. Having worked in Youngstown Ohio, I was well aware of the football program at the Warren Harding High School in Warren, Ohio, just 13 miles away, where Bill starred. I believe that Bill was the first African-American TV sports anchor in Philadelphia, and the first African-American play-by-play broadcaster in baseball. He was there because of his ability. His '64 St. Louis Cardinals were world champions and had a tremendous social impact with Bob Gibson and Curt Flood. After 17 years as a Yankee broadcaster (1971–1988), Bill became the president of the NL from 1989 to 1994, the first African American to hold such a high position in American professional sports.

My favorite story about Bill was that he was recruited by Hiram College in Hiram, Ohio. I knew about Hiram because I covered Cleveland Browns training camp, held at Hiram. Bill was told that if he came to Hiram College, the school would start a baseball team. They did and Bill played for Hiram. Then he was recruited and signed by the New York Giants.

Bill had a near Hall of Fame playing career and I think should be a Hall of Fame broadcaster. His recent book, *Uppity*, is a brutally honest account of his years as a player, a broadcaster, and baseball executive. As blunt, direct, and honest as Bill is in person, he is just the same in his book. I love it.

Bill's warm and sensitive nature was evidenced by his close friendship with Phil Rizzuto. During the 18 years they worked together on Yankee broadcasts, they never had a cross word and shared many laughs, such as about Phil's unique scorekeeping. Phil used "WW" on his score sheet for "wasn't watching." In his final days, when Phil was dying in a New Jersey nursing home, Bill visited him and would hold his hand for hours.

John Sterling

John Sterling of the Yankees is a good friend. He's frequently imitated—a great form of flattery—and is certainly not inhibited in his expressions. He gives the Yankees a certain style, as does his broadcast partner, Suzyn Waldman, who used to record songs with Ken Coleman. Suzyn has performed on Broadway. She's done very well as a broadcaster, the first and still the only woman doing major league games.

Bill O'Donnell and Chuck Thompson

Two of my all-time favorites are in Baltimore. The first was my mentor, Bill O'Donnell, who did Oriole baseball from 1966 to 1982. I met Bill in January '65 at the old Huntington Gym at Colgate University. Bill had been a TV sports anchor and the voice of Syracuse sports for many years. That evening, we had a tremendous game between archrivals Syracuse, led by Dave Bing, later an NBA star, and now the mayor of Detroit, and Colgate, which seldom had a good basketball program. (Colgate lost twice as many games as they won that year.) Syracuse prevailed in that game in triple overtime in the most exciting game I've ever done. With about three seconds left, Syracuse made one of two foul shots, but we had an old-fashioned scoreboard, which didn't register the one point, so it looked like Syracuse still had a one-point lead. Colgate came down and George Dalzell hit a long shot. Today it would have counted for three points, but there was no three-point shot at the time, so it only counted for two. The entire gym thought that Colgate had won. But I knew the score because I keep my own book.

I knew that the game was tied. The players carried the 24-year-old coach Bob Duffy, a Colgate grad, off the court and into the locker room. Duffy had played for the Detroit Pistons and the St. Louis Hawks. But I saw the head referee, Johnny Gee, who, at 6'9" had been the tallest pitcher in major league baseball. He was waving everybody back onto the court. The game was not over. In the first overtime Jim Boeheim hit a rebound shot to send it to double overtime. Then, in triple overtime, Colgate star George Dalzell fouled out. Syracuse finally won the game. A disappointing loss.

After the game, I picked up Bill O'Donnell's gloves by accident. I met him when I returned his gloves and we had a great relationship ever since.

Whenever he heard about a job opening up in broadcasting, he'd call to let me know. He actually offered me an opportunity to fill in for Chuck Thompson and Bill in Baltimore during their vacations. Unfortunately, I wasn't ready. My audition tape wasn't very good and I knew it. But Bill always kept tabs on me.

I kept the out-of-town scoreboard for Bill and Chuck when they came to Cleveland with the Orioles, and we had a great relationship. I'd go out to lunch with Bill when he was in town. Bill was the first person outside of my family I called when I got my first baseball job with the Indians in 1979. He lost a courageous battle with cancer in '82.

His partner, Chuck Thompson, was a wonderful guy. When he was broadcasting for the Orioles into his seventies, he still sounded as if was in his thirties. Chuck also broadcast games for the Baltimore Colts. Bill told me a story about Chuck's generosity. In '69 when the Orioles won the AL pennant again, NBC asked Chuck to broadcast the World Series against the New York Mets. Chuck said no, Bill should do it. "I've already done a World Series."

I used to see Chuck at St. Leo's church in Baltimore's Little Italy where he and his wife Betty went. When Chuck passed away, the pastor of St. Leo's, Father Mike Salerno, a Brooklyn native, said at the funeral Mass, "I don't know nuttin' about baseball but I know Chuck got us a new roof on the church" (through a fund-raiser.) Chuck was given the Ford C. Frick Award for broadcasting at the Baseball Hall of Fame in 1993.

The current Orioles radio team of Fred Manfra and Joe Angel are great successors and the TV team is excellent. Hall of Famer Jim Palmer gives excellent scouting reports and Gary Thorne and I share many experiences—especially about the '86 World Series, when he was a broadcaster for the New York Mets.

Tom Hamilton

Tom Hamilton with the Cleveland Indians has been a great broadcaster and a good friend for many years. I was very happy for Tom when he finally had some good clubs to work with in the mid-1990s. I had been there with bad teams.

Dan Dickerson and Jim Price

Dan Dickerson fit right into the Tigers broadcast booth after Ernie Harwell retired before the 2003 season. Even though Ernie was a very tough act to follow, Dan's a true professional. I remember calling Dan to wish him well before the Tigers-Cardinals World Series in '06 and how excited he was.

His partner, former catcher Jim Price, is an excellent baseball analyst. There is a photo of the 1968 world champion Tigers in the visitors' broadcast booth in Detroit. Jim loves to come into the booth and tell stories about all the players on that team, including himself.

Dan Gladden

Former Twins outfielder Dan Gladden, called "Dazzle Man" by his broadcast partner John Gordon, scored the winning run for the Twins in Game 7 of the 1991 World Series against the Atlanta Braves, a 1–0 victory. Dan is a very colorful guy. He stays at the same complex as we do in Ft. Myers, Florida, during spring training for the Twins and the Red Sox. I'll never forget that one day he came zooming up to the little pool at the end of our block on his big motorcycle. He parked it with a lot of noise, and came into the pool area. A number of older women wondered aloud, "Who is this guy with the long blond hair and the big motorcycle?" Said Dan, "I heard that. In five minutes, you'll love me." And they did. He had them eating out of his hand because he's such a charming guy. My wife always enjoys the Dazzle Man.

Dave Niehaus

In Seattle, they really miss Dave Niehaus, a Hall of Fame broadcaster. Even when the team was dreadful during its formative years, Dave brought a sense of excitement to baseball in the Pacific Northwest. Dave was so well respected and loved in Seattle, that when Safeco Field, the Mariners' new ballpark opened on July 15, 1999, Dave Niehaus was selected to throw out the ceremonial first pitch.

Dave broadcast Mariners games from their first game in 1977 until his death in 2010—more than 5,000 Mariners' games, and only missed 81 games in 31 years. It was Dave Niehaus who gave Alex Rodriguez his "A-Rod" nickname when he played for the Mariners.

Dave and his partner of 25 years, Rick Rizz, had a terrific working relationship, as they had with their producer Kevin Cremins. Rick does a wonderful job. It was always great to see Dave, and his death was a great loss for all of us in baseball.

Tim McCarver

Tim McCarver and I share a bond through our friendship with Joseph Michael Morgan, former manager of the Boston Red Sox. Tim roomed with Morgan in 1964 when they were both with the St. Louis Cardinals. They remain very close. His playing career spanned four decades: 1950s, '60s, '70s, and '80s. Tim spent a little time with the Red Sox, and he has been broadcasting games since '80. He does an excellent job preparing for the games, and he brings a sense of joy and enthusiasm to the game, which is special. Through 2011, Tim has broadcast 22 World Series on television. I was very happy to learn in December 2011 that Tim had won the Ford C. Frick Award from the Hall of Fame. He richly deserves it.

Jerry Remy

Jerry Remy, a native New Englander, has become very popular in the broadcast booth on NESN-TV, probably even more than when he was a player for the Red Sox. I first knew Jerry as a player. He was the second baseman when I first came to the Red Sox. Jerry and his family had the room at the Holiday Inn in Winter Haven, Florida, as I did. So we would see Jerry, his wife Phoebe, and their children on a regular basis during spring training. Jerry had a series of knee problems that set him back. He's become a big TV celebrity as a broadcaster. He's from New England, he sounds like he's from New England, and he played for the Red Sox. He's a very good analyst. He also has a lot of fun in the booth first with Sean McDonough and recently with Don Orsillo. There's always lot of laughter in the TV booth.

Buck Martinez and Jim Kaat

I usually learn something when I listen to Buck broadcast either a network game or a regular season game, which he now does for the Toronto Blue Jays. I believe that Buck, Tim McCarver, and Jim Kaat are the best analysts around, because whenever I watch them I learn something I didn't know before about the game of baseball. You never know it all in baseball. Jim Kaat, who remains so contemporary, can really communicate both with the expert and the casual viewer, especially about pitching, the heart of the game. Kitty's at his best when the TV camera shows him demonstrating the different grips and pitching deliveries.

Duane Kuiper and Brothers

I love to see my old friend Duane Kuiper, now with the Giants, and his brother Jeff, who produces the Giants broadcasts. Duane had a 12-year major league career, and he's been doing Giants games for 17. I was at Cleveland Stadium on August 29, 1977, when Kuip hit the only home run of his career off Steve Stone. When we were starting a cable station in Cleveland for the Indians, Duane was playing second base for the Indians, and Jeff was looking for a job. We hired him at the SportsExchange. While that didn't last very long, Jeff had the experience to become the producer for Giants baseball. Along with Mike Krukow, Duane has become one of the most popular baseball announcers in the Bay Area.

CHAPTER 13

"Get Together"
Introductions

Chuck Tanner and Daniel Nava

CHUCK TANNER PLAYED FOR THE BRAVES, CUBS, INDIANS, AND ANGELS. Chuck had managed the Hawaii Islanders. In the off-season he did TV sports in Youngstown, Ohio. I replaced him there in 1970 at WFMJ. At the studio, guys would stand behind the TV camera trying to make Chuck laugh. And they did. He laughed through many an obituary. I came in to do the sports at 6:00 and 11:00 PM, which he had done, and the play-by-play for the high schools and Youngstown State which Chuck had not done. Once the minor-league season started again, Chuck went back to Hawaii to manage, and I continued at WFMJ.

In September '70, at the end of the season, Chuck was named the manager of the Chicago White Sox. He was very loyal to Youngstown. Chuck Tanner was from New Castle, Pennsylvania, just 20 miles from Youngstown. Chuck gave the news of his hiring to Larry Stolle, the sports editor of the *Youngstown Vindicator*, who broke the story—big news at the time. During the off-season, Jan and I went to a testimonial dinner in Chuck's honor, held in the Holiday Inn in New Castle. We continued to have a very close relationship with Chuck and used to see him when the White Sox were in Cleveland.

In '75, Chuck was managing the White Sox. Chuck got seats for us right by the visitors' dugout at Fenway Park. Jan and my brother, Charlie, were with me. Later, Chuck moved on to manage the Pittsburgh Pirates. In '79, I went to Game 5 of the World Series (Pirates vs. Orioles) in Pittsburgh. Chuck's mother had passed away late the night before or early that morning. The Orioles led the Pirates three games to one. With their backs against the wall, the Pirates started journeyman left-hander Jim Rooker. Chuck told the media, "Mom's in heaven, taking care of the Pirates." Rooker pitched five strong innings, and was replaced by future Hall of Famer Bert Blyleven who shut down the Orioles the rest of the way. The Pirates rallied to win and lived to play at least one more game. As Sister Sledge's song "We Are Family" blared through the stadium, the players' wives danced on top of the Pittsburgh dugout—a sight I'll never forget. At the time, Sister Sledge was in Europe, and had no idea that the song had become the theme song for the '79 Pirates.

The Series shifted to Baltimore, where the Pirates won Game 6 to tie the Series at three games each. Scott McGregor started Game 7 for the Orioles against Jim Bibby. Willie Stargell hit a two-run homer in the sixth inning to make the score 2–1 Pirates. Pittsburgh won the game 4–1 and the World Series.

After that, I didn't see Chuck for a while, but his presence was always there because he was the first guy I ever knew in baseball. One thing Chuck told me, and he was very proud of it: he hit the first pitch of his major league career for a home run when he was with the Milwaukee Braves on Opening Day, April 12, 1955. He pinch-hit for Warren Spahn. (Spahn's numbers are easy to remember: 363 wins, 363 hits.) Chuck's homer was off a right-handed pitcher named Gerry Staley, then with Cincinnati, who later was with the Go-Go White Sox of '59.

Chuck used to tell young players, "Swing at the first pitch and hit it out. You'll never have another chance to do that." Chuck was the seventh player in major league history to hit the first pitch of his career for a home run.

Chuck was a very special man. To this day, whenever I meet a Red Sox rookie, about to get his first big league at-bat, I tell him what Chuck told the players on his teams: "Why don't you try to hit the first pitch for a home run? You'll never get another chance."

When the Red Sox opened the 1986 season at Tiger Stadium in Detroit, Dwight Evans did something similar: he became the first player ever to hit the first pitch of the season for a home run. Evans was not a rookie, but it was still quite a moment.

Daniel Nava is a switch-hitting outfielder from Redwood City, North of San Francisco, who went to St. Francis High School in Mountain View, and then Santa Clara University. He tried out for the baseball team but was cut. Although he wasn't playing, he still wanted to stay close to the game. So he became the team manager. He washed the uniforms after games and practices. He transferred to junior college, where he excelled, and then went back to Santa Clara. There, he played for one year and hit very well. But when the season ended, he was not drafted.

In 2006, Nava played ball for the Chico Outlaws of the independent Golden Baseball League. He was cut. He came back the next year and won the batting title, hitting .371 with 12 home runs in just 72 games. Then the Red Sox signed him and assigned him to the Lancaster Jethawks in the Class A Advanced California League. He hit .341 and won the league batting title. In '09, he was promoted first to Salem in the Carolina League, where Nava hit .339, and then to the AA Portland (Maine) Seadogs, where his batting average in 32 games was .364. He moved up to the Red Sox AAA team, the Pawtucket (Rhode Island) Red Sox in 2010, as part of his quick ascent through the minors. There, he hit .289. We didn't see much of him in spring training that year, and didn't know much about him. But after just 19 games at Pawtucket, he was called up to the Red Sox on June 12, 2010, a Saturday afternoon. The Philadelphia Phillies were at Fenway Park. I went down on the field to do a normal pregame show with Daniel. I remembered what Chuck Tanner told me.

Nava is one of the rare switch hitters who throws left. Before the game, I did an interview with him, and at the end of our talk, I said, "Hit the first pitch out, kid—you'll only have one chance."

In the bottom half of the second inning, the Red Sox loaded the bases against Phillies pitcher Joe Blanton. Dave O'Brien, doing play-by-play, asked me on the air, "Joe, you told him to hit the first pitch out, right?" Then came the pitch. O'Brien: "Here's the pitch. Swing and a drive—deep right center. There it goes! Over the bullpen! A grand slam! Daniel Nava has hit the first pitch of his career for a grand slam home run, becoming the third major leaguer to hit a grand slam in his first at-bat and the first to do it on the first pitch."

We had Daniel on the postgame show. He was flying high.

It all goes back to Chuck Tanner. I took my bows. I was in the right place at the right time. But I believe I was just a conduit. I think it was a spiritual experience to be the intermediary between Chuck Tanner and Daniel Nava.

In the middle of the seventh inning, I took a break to go to the men's room just behind the broadcast booth at Fenway. There's Tim McCarver, broadcasting the game on Fox-TV. I told Tim the story. I said, "Tim, the reason I told Nava to hit the first pitch for a home-run was because Chuck Tanner, a wonderful guy, told me to do that." Tim put the story on the air. Later, I called Chuck Tanner. He told me that he got many letters and phone calls. At the time, Chuck was struggling with congestive heart failure. He missed most of the '10 season, but occasionally saw the Pirates in Pittsburgh in their beautiful new stadium, PNC Park.

The story of how, through me, Chuck had told Nava to swing at the first pitch and hit a grand slam made Chuck very happy. I spoke with him a few more times before he passed away in February '11. I was very glad that we had brought some joy to one of the sweetest baseball men, one of the most giving people I've ever met. Chuck Tanner was a very positive person. He could make you feel 10-feet tall. He did that with players, too. When the White Sox acquired the enigmatic Dick Allen in late '71 from the Dodgers, Chuck went to Allen's hometown of Wampum, Pennsylvania, not far from New Castle, to speak with Dick's mother, Era Allen, the only person Dick would listen to. Chuck won her favor.

Allen performed well for Tanner in '72, and had a banner year: he led the AL with 37 home runs, 113 RBIs, 99 walks, a slugging percentage of .603, and an on-base percentage of .420. He was the MVP in the AL. He was an All-Star that year. He was second in total bases, sixth in doubles, 10th in triples, and third in intentional walks. The White Sox finished second in the AL West. Why? Because Chuck Tanner knew how to deal with people.

Chuck also had Dick's older brother, Hank, who had played for several clubs including the Washington Senators, Milwaukee Brewers, and the White Sox. Chuck helped extend his career to seven years by making him a third-string catcher—a position he never played. Hank got his pension. Now a scout for the Washington Nationals, Hank told me in April '11 that Chuck had attended their mother's funeral several years before. Chuck always loved her name, Era Allen. Hank said that he and his brothers, Dick and Ronnie, all attended Chuck's funeral.

Chuck had tremendous people skills. Not only was Chuck great to me, but he actually talked Terry Francona into managing. Terry has told me this story many times. There is a very strong bond among the players from western Pennsylvania. Although Terry was born in Aberdeen, South Dakota, he grew up in New Brighton, Pennsylvania. Chuck was a contemporary of Terry's father, Tito, who played in the majors for 15 seasons. I had Tito's baseball card as a kid and was thrilled to get to know him. It's so much fun to get together with him at spring training or when we see him in Cleveland or Pittsburgh. When Terry's beloved mother passed away, Chuck went to the back of the church after the funeral and went nose-to-nose with Terry—as he did with everyone—telling him, "You have to manage. You have to do this." As always, Chuck was straightforward and direct. Terry listened. Terry managed Michael Jordan in '94 on the AA Birmingham Barons in the White Sox organization. He also managed the Phillies from 1997 to 2000, a very tough task with a very bad team. And in '04, he was hired to manage the Red Sox. He led them to their first world championship in 86 years—again, a Chuck Tanner connection.

The Daniel Nava story has so many tentacles. Chuck brought so much joy to so many people. I really believe that God put me in a place to be an intermediary to set this up—to make this connection—so point A could reach point B and point C and so that Chuck Tanner would have some joy in his final months on this Earth.

I hope that all the letters and phone calls he got after Nava's home run gave him some pleasure and comfort in his failing health. He died at age 82. I only regret that Daniel never had the chance to meet Chuck Tanner.

Rich Rollins

Rich Rollins was a hard-hitting third baseman for the Twins, Pilots, Brewers, and Indians. Rich grew up in Parma, Ohio, near Cleveland. He was a close friend of mine when we worked together in Cleveland, where he was the director of advertising and group sales for the Indians. I also worked with Rich when I did television for the Cleveland Cavaliers, when he was the director of advertising and sales.

Rich was an outstanding player, first at Parma High School, then at Kent State University, where he played with Gene "Stick" Michael. Rich was invited to a Washington Senators tryout camp, where he hit a couple of bombs. It was 406' to left field at Griffith Stadium, the Senators' park, and he hit them out. The Senators offered him a contract in 1960 to start his career at Wilson, North Carolina, in the Class-B Carolina League. He was promoted to Class A Charlotte in the Sally League, and then AAA Syracuse in the International League where he appeared in only three games before making his major league debut with the Minnesota Twins, after the Senators moved to Minneapolis, on June 16, 1961.

He hit .307 in '63, and was an outstanding player. Rich was part of those really good Twins teams of the '60s, including the one that won the pennant in '65. In fact, in the World Series that year he connected for a long fly ball off Sandy Koufax of the Dodgers, which almost left the park. But Koufax dominated in that game. Rollins' teammates included Rod Carew, Harmon Killebrew, Bob Allison, Jim Kaat, Mudcat Grant, Bernie Allen, Tony Oliva, Zoilo Versalles, and Cesar Tovar.

Rich and I have remained friends through the years. My son Duke went to the Rich Rollins–Garry Roggenburk Camp. Roggenburk was an outstanding pitcher with the Red Sox, Pilots, and Twins. It later became the Rollins-Bova camp.

I was hosting Pete Franklin's sports talk show on the Indians' flagship station then and said that Lebovitz was being totally unfair to Rollins. Rich had no contract with the Indians. He left because he got a better offer from the Cavaliers, and took it because he was free to do so. Rich was happy that I was so loyal to him.

Rich is well-known in Red Sox history because he popped out to Rico Petrocelli, facing Jim Lonborg, to end the Red Sox's "Impossible Dream" season in '67. Rich was honored years later at a Jimmy Fund dinner as that pop-up was commemorated. In fact, we have a photograph of Rico making the catch and Rollins leaving the field posted outside our broadcast booth at Fenway Park.

The Twins and Red Sox went into that game tied for the AL lead. The Red Sox won the game and the pennant when the Tigers were eliminated by the Angels a short time after the Red Sox game ended.

I had a chance to do something very nice for Rich in spring training 2011. Rich called me during the previous winter, and said he'd be spending some time in Naples, Florida, during spring training. I said great, we'll get together. He told me that he had a baseball that had been signed by Hall of Famer Paul Molitor, a player he really admired. It came from a mutual friend, who also told Rich that Rich had been Molitor's hero when Molitor was growing up in St. Paul and Rich was playing third base for the Twins.

So Rich came up with our friend Andy Kosco, a terrific outfielder with the Twins. He and Rich had been teammates. I knew Kosco because he was one of the first major leaguers I ever interviewed when I was doing TV and radio in Youngstown. Kosco was born in Youngstown, but grew up in nearby Struthers, Ohio. It was the home of the open hearth and steel mills—a tough, blue-collar town with a very good high school sports program. After high school, Andy signed with the Detroit Tigers for a big bonus. Kosco later went to the Yankees and I met him when he was with the Los Angeles Dodgers in 1970, when I interviewed him in Pittsburgh. Andy also played for the Red Sox in '72.

I invited Andy and Rich to meet me in Ft. Myers, which is only about 25 miles from Naples. I took him to the Twins' spring training camp, and then to the Red Sox camp. I knew that Molitor had been at the Twins camp as a special spring training instructor. When we got there I spotted Molitor on one of the practice fields. I had known Molitor when I broadcast games in Milwaukee and he was with the Brewers. I mentioned that I had both Andy Kosco and Rich Rollins with me and he asked me to bring them onto the field. It was so neat. I introduced Rich and Andy to Paul Molitor. Rich and Paul were both really thrilled to meet each other. Rich had said that he really admired Molitor because of his great hitting style. Molitor was also thrilled to meet Rich, and a true bond was formed.

A few days later, I saw Molitor again at the Twins' training camp and I told him how thrilled Rich had been to meet him. No, he said, he was the one who had been thrilled to meet Rich Rollins. "He was my hero," said Molitor. I was very glad to have brought these two terrific players, who had never met, together.

Ernie Harwell and Pedro Martinez

I also introduced one of the great broadcasters to one of the great pitchers. The Red Sox were in Detroit at Tiger Stadium. We were on the field before the game. Ernie Harwell, the Tigers' Hall of Fame broadcaster who started doing their games in 1960, said to me, "Would you please introduce me to Pedro Martinez? I'd like to meet him." I was happy to oblige. Pedro was coming up through the Red Sox dugout. I said, "Pedro, I'd like you to meet Ernie Harwell." Pedro, a player with a deep appreciation of the game, knew exactly who Ernie Harwell was and what he meant to the game. He was very gracious and humble. Pedro told Ernie how much he had heard about him and how much respect he commanded throughout baseball. I was very proud to have introduced two of my favorite people, and two baseball giants, to each other—one of the greatest broadcasters ever, and the greatest pitcher I ever covered on a day in, day out basis. Pedro was also the most charismatic athlete I ever covered.

Pedro Martinez and Roger Clemens were the greatest pitchers I have ever covered. Both were dominant and in total command. Both were larger-than-life personalities and divas to a certain extent, but both are good friends. On the mound, both were the boss and never gave an inch: hitters beware. Pedro had a smoother delivery and an easier motion. Roger muscled the ball and overpowered the hitters. I would love to have either in a big game, but if a gun were held to my head, and I had to choose, I would take Pedro because of his coolness under pressure.

Brian Daubach

Then there is the Brian Daubach–Chrissie Geppi story. One of my favorite stops in the league is to visit Little Italy in Baltimore. It has wonderful Italian restaurants, such as Chiapparelli's and La Scala, owned by Nino Germano, who has become a good friend of mine. Nino and his mother are from Sicily. In addition to excellent Sicilian cooking and a fine wine cellar, La Scala has an indoor bocce court. They make *spada* (Italian for swordfish) with red sauce, capers, and olives the way my *nonna* (grandmother) made it.

It was because of my journeys to Baltimore's Little Italy that I got Brian Daubach from Belleville, Illinois, together with the woman he would marry.

When I needed a haircut in Baltimore, I went to Geppi's on Eastern Avenue in Little Italy. The woman who cut my hair was Chrissie Geppi, a beautiful young lady who looked like a young Sophia Loren. Geppi's was within walking distance from our team hotel in Baltimore, so it was very convenient. I told Brian Daubach that he ought to get his hair cut at Geppi's by Chrissie, who was also the owner. On April 4, 2001, he took my advice and went to Geppi's to have his hair cut. I remember the date, because in our game that night against the Orioles, Brian hit two home runs (both off Sidney Ponson), and Hideo Nomo pitched the first Red Sox no-hitter since Dave Morehead did it in 1965. Naturally, being superstitious and creatures of habit, ballplayers want to repeat whatever they did on a day when, for example, they hit two home runs. Both Brian and Chrissie had other people in their lives at that time but there was some communication. After September 11, the Red Sox returned to Baltimore to finish the season. That was the weekend of Cal Ripken Jr.'s final games as a player. Brian and Chrissie continued to speak with each other during the off-season. Then Chrissie came to Ft. Myers for spring training in '02. They became very close and their romance blossomed.

Chrissie came to Boston and sat with Jan during a game. Jan told her some of the ins and outs of the lifestyle of a baseball spouse. Brian and Chrissie became engaged. Even though I wasn't a player, Jan's life—with her husband away half the year, and having to be both mother and father to three young children—was almost identical to that of a player's wife. The main difference was my salary.

Brian became a free agent after the '02 season, and signed with the Chicago White Sox. One day that season when the White Sox were in Boston, Chrissie came up to the broadcast booth and asked me if I would do a reading during their wedding. I talked it over with Jan. *Why not?* I thought. The wedding was to be in December in St. Louis, and I was pleased to accept. It was a lovely wedding ceremony in an old Catholic church in St. Louis. I did the second reading.

Chrissie's parents had become good friends of ours. Her dad, Toodie, was a very colorful and funny guy. (In early 2010, when Toodie was dying of cancer, Chrissie called to ask me to talk with him. We had a nice conversation and I wished him well. That was the last time I spoke with Toodie, as he passed away in April '10.) He owned a print shop five or six doors from Chrissie's hair salon in Baltimore.

Just after Christmas '03, we got a call from Chrissie to let us know that she and Brian were returning to the Red Sox for the '04 season. He had signed as a free agent after his year in Chicago. He made the club after spring training, but Brian got caught in a roster situation and he was sent down to Pawtucket after the Red Sox's home opener. He came back up briefly later that season but spent most of the year in the minors. Then he moved on to the Mets and wound up his career in the Cardinals' organization.

Brian and Chrissie came to see Jan and me at the hotel the day of Game 3 of the '04 World Series. They told us that Chrissie was expecting their first child. Brian was disappointed that he wasn't in uniform, but he was on the field for the celebration of the Red Sox's first world championship in 86 years. Brian had been part of the team, playing in 30 games for the Red Sox, so he got a world championship ring. Just as we were about to take off on the plane home to Boston at about three in the morning, I got a call from Brian wishing us well and congratulating us.

Chrissie called us again on November 27—our wedding anniversary—to let us know that they had had a son. They named him Caden Daubach. A few years later they had another child, a girl named Tatum. In the long run, Brian and Chrissie's marriage did not work out. But when we go to Baltimore now, I still see Chrissie, her kids, and her mother, Diane. I see Brian at Red Sox Fantasy Camp or in Boston, and I speak with him on the phone quite frequently. Brian is back in baseball, having managed independent league teams in Nashua, New Hampshire, and Pittsfield, Massachusetts. In '11 Brian returned to organized ball, managing the Hagerstown (Maryland) Suns, the Washington Nationals' affiliate in the Single-A South Atlantic League. Jan and I have maintained our friendship with both Brian and Chrissie and we've been able to watch their kids grow.

CHAPTER 14

"Glory Days"
My Favorite Players, Coaches, and Managers

Catchers
Rich Gedman

RICH, A POWER-HITTING LEFTY, WAS WITH THE BALLCLUB WHEN I JOINED THE RED SOX IN 1983. We spent a lot of time together on buses and planes. I remember one time when he was not playing much and was struggling when he was in the lineup, he said, "Maybe I should ask to be sent down to Pawtucket [the Red Sox AAA team] so I can play every day." I told him that if he went down to the minors, something might happen and he might never get back. He did not do it. Gedman stayed with the big club and between '84 (24 home runs) and '86, nobody hit the ball harder or with more authority. He caught the great pitching staff of '86, including Roger Clemens, Oil Can Boyd, and Bruce Hurst. Rich, a native of Worcester, Massachusetts, has remained a good friend for many years. Rich and I get together every winter at Red Sox Fantasy Camp. Rich is now a coach in the Sox's minor league system.

John Marzano
The late John Marzano, a tough South Philly kid who went to Temple University, came up in 1987. We had an instant bond. I called his first home run—a three-run blast at Arlington Stadium, then the home of the Texas Rangers—on August 3, 1987. John later told me that he kept a tape of that call in a safe deposit box. John was a friend of the stars: in Boston, he was a friend of Roger Clemens. When

John was with the Seattle Mariners, he hung out with Ken Griffey Jr. When Griffey left Seattle, John hung out with Alex Rodriguez. He later went to Texas and still later did a talk show in Philadelphia. Unfortunately, John died of a heart attack in 2008 at the age of 45. I loved his passion for the game and his loyalty. He was a guy who never forgot his roots.

Tony Peña

Tony came to the Red Sox in 1990 and stayed through '93. Tony was a great defensive catcher who always played with a lot of fire and enthusiasm. He's a wonderful guy and worked with my son Duke, who was a catcher in high school and college. Tony did a lot of volunteer work for the Jimmy Fund.

One time, I asked Tony to attend a Jimmy Fund softball game and function. It was in Worcester, about an hour away, after the Red Sox game. I told him he would only have to stay a short time. Tony had played in a Saturday game at Fenway, going 0–4, then he went to the event. He was kept for almost four hours. The next day, he said, "You lied to me. You told me half an hour, but I stayed for four hours." I said, "Tony, you could have left." He replied, "I couldn't leave—they honored me." Tony forgave me, and we've remained good friends to this day, even though he is now the bench coach for the Yankees.

I always ask Tony about his sons. Tony Jr., a former major league shortstop, is now a pitcher in the Red Sox's farm system. Tony's second son, Frankie, is a catcher in the Mets' farm system. Tony's daughter, Jennifer, graduated from the University of Hartford and now runs Tony's water treatment plant in the Dominican Republic.

Jason Varitek

Jason is a rock. He joined the Red Sox in 1997. He was a catcher on the Red Sox world championship teams in 2004 and '07. Jason caught a record four no-hitters (Nomo, Lowe, Buchholz, and Lester). Jason is a great handler of pitchers and is one of the most respectful players I have ever seen. I have often seen him give up his seat at Baseball Chapel for his elders (like me). In the clubhouse he has his notebook out, studying the hitters. Jason is a guy whose opinions I greatly respect.

He's also very good at summing up individual talents, especially pitchers. I asked him once to describe the difference between Pedro Martinez and Derek Lowe, besides their stuff. The answer was a classic: "One was high maintenance;

one is no maintenance." Jason could just put down the glove and Pedro (low maintenance) would hit it. Lowe (high maintenance), on the other hand, was very emotional on the mound.

First Base

Bill Buckner

Bill Buckner came to the Red Sox in 1984 in a trade engineered by Boston general manager Lou Gorman that sent Dennis Eckersley and Mike Brumley to the Chicago Cubs. Bill was a great hitter who won an NL batting title with the Cubs in '80, hitting .324. He finished his career with 2,715 hits. He was a big factor in the Red Sox's AL championship season of '86.

Unfortunately, Bill was branded as the goat in the '86 World Series, one of the most unfair labels I've ever seen. When the ball went through Buckner's legs in the 10th inning, the game had already been tied. Boston had a two-run lead in the bottom of the 10th inning. The game was tied before Mookie Wilson's ground ball ever got to Buckner at first base. The biggest play was the wild pitch (or passed ball) that let the Mets score the tying run and put the winning run at second base.

Some of the fans reacted very poorly over the next few years. The hostility was so bad that Bill and his family moved out of New England entirely and settled in Idaho, but Billy Buck came back to Boston in '90. He won a job in spring training, played in 22 games, and was released. He ended his career as a member of the Boston Red Sox. After the Red Sox won the World Series in 2007, Buckner was invited back to Fenway to throw out the first pitch of the '08 season. Red Sox Nation gave the impression that "all was forgiven," but to me, there was nothing to forgive: he never should have been treated that way in the first place.

Sean Casey

Sean Casey, known as "The Mayor," was with the Red Sox for only one year, 2008. Sean was one of the friendliest, most outgoing guys in baseball.

Brian Daubach

Brian and I have many connections, including my arranging his meeting with Chrissie Geppi, who would become his wife. We have stayed in touch over the years since he left the Red Sox and during his post-playing career. He's now managing the Hagerstown Suns, the Washington Nationals' affiliate in the Class-A South Atlantic League. Brian has the potential to be an outstanding major league manager.

Brian and I communicate regularly by phone and text messaging.

Mo Vaughn

Mo Vaughn is one of my all-time favorites, and one of the great people the Red Sox have ever had. He was a highly touted player from Seton Hall University when he joined the Red Sox in June 1991. Mo was a great power hitter who usually hit .300. Mo had very broad shoulders in many ways. He was the go-to guy when a reporter needed a story or when the game was on the line. Mo was also the go-to guy for charity. I tell the story of Mo Vaughn's relationship with Jason Leader in the chapter on the Jimmy Fund.

Mo was loved by the fans, not only for his home runs, but also for his relationship with the Jimmy Fund and the Mo Vaughn Learning Center. He has always been a stand-up guy. Mo was once involved in a scrape in a night club. He was protecting the honor of an innocent woman who was being insulted. When we got to Fenway, Mo was afraid that the crowd would react negatively when he took the field at first base because of it. But the fans' reaction was quite the opposite: the Fenway fans gave Mo a tremendous standing ovation. That was a true indication of how much Red Sox fans loved Mo.

Mo had some very big years in Boston, including the MVP in '95, when he led the league with 126 RBIs. He could carry a club on his back both with his bat and spiritually and emotionally. I thought it was very sad when he was forced to leave town when Red Sox management showed very little interest in keeping him after the '98 season. That year, Mo hit 40 home runs and had 205 hits, driving in 115 while scoring 107 runs. The Red Sox made him an offer to stay in Boston, but it was a low-ball offer. He signed with Anaheim as a free agent. Mo batted left and threw right. He had a made-for-Fenway swing. In my opinion, had he finished his career in Boston, not only would Mo Vaughn have landed in the Red Sox Hall of Fame—which he did in 2008—but he would be in the Baseball Hall of Fame in Cooperstown.

Mo has been a friend of mine for 20 years. The night I emceed his Mo Vaughn Night Out for the Mo Vaughn Learning Center, the team was leaving on a trip. Mo took care of my travel arrangements. He flew with me first class to our next city. I also have an ongoing friendship with his parents, Shirley and Leroy. Mo is one of the real pillars of my 30 years with the Red Sox.

Adrian Gonzalez

After coveting him for many years, the Red Sox acquired first baseman Adrian Gonzalez in a trade with the San Diego Padres in December 2010. In addition to swinging an MVP-type bat and playing Gold Glove defense, Adrian brings a quiet sense of leadership to the ballclub. He is always calm and even-keeled. He is also a man of strong faith.

Second Base

Marty Barrett

Marty played in 33 games for the Red Sox in 1983—my first year—and by the next year, he had become the regular second baseman. Marty was a very good hitter and a very steady second baseman. Although he did not have great range, he was a very smart player. He pulled the hidden ball trick twice during his nine years with the Red Sox.

In the '86 postseason—which then consisted only of the ALCS and the World Series—Marty had 24 hits, a record at the time. Marty was a very shrewd guy who got everything he could out of his tools. Marty was only 5'10", was not very fast, and did not have much power. But he was an excellent hitter who knew how to play the game. During his years with the Red Sox, he lived near me in Pembroke, and we'd often ride to the ballpark together. During those rides, we shared many baseball opinions.

Lou Merloni

In his first at-bat at Fenway Park, Lou hit a home run into the left-field screen. It was one of the great thrills I had as a broadcaster, partly because Lou is a hometown guy from Framingham, Massachusetts, and partially because his name ended in a vowel. Lou and I have remained good friends over the years. He does a radio talk show now on WEEI, the Red Sox flagship station. Lou also worked a game with me. He's a very smart baseball analyst.

Dustin Pedroia

One of the grittiest and best players I think I've ever seen in a Red Sox uniform, Dustin was the AL Rookie of the Year in 2007, and AL MVP in '08. Dustin hit a home run in his first World Series at-bat in '07 after getting the hit that broke open Game 7 of the ALCS against the Cleveland Indians. Pedroia plays tremendous defense and has the ability to dive and then get up to throw faster than anyone I have ever seen. A Gold Glove winner at second base in '08, he always makes the spectacular play with the game on the line.

Former Red Sox manager Joseph Michael Morgan says that Pedroia is as good defensively as Roberto Alomar. He makes all the plays. He makes his biggest plays when they matter the most. Pedroia calls his hitting "a laser show," because he hits line drives everywhere.

David Ortiz had a quote about Pedroia—who is listed officially as 5'9", but stands somewhere between 5'6" and 5'7"—"Most of us play the game because we love it. And then we play it for the paycheck as well. Pedroia plays it because he loves it and because he wants to prove you're wrong."

Shortstop
Nomar Garciaparra

Nomar Garciaparra was the best all-around player whom I have covered in a Red Sox uniform—combining offense, defense, and baserunning. Nomar won two batting titles and hit the ball as hard and as consistently as anyone I've ever seen. One year, manager Jimy Williams—who spells his name that way just to be different—had me count the number of line-drive outs that Nomar made. They totaled close to 50. If even half of them had fallen for hits instead of being caught, Nomar would have hit .400.

I don't think I ever saw Nomar break a bat. He played hard and he played smart. He made spectacular plays defensively, especially the play where he went to his right, toward the third base stands and made the turnaround jump throw to get the runner at first base.

It's unfortunate that Nomar had surgery on his right wrist that set him back. Before the operation, he could smack the ball into right center so well. Then there was the unhappiness with his contract situation that led to his departure after eight and a half years in Boston for the Cubs and then the Dodgers. He wound up his playing career after a brief stint with the Oakland A's because of a muscular problem in his legs.

It's also unfortunate that he had the condition with his leg muscles that didn't bounce back after playing a certain number of days; they just stayed fatigued. That really cost him the Hall of Fame. Nomar will be in the Red Sox Hall of Fame, but he could have been in Cooperstown without the injuries and the strange illness that affected his legs. Nomar's parents, Ramon and Sylvia, are good friends of mine. His given name is Anthony, but he went by his father's first name spelled backward.

These days, Nomar is doing an excellent job on ESPN doing *Baseball Tonight* and working as an analyst on their Wednesday night games.

Nomar and his wife, former soccer star Mia Hamm, are the proud parents of twin daughters.

Jackie Gutiérrez

Joaquin Jackie Gutiérrez, known as "The Whistler," was a very colorful player who was the Red Sox's primary shortstop in 1984.

He made spectacular play after spectacular play. Jackie had a shrill whistle on the field that could be heard all over the ballpark. He was a very engaging player, the third of only 10 major leaguers from Colombia.

Jackie was a special favorite of my daughter, Kate. Early in the '84 season, Jackie, pitcher Al Nipper, and Jackie's mother who was visiting from Colombia came to our home for dinner following a Sunday afternoon game. Ken and Ellen Coleman joined us. Ken spoke not a word of Spanish. Nevertheless, he was trying to communicate with Senora Gutiérrez, who spoke no English. He spoke slowly in English and used his hands a lot. He got lots of smiles, but not much reaction otherwise. It was one of the funniest things I've ever seen.

Jackie's stay with the Red Sox was brief ('83–85), but he remains a personal favorite and a favorite of my family's.

Luis Rivera

Little Looie. A shortstop for the Red Sox in the 1990s. Joe Morgan described him as a little man (listed at 5'9") with a big swing. He was a good shortstop with a little power. Luis was fun guy with a great sense of humor. He had a beautiful little daughter who was about four.

Luis was not a great hitter. Joe Morgan, the Red Sox manager at the time, told me that he once went up to Rivera and said, "Luis, next time we're going to pinch-hit." Rivera looked deadpan at his manager and said, "What, for Boggs?"

John Valentin

John was a teammate of Mo Vaughn at Seton Hall University. Both are now in the school's hall of fame. John batted eighth or ninth in college. When he came up to the Red Sox, the feeling was that he'd be a defensive shortstop and not hit a lot, and certainly not for much power. But he developed into a power-hitting shortstop—a right-handed pull hitter who could pepper the Green Monster in left field. He drove in a lot of runs—102 in 1995. Johnny Val was a very quiet guy. I got to know John and I found him to be a very engaging guy with a nice family. John grew up in a tough area of Jersey City, and eventually bought his parents a new home. He was always very generous in giving of his time to the Jimmy Fund. He had a number of special relationships with patients. Valentin was what Jimy Williams called a "big game player." I'll never forget his seven-RBI game against the Indians at Fenway Park in Game 4 of the '99 ALDS that Boston won 23–7. John hit .347 in three postseasons.

Third Base

Wade Boggs

It was amazing to watch Wade Boggs play third base every day from 1983, my first year with the Red Sox, until he left for the Yankees after the 1992 season. Wade was a rookie in '82. He was the best two-strike hitter I've ever seen. He'd hit the ball out of the catcher's mitt, or so it seemed, as he waited and waited. He hit the left-field wall so often. A truly great hitter, Boggs could have hit for a lot more power. But he apparently decided that he'd be better off hitting .328 over 18 seasons. In '87, there was some speculation that the regulation major league baseball was somehow juiced to increase hitting—particularly home runs in major league games. I have no idea if that is true, but that year, Boggs hit 24 home runs. He was elected to the Baseball Hall of Fame in 2005 with nearly 92 percent of the vote.

I keep my own stats for some players—stats you can't look up, even on the Internet. Boggs loved some of the stats I kept for him. When he led the AL and set a Red Sox record with 240 hits in '85, for example, my stats showed that Boggs didn't pop up to an infielder until August.

Mike Lowell

Mike Lowell was one of the most solid people the Red Sox ever had. He came to Boston in a trade with the Florida Marlins. The Marlins wanted to unload his big contract after a tough year in 2005. He had a great career over his five years with the Red Sox, and was the MVP of the '07 World Series.

Mike and I shared many bonds. He was very honest and analytical in assessing the talents of players—both teammates and opponents. It's often been said that active players are the worst scouts because they judge talent based on friendship and their likes or dislikes for a particular player. But not with Mike Lowell. He will make an excellent manager should he choose to stay in baseball. Mike was one of the most mature players I've ever been around and he was a great third baseman—a tremendous glove, perhaps the best I've ever seen at Fenway for the Red Sox.

I helped Mike arrange to stay at the home of my friend Neil Calisi in our neighborhood in Ft. Myers. Jan tutored the Lowells' young daughter, Alexis—an outstanding student—for the last three years he was with the team during spring training when she was out of school. Jan really enjoyed it.

Mike's bad right hip which had been surgically repaired forced him into retirement in 2010 at the age of 36.

Tim Naehring

Tim played shortstop and third base for the Red Sox. He went to Miami University in Oxford, Ohio, and came up through the Red Sox minor league system. Tim was a solid, down-to-earth guy. A very respectful young man and an excellent clutch player. Tim was a great defender at third base after he came up as a shortstop. He was a true team player—very unselfish. He got some very big hits for the Red Sox. I remember a two-run game-winning home run he hit in the 19th inning at the Indians' home opener in '92 off Eric Bell. At six hours and 30 minutes, that was the longest game I ever broadcast. There were 34 hits, 29 strikeouts, seven doubles, nine double plays, and 28 runners left on base.

The temperature had dropped from the mid-60s to the high 30s, and most of the crowd of 66,000 had departed by the end of the game. But the Red Sox won, and the fans who stayed until the end of the game sure got their money's worth!

He also had a big home run in Game 1 of the '95 ALDS against the Indians that put the Red Sox ahead in the 11th inning. But Cleveland went on to win the game 5–4 on a home run by my old friend Tony Peña and won the series.

Unfortunately, a serious back injury ended Tim's playing career. He was the Reds' farm director. Today, he's a scout for the Yankees.

When the Red Sox clinched the division title in '95, while teammates were whooping it up on the field, Tim looked up to Jerry Trupiano and me in the broadcast booth and saluted us, something you really don't expect a player to do, especially after a clincher. I'll never forget it.

Kevin Youkilis

Another Cincinnati native, a product of the University of Cincinnati, Kevin is a self-made player—a very hard-nosed guy whose true grit, hitting ability, and amazing knowledge of the strike zone have made him an outstanding big league player. In the book *Moneyball,* he was called the "Greek God of Walks," but he's much more than that. He can drive the ball for power and he can hit for average. Youkilis has done it all. He came up as a third baseman and later moved to first. He won a Gold Glove, set an errorless streak record, then moved back to third base seamlessly. Kevin plays the game with tremendous passion and fire. I really respect what Youk has done to make himself an outstanding big leaguer. I know his parents, Mike and Carolyn, very well. They watch a lot of his games in person at Fenway and on the road. He has a great support system.

Kevin has also done a great deal for charities, including his own, Youk's Hits for Kids, around New England.

Designated Hitter

David Ortiz

David "Big Papi" Ortiz is beloved by Red Sox fans for his walk-off hits and heroics. He is loved by those of us who know him just as much for his warmth and his personality. He always has a smile and hug for his teammates. David seems to like everybody. He has big shoulders and can carry a ballclub with his bat and has since he arrived in 2003. What a great ambassador for the game! David treats everyone with respect and fondness whether they're the star player or the 25th guy on the roster.

After he won the Home Run Derby before the 2010 All-Star Game, David auctioned off his bat, cleats, and batting gloves to benefit the David Ortiz Children's Fund. It provides critical pediatric services to young patients in David's native Dominican Republic and in New England.

David has a great sense of humor and it's always fun to be around him. He's one of the most popular players in Red Sox history, primarily because of his late-game heroics—winning two games with walk-off hits in the '04 ALCS against the Yankees—and his timely home runs. Another factor is David's engaging personality. He is one of the warmest, friendliest, most outgoing people I've ever met. He likes every teammate, even those who are not considered popular with other teammates. Anyone he was with on the Twins or the Red Sox, anyone who has been his opponent, he likes.

This attitude translates to the way he is with the fans. It shows up when he is doing a function for the ballclub. I'll never forget in 2011 on the "Run to Home Base 9K," which raised money for trauma and stress victims of the wars in Afghanistan and Iraq. There was a run to Fenway Park. Before the game, a soldier who had lost a leg in Afghanistan was running the bases with a prosthetic leg. David Ortiz was the first player out of the dugout to bear hug this soldier at home plate. That's David Ortiz. He has a constant smile.

David has a wonderful family: his wife, Tiffany, and his daughter, Alexis, whom Jan tutored because she was missing school to be in Ft. Myers for spring training, and his son, D'Angelo, who is always around Fenway Park having a catch or swinging a bat. David won the Roberto Clemente Award in 2011 for his charity work.

Outfielders

Tony Armas
Tony came to the Red Sox in 1983, my first year with the club. In '84, he led the AL with 43 home runs and 123 RBIs. I spent a lot of time having postgame refreshments with Tony who was a very humble guy from Venezuela. In addition to his home runs, Tony struck out a lot. When he'd make a great catch, we'd always compliment him on it, to which Tony replied, "If you don't hit, you've got to do something." He was a very team-oriented guy. By '86, he was fading, but he did appear in the '86 postseason with the Red Sox.

Ellis Burks
Ellis came up in 1987, when he hit 20 home runs and stole 27 bases. He was a tremendous talent and a wonderful gentleman. He was very calm, always on an even keel. Ellis was a personal favorite of my daughter, Kate. Between the time he came to the Red Sox and the time Kate got married in 2005, she kept his photograph hanging on the wall in her room. I got to know Ellis' mother in Ft. Worth when we played in Texas. Ellis was a fun guy to be around because of his cool presence and his great ability. We were all very excited that Ellis came back to the Red Sox in time for the '04 world championship. Even though he was hurt that year, he had a tremendous influence on that team.

In fact, he told me a story that there was a rain delay before Game 6 of the ALCS against the Yankees, with the Red Sox down three games to two. Neither team was able to take batting practice. Ellis got Johnny Damon to come down to the batting cage to work with "Papa Jack," Ron Jackson, the hitting instructor. They discovered a flaw in Damon's swing and corrected it. In Game 7, Damon hit two home runs, including a grand slam in the second inning to help the Red Sox win. Damon also opened Game 4 of the World Series—the final game—with a lead-off home run.

During the '04 Duck boat parade, nobody was happier than Ellis Burks, who was retiring. What a way to end a career! Even though he was hurt and unable to play in the postseason—he had played in only 11 games that year—it was great to have him on the team. And he appreciated it. After 18 seasons in the majors, '04 was his only World Series victory.

Jacoby Ellsbury

A talent like we've never seen before with the Red Sox. Jacoby has blazing speed. He burst on the scene in 2007 and had an excellent World Series, with three doubles in Game 3. He added speed, a dimension the Red Sox had not featured for a long time. He has led the AL in stolen bases twice in his first five years in the majors and broke Tommy Harper's team record for stolen bases in a season with 70 in '09. Tommy mentored Jacoby throughout his minor league career and is very proud of his accomplishments. Now, he has shown outstanding power.

Jacoby is also a very nice young man, the first major leaguer of Navajo heritage. I met his family, all nice people. His offense and his defense in center field have been a tremendous asset to the Red Sox.

Dwight Evans

Dwight Evans is a member of the Red Sox Hall of Fame. He had a penchant for hitting late-inning home runs to win games, especially on Saturday afternoons. Dwight is probably the best right fielder in Red Sox history, with a tremendous throwing arm. I was with Dwight during my first eight years with the team, and later, when he was a hitting coach.

Dwight and I always shared information about our families. Dwight never wanted to know his statistics, but he had some good ones: 385 career home runs; he led the league in walks three times, won eight Gold Gloves, two Silver Sluggers, and was a three-time All-Star.

In 1986, he did something that had never been done before: batting against Jack Morris at Tiger Stadium on Opening Day, he hit the first pitch of the season for a home run! Dwight later admitted he had thought about it during the winter. It is always great to see Dwight, who still consults for the Red Sox and works with minor league hitters in spring training.

Dave Henderson

Hendu was the ultimate big-game hitter. In 1986, Dave hit a two-out, two-run home run in the ninth inning in Anaheim in Game 5 when it looked like the Red Sox would be eliminated in the ALCS. But they won that game (on a sacrifice fly by Henderson, scoring the winning run) and Games 6 and 7 to go to the World Series against the Mets. In Game 6, Dave homered to give the Red Sox a 4–3 lead and what looked like the world championship. Dave played the game with a smile and always had a lot of fun. Sometimes his managers thought he wasn't serious enough, but I think it was his personality and his looseness that helped him do the great things he did in the clutch.

I will never forget broadcasting the '88 ALCS against the Oakland A's. The broadcasters were stationed behind the screen, about 30 feet from the on-deck circle. In Game 3, men were on base. I happened to make eye contact with Henderson in the on-deck circle. He waved to us. I couldn't believe it. That's the type of guy he was. Staying loose helped make him successful.

Darren Lewis

Darren was the best-prepared player I've ever been around. He set records for consecutive errorless games in the outfield. He was an outstanding center fielder—a self-made player who never expected to be a big leaguer. He went to college in his hometown of Berkeley, California. He got to the majors not only through his natural athletic ability, but through his hard work, determination, and intelligence. He was one of the brightest guys I've ever been around.

Darren had a 13-year major league career and brought a lot of character to the Red Sox clubhouse. He was one of the few players I've ever exchanged books with. In fact, after his playing career was over in 2002, he went back to the University of California to finish his degree, studying under the great sports psychologist Harry Edwards. Darren sent me a copy of his thesis, called "The Globalization of Baseball." I think it speaks volumes about Darren Lewis. He's now an investor in airport restaurants. He lives in the Bay Area, but he travels a lot, and we see him when he comes to Boston.

Steve Lyons

Steve Lyons is a real favorite of mine. Steve had four different tours with the Red Sox. (1985 and part of '86, 1991 and part of '92, and '93) He loved to play to the cameras. Steve had a lot of trouble with lefties, but he could play a lot of positions:

first base, second base, third base, shortstop, and all three outfield positions. He also caught two games and pitched in two in the big leagues. Steve had some speed and he brought a certain bravado to the game. He wound up on TV with Fox and with the Dodgers for a time. He was very helpful to my son Duke when he was trying to get on Fox. His nickname, "Psycho," was well-earned.

Darnell McDonald

Darnell had been the No. 1 draft pick of the Baltimore Orioles in 1997 and spent 14 years in the minors, including 11 at AAA. He had a couple of cups of coffee with Baltimore and the Minnesota Twins and played 47 games for the Reds in 2009, but he came into his own as a major leaguer with the Red Sox in 2010 at the age of 31. He can bunt, steal a base, play the outfield, and hit with occasional power. McDonald had a pinch-hit two-run home run in his Red Sox debut against the Texas Rangers on April 20, and also had a walk-off hit off the wall in the bottom of the ninth to give Boston a 7–6 win.

Darnell McDonald is a great study in perseverance. He was a tremendous high school running back in Englewood, Colorado. He was recruited by the University of Texas, but signed by the Orioles. Darnell has adjusted well, making the transition from No. 1 draft pick to utility player.

Rick Miller

Rick Miller was in his second tour with the Red Sox when I joined the team in 1983, and he set the team record for pinch hits that year. He'd been a second-round draft pick out of Michigan State in 1969. He was an excellent outfielder (Gold Glove, 1978). Rick invited me to Red Sox Chapel. We're about the same age and socialized on the road. We went to Snoqualmie Falls and Mt. St. Helen's near Seattle together. Rick is a very solid, classy guy. Rick remains a good friend to this day.

Reid Nichols

Like Rick Miller, Reid was with the Red Sox when I joined the team in 1983. Reid was a utility outfielder, sometimes platooned in left and center. Also like Rick Miller, Reid invited me to join the Red Sox Baseball Chapel. He later became the farm director for the Texas Rangers and the Milwaukee Brewers. Our families occasionally got together during his stay in Boston before his trade to the White Sox.

Trot Nixon

The original "Dirt Dog" was the No. 1 draft pick in 1993. Christopher Trotman Nixon is from Wilmington, North Carolina. The Red Sox had to pry him away from North Carolina State University, where he was due to play quarterback. He played the game with tremendous drive and desire. He didn't hit lefties very well when he started, but he worked hard with manager Jimy Williams. He had some huge hits for the team in 2003 and '04, including some big hits in the ALCS and a big double in Game 4 of the World Series in St Louis that broke open the game.

Trot's wife, Kathryn, was one of the nicest players' wives. She was very good to the Jimmy Fund. Both Trot and Kathryn are very strong Christians. Trot's dad is a nephrologist. I'll never forget the day Trot's dad, at the age of about 55, hit one over the fence at Red Sox fantasy camp. Absolutely amazing!

Troy O'Leary

Troy was a very quiet guy, obtained from the Milwaukee Brewers, who developed into a power hitter playing left field. I spoke to Troy often. Troy had some very big hits, including a grand slam and a three-run homer in Game 5 of the ALCS in 1999 in Cleveland, after the Indians walked Nomar Garciaparra twice to get to him. Troy went with me to the Negro League Museum in Kansas City.

Jim Rice

I think that with the possible exception of Tim Wakefield, I traveled more with Jim Rice than with any other player or coach. I was with Jim on the Red Sox from 1983–89, and then when he coached from 1995–2000. Jim—big, strong, powerful—was a stoic guy, a first-round pick in the 1971 draft. Jim was a guy you really wanted in the trenches. He never made any excuses. At times, Jim had a tough exterior, but he seems to have relaxed a good deal since his election to the Baseball Hall of Fame in '09, his final year of eligibility. Jim was always very cooperative and cordial with me, but not necessarily with the rest of the media. Jim was not a guy a lot of people knew intimately.

Dave Roberts

Dave Roberts had the biggest stolen base in baseball history. Dave will forever be a hero in Boston and with Red Sox Nation. He was only with the Red Sox for about half a year, but Dave Roberts deserves everything that comes his way. Dave is one of the sweetest, nicest people in the game. He has outstanding speed and stole that base in Game 4 of the 2004 ALCS. The Yankees led 4–3 in the bottom of the ninth. Pinch-running for Kevin Millar, Roberts stole second and scored on a single by Bill Mueller. The Sox went on to win the game 6–4.

Dave played the game with a smile. He appreciated what he did and the way the fans reacted to him.

After he retired from baseball in '08, he did some broadcasting for the Red Sox. Dave was diagnosed with lymphoma. He was treated during the summer of 2010 in Boston and has been a great spokesman on our Jimmy Fund radio telethon. Dave, one of only three players born in Naha, Okinawa, is now a coach with the San Diego Padres. He gets a hero's welcome whenever he returns to Boston. We communicate often by text message.

Johnny Damon

Johnny Damon always plays the game hard. He plays hurt, and he always goes to the post. Johnny led the league in broken bats, but he's closing in on 3,000 hits. He was a huge part of the Red Sox's 2004 world championship season, especially with his grand slam off Javier Vasquez in Game 7 of the ALCS at Yankee Stadium. Johnny is a very pleasant guy who was always cooperative when I asked him to do a pre- or postgame show, asked a question, or needed a quote.

Mike Easler

Mike Easler was known as "the Hit Man." I first met Mike in 1977 when I was working in Cleveland. We've been friends ever since. In '77 and '78, he was with the Columbus Clippers, then the Pittsburgh Pirates AAA team in the International League. I did a story on him: why isn't this guy who tears up AAA in the big leagues? Mike had brief trials with the Astros and the Angels, but finally made it with the Pirates as part of their world champion "We Are Family" team in '79.

Mike came to the Red Sox in a trade for John Tudor in 1984. He had a tremendous year as a DH (27 home runs, .313 batting average, 91 RBIs, and 188 hits). Nobody hit the left-field wall any better as a left-handed batter. He peppered the wall more than 20 times in '84. He was right up there with Mo Vaughn, Adrian Gonzalez, and Wade Boggs.

The next season, he got hit in the face with a pitch. He was never really the same after that. After two years in Boston he moved on to the Yankees.

The Hit Man came back to the Red Sox as the hitting coach in 1993–94. Mike had tremendous enthusiasm for the game. He was also a good teacher who helped a lot of hitters with his theory: "See, read, explode!" See the ball, read the pitch, hit it explosively. Mike, a man of strong faith, always wears a smile. He's also one of those rare players whose brother-in-law was a major leaguer: Cliff Johnson.

Recently, Mike has been the hitting coach for the Mets' AAA team at Buffalo, New York. Mike is always very positive. I see him at Red Sox Fantasy camp every winter. Mike Easler, a very solid guy.

Carl Yastrzemski

My first year with the Red Sox, 1983, was Carl's last. He's one of those rare Hall of Famers who spent his entire career—23 seasons—with just one team. It was sort of fitting. Ned Martin had 32 years with the Red Sox. His first year was Yaz's first year. I'm very glad that I had the opportunity to be with Yaz even for that one year. He was always very cooperative with me. He treated me as he would any member of the ballclub. I remember sitting with Carl on a bus a couple of times and having some great conversations.

To me, Carl Yastrzemski is the most important figure in Red Sox history; more important than Ted Williams. Why? Because 1967, the year the Red Sox won the AL pennant—the "Impossible Dream" team—was the most important year in Red Sox history. Without Yastrzemski, the team would not have won the pennant, and none of the modern Red Sox Nation would have happened. Yaz made it happen. He carried the team. He won the AL Triple Crown that year, leading the league in batting average (.326), RBIs (121), and home runs (44). He also led the league in total bases (360), runs (112), hits (189), extra-base hits (79), and on-base (.418) and slugging percentage (.622). He was the AL's MVP, an All-Star, major league's Player of the Year, and won a Gold Glove in the outfield. Yaz's '67 season was one of the best any player ever put together. He did everything in the clutch with the game on the line. As Ken "Hawk" Harrelson marveled, "It was when he got his hits that really mattered."

There really should be a statue of Carl at Fenway Park. I think Carl deserves it. He's a very private man. He comes to spring training where he works with Red Sox minor leaguers, rarely venturing to the big-league camp. He does not like to reminisce about his career. But he loves to talk about the current hitters, and he's very proud of his grandson Michael who plays at Vanderbilt University and is a real pro prospect.

I will never forget that in Yaz's final year, on his 44th birthday, he lined a game-winning double around Pesky's Pole.

Yaz craves his privacy but he really opened up during the final weekend of the season with the ceremonies on the field. My son Duke was working in the clubhouse. He ran Jean Yawkey's chair out to the field. Yaz was great. He gave a brief speech on Saturday, thanking the Fenway fans, then ran around the warning track. He did the same thing on Sunday. I deferred to Ken Coleman to call Yaz's last at-bat because he had been with Yaz in '67 and had shared so much of his career, including many Jimmy Fund events.

The Indians' pitcher was Dan Spillner. He tried as hard has he could to throw a strike to Yaz. He went to 3–0, and finally threw one eye-high. Yaz popped up to Jack Perconte. At the end of the game, Carl ran around the field again.

Being with Carl Michael Yastrzemski during his final year with the Boston Red Sox was a memory I will always treasure.

Utility Infielder
Alex Cora

Alex, a very bright guy, is the brother of Joey Cora, who played for the Seattle Mariners and is now the third-base coach with the Marlins. Alex was a starter with the Dodgers, and was a big part of the Red Sox 2007 world championship team, primarily as a utility man. He's very versatile and can play many positions. He also gave the team very good defense when he came off the bench. Alex, a native of Puerto Rico, went to college at the University of Miami. He did a pregame show with me during the '08 postseason. He speaks very well and understands the game. One day, I think he'll be a major league manager, if that's what he wants to do.

Starting Pitchers
Pedro Martínez

Pedro Martínez may be the most charismatic and articulate athlete I have ever known. Pedro spent two years with the Dodgers and four with the Montreal Expos before coming to the Red Sox in November 1997 in a trade involving Carl Pavano and Tony Armas Jr.

A native of Manoguayabo, near Santo Domingo in the Dominican Republic, Pedro speaks as well or better in English, his second language, than most of us do in our native tongues. Pedro told me that he was taught by his older brother

Ramon Martinez, an outstanding pitcher in his own right with the Dodgers, that if you cannot communicate, you have very little going for you. Though he was a teenager when he signed his first professional contract, Pedro considered a career in dentistry, just like one of his uncles.

Pedro spent seven years (1998–2004, 117–37) with the Red Sox. I called every one of his games. Then he went to the Mets and finished his career with a brief stint in Philadelphia (nine games in '09) and had two outstanding starts in the postseason.

On the mound, Pedro was the best pitcher I have ever seen. His fastball was in the mid- to high 90s. His curve was knee-buckling. And his changeup was unhittable. Many an opponent said that even if you knew it was coming, there is no way you could hit it. It faded away from a left-handed hitter like a screwball.

Pedro's day to pitch was always special. Dominican flags flew all around the ballpark, which had an electric atmosphere. Pedro was truly an artist on the mound. With a mean streak he controlled the inside part of the plate and woe to the hitter who crowded the plate or dived into a pitch. Pedro either led the league, or finished second or third for hitting batters in five different years.

To me, Pedro's greatest games with the Red Sox were 1) his one-hit, 17-strikeout victory over the Yankees in New York on September 10, 1999, before 55,000 fans, marred only by Chili Davis' home run and 2) his relief performance to beat the Indians in the fifth and deciding game of the '99 ALDS on October 11. In that game, before a crowd of 45,000 in Cleveland, Pedro came on in the fourth inning in relief of Derek Lowe (who'd relieved Bret Saberhagen in the second). He pitched six scoreless innings without surrendering a hit, striking out eight to get the 12–8 win and send the Red Sox to the ALCS against the Yankees.

On the mound, Pedro could be a diva but he was in complete command. Off the mound, he is pensive, thoughtful, and charming. He and I became very close, discussing families, faith, and other private matters. When my son Duke and his wife, Kiki, vacationed in the Dominican Republic, Pedro gave them the use of his yacht and assigned his captain to take them around Santo Domingo's harbor. He also had his bodyguards accompany Kiki to a shopping mall.

Pedro was always very accommodating when I asked him to help with Jimmy Fund events and promotions.

I was so happy when he won Game 3 of the '04 World Series. It was his final appearance in a Red Sox uniform. The Red Sox were concerned about the condition of his shoulder, so he signed with the Mets as a free agent. Pedro was thrilled when I stopped by Citizens Bank Ballpark in Philadelphia to see him in the Mets clubhouse on a Red Sox day off in '05. I also went to Game 2 of the '09 World Series just to see Pedro pitch. While he spun a beauty for the Phillies, he lost a close game. After his postgame news conference at the new Yankee Stadium, we embraced and had a great reunion.

Pedro graciously wrote the foreword to my first book, *Broadcast Rites and Sites*.

Pedro was selected for eight All-Star teams; he won the Cy Young Award three times; the *Sporting News* selected him as the Pitcher of the Year three times; in '99 he won the Triple Crown of Pitching; he had the lowest ERA in the league five times; he had the best won-lost record in the league three times; he led the league in strikeouts three times, and in shutouts and complete games once each; twice he led the league with a fielding percentage of 1.000. He was the best pitcher of his era. Not only did he win more than 100 games than he lost (219–100), but his earned-run average (2.93) while pitching in the ultimate steroid era was often better than three runs less than the league average.

There is no doubt in my mind that Pedro Martínez should be a unanimous first-ballot selection to the Baseball Hall of Fame.

Dennis "Oil Can" Boyd

He was called "Oil Can" because in Meridian, Mississippi, where he grew up, beer was known as oil. Dennis wasn't selected until the 16th round of the 1980 draft, and debuted with the Red Sox two years later when he was just 22.

A song was written about him, "The Ballad of Oil Can Boyd" by John Lincoln Wright and the Designated Hitters. We played it during a game once. Our station owner, who liked only big band music, was not happy.

I enjoyed talking pitching with Dennis. He loved to expound on the subject. Oil Can was an artist on the mound, featuring a variety of pitches. He really knew how to pitch, how to set up hitters and get them out. He had good but not overpowering speed.

The Can Man won 15 games in '85 and 16 in '86, when he was a big part of the Red Sox's pennant-winning team. When I stopped by his locker in the clubhouse he would talk pitching for 15 to 20 minutes. I learned a lot about pitching from Dennis. He won some very big games for Boston, including the AL East–clinching game, a 12–3 win over Toronto on September 28 and Game 6 of the ALCS against the California Angels. Dennis was very disappointed when

And with Mr. and Mrs. Einar Gustafson in 1999. Einar was the original "Jimmy" for whom the Jimmy Fund was named.

The great Ned Martin, who broadcast Red Sox games for 32 years. (Courtesy of Boston Red Sox)

Die-hard Red Sox fan Stephen King stops by the booth with Jerry Trupiano and myself.

In the booth before the start of the 2004 World Series. (Courtesy of Boston Red Sox)

Celebrating with my daughter, Kate, and Pedro Martinez at the 2004 World Series parade.

Jerry Trupiano and I posing with the World Series trophy. Jerry and I have been calling games together since 1993.

In 2007, we once again boarded the Duck boats for a World Series Parade through the streets of Boston.
(AP Images)

On the field for the 2010 home opener pregame ceremonies. (Courtesy of Alainna Chiklis)

Game 7 of the World Series was postponed by rain. He was supposed to start, but with the extra day's rest, he was bypassed for Bruce Hurst.

Dennis was a very emotional person who created some turmoil in the clubhouse, but I always found him engaging. After eight years in Boston, he moved on to Montreal and Texas, where he finished his career. He now plays shortstop in a senior league in Rhode Island.

He still loves the game of baseball, and we stay in touch. I see him at Red Sox fantasy camp and I consider Dennis a good friend.

Roger Clemens

He was a first-round pick in the 1983 draft, and made his debut with the Red Sox in May '84.

I saw every one of Roger's Red Sox starts, and called every one of his Red Sox games including all 192 of his Boston wins. Clemens was 192–111 with the Red Sox. Cy Young was 192–112. I also called the games Clemens pitched against Boston when he was in a Blue Jays and Yankees uniform. I did the game when he tied Cy Young for the club record: most wins by a Red Sox pitcher. I was with the Sox for the three seasons in which Clemens won the Cy Young Award as the outstanding pitcher in the AL in '86, '87, and 1991, and when he was named the AL's MVP, also in '86.

I will never forget the first time I saw Roger Clemens. It was in spring training '84 in Winter Haven, Florida. The Sox were playing their nearby rivals from Lakeland, the Detroit Tigers, who went wire-to-wire to win the world championship that year. Roger came out of the bullpen to face three of the Tigers' prime hitters: Tom Brookens, Larry Herndon, and Chet Lemon, all righty starters on a championship team. Clemens struck them out on 10 pitches, all fastballs. It was absolutely overwhelming. I'd never seen anything like it. He really opened a lot of eyes that day. People were awestruck.

Roger came out of the University of Texas with less than a full season (9–5) in the minors. (Winter Haven, New Britain, Pawtucket). Roger pitched much of that year, but was shut down in September, then had arm surgery, in '85. In '86, he had one of the greatest years I've ever seen. He led the majors, going 24–4, and led the AL with an ERA of 2.48. He struck out 238 and walked only 67. In addition to being an All-Star, he was the MVP of the All-Star Game. He was named the *Sporting News'* Pitcher of the Year, the major league Player of the Year, and the AL's MVP.

He started the season 14–0. He won Game 7 of the ALCS against the California Angels to send the Red Sox to the ill-fated World Series against the Mets. The controversy about whether he took himself out of Game 6 of the World Series or whether John McNamara did remains.

I always had an excellent relationship with Roger. He came on the postgame show after his 20-strikeout game on April 29, 1986, against the Mariners. A decade later, on September 18, 1996, he K'd 20 Detroit Tigers. He always treated me with respect.

I would vote for Roger for the Hall of Fame because of what he did with the Red Sox. What happened afterward is a different question. After a few down years with Boston, he went to Toronto, where he won back-to-back Cy Young Awards in '97 and '98. Clemens accomplished an extremely rare feat in Toronto. He won the Triple Crown of pitching, leading the league in wins, strikeouts, and ERA in both '97 and '98. After Toronto, Roger was traded to the New York Yankees, where he won another Cy Young Award in 2001. He set the record for most strikeouts by a pitcher in the history of the AL (4,167). In his later years, he broke his own record every time he recorded a strikeout. That record would have been greater, but for the three years he spent pitching for the NL Houston Astros.

One day in 2010, Roger was in Boston for a golf tournament. He came to Fenway despite all the controversy and legal entanglements and came up to the broadcast booth unannounced to see me before going out to sit in the Monster seats. I'll never forget that.

I don't know whether Roger used steroids, but knowing him I know that in his own mind, he's convinced he did not. In my view, he's a Hall of Famer based solely on his 13-year Red Sox career: 192–111, 2,590 strikeouts, and an ERA of 3.06 with more than 100 complete games. If I had a vote, he'd get it.

Bruce Hurst

Bruce was a left-handed pitcher for the Red Sox in the 1980s. Jan said that he was the nicest player she had ever met, up to that time. He was from Utah, a first-round draft pick by the Red Sox in 1976. He had a big run in '86 when he pitched very well, especially late in the season and in the postseason. Had the Red Sox won the World Series, he would have been the Series MVP. He won Game 1 and the pivotal Game 5. In the bottom of the 10th inning of Game 6, the Shea Stadium scoreboard mistakenly flashed "CONGRATULATIONS BRUCE HURST—WORLD SERIES MVP."

Bruce became a very good competitor and won 18 games for Boston in '88. He completely disproved the theory that lefties can't win at Fenway by going 13–2 at home. Bruce loved the big moment. Unfortunately, he left the Red Sox for San Diego and then the Colorado Rockies and Texas Rangers but he told me later that he wished he'd spent his entire career with Boston. Bruce is a member of the Red Sox Hall of Fame and deservedly so, one of the winningest left handers in Red Sox history. Bruce is a real gentleman.

Jon Lester

Jon, a left-handed pitcher, is a real stoic—he rarely shows emotions and is never satisfied with his performance. He's always trying to improve some aspect of his game. A second-round draft pick from Tacoma, Washington, Jon came up and made an immediate impression in 2006. He was diagnosed with lymphoma, which he battled very courageously first in Boston and then at the Fred Hutchinson Institute in the state of Washington. Jon has outstanding stuff, and is certainly on a path to Cooperstown. He has the second-best winning percentage of all time (behind Yankee Spud Chandler .717) of any pitcher with at least 50 decisions: .691. Jon knows how to win. I have tremendous respect for Jon.

Jamie Moyer

Jamie Moyer, another left-hander, was only with the Red Sox for half a season in 1996, his sixth year in the big leagues. Jamie was 33 at the time. The team got off to an 0–5 start that season, and Jamie got them their first win. By late July he was 7–1. The club was struggling. I remember that the front-office management people decided, "Let's trade him now, because he'll never do this again." They traded him to the Seattle Mariners for Darren Bragg, who helped the Red Sox. But Jamie went on to win 201 more games in the final 14½ years of his career. He sparkled for the Mariners, becoming the oldest man to win 20 games for the first time, which he did in 2001 when he was 38. He was the oldest player in the AL for five seasons. He finished his career with a 267–204 record with more than 4,000 innings pitched and more than 2,400 strikeouts. As of 2011, although he's not pitching, he has not actually retired.

Al Nipper

A St. Louis area product, Al came up in 1983, my first year in Boston. Before he got to the big leagues, he told me that he had read 26 books about pitching. He won the last game in which Carl Yastrzemski played. In '84, he became part of the Red Sox pitching rotation. He was a very studious guy who got the most out of his pitching ability. I spent a lot of time with Al, who came over to my house. He and Gutierrez were favorites of my daughter, Kate. (Al taught Kate to roller skate at the Holiday Inn in Winter Haven, Florida.) Al was part of the '86 AL champion team.

I'll never forget the game in '86 when Al had a terrible injury. Larry Parrish of the Rangers caught him with his spikes sliding into home. Al went to the hospital with what looked like a very serious gash on his leg. But he was back in the rotation three weeks later and won a big game for Boston in his first start back.

Al lost Game 4 of the '86 World Series and pitched in relief in Game 7. He went to the Cubs in '88 and eventually returned to the Red Sox as a pitching coach. He was a good coach and a very thoughtful guy.

Tim Wakefield

I've been with Tim Wakefield more than any other uniformed Red Sox employee. He came to the Red Sox in 1995, so we've been together for 17 years. Tim was signed after spring training, so he worked out in Ft. Myers. Tim had had some success with the knuckleball during his two years with the Pittsburgh Pirates and won two games in the '92 NLCS. He worked with Joe and Phil Niekro to perfect it. He won two games in four days for Boston in his first two starts. Tim's 14–1 start was the biggest reason that they went from a sub-.500 team in '94 (54–61 under manager Butch Hobson) to the AL East title in '95 with new manager Kevin Kennedy. He finished that season 16–8 with an ERA of 2.95 and 119 strikeouts. Wake's knuckleball has been a thing to behold over the years. He's kept it going. As I write this, he is No. 3 on the all-time Red Sox win list, behind Clemens and Cy Young. Tim holds the team records for most games started and most innings pitched. Now, he breaks those records every time he pitches.

While Tim has been primarily a starter with the Red Sox at the top of the rotation, or at the back of the rotation, he has also been a closer and a long reliever. No matter what the Red Sox ask him to do, he has always responded well.

I felt so badly for Tim in 2003 when he gave up the home run to Aaron Boone of the Yankees in the bottom of the 11th inning of Game 7 of the ALCS. Tim was afraid that the fans would make him the goat of the series. He didn't deserve it. But the Red Sox fans rallied to his defense and never blamed him for the loss. Grady Little got the heat (and the boot) for not taking Pedro Martinez out of the game in the eighth inning. Tim bounced back from that, and in '04 he was one of the big reasons that the Sox came back to beat the Yankees in the ALCS. Tim took the ball in relief and saved the bullpen in Game 3, the 19–8 blowout, keeping the bullpen fresh, and part of the greatest comeback in history. He won Game 5 of that series.

Tim is always a team player who has done a great deal for charity. He won baseball's highest humanitarian award, the Roberto Clemente Award in 2010. He's come to many Jimmy Fund events. Tim and his wife Stacy are very active in other charities. Tim's own charity, the Wakefield Warriors, helps patients at the Franciscan Hospital for Children and the Jimmy Fund. He also hosts a golf tournament annually for the benefit of the Space Coast Early Intervention Program in his native Melbourne, Florida.

Tim was awarded the Bart Giamatti Award by the Baseball Assistance Team in '10 in recognition of his charitable work.

Tim will certainly wind up in the Red Sox Hall of Fame.

Daniel Bard

Daniel Bard throws an easy and seemingly effortless 100-mph fastball. He has a devastating slider and a wonderful demeanor. He's always calm and under control. Daniel is a leader of Baseball Chapel. He grew up in North Carolina and pitched at the University of North Carolina, but his grandfather, Fran O'Brien, an old friend of mine, is a Bostonian. Fran was the athletic director at MIT, baseball coach at Holy Cross and even now in his eighties is assistant baseball coach at Brandeis.

Relievers

Mike Gardiner

A red-headed native of Sarnia, Ontario, Mike came to the Red Sox in 1991 in a trade with Seattle. He grew up rooting for the Detroit Tigers. On occasion, he'd work out with my son Duke. Mike got everything he could out of his pitching tools. He was 13–20 with the Red Sox ('91–92), then left for Montreal. He finished his six-year major league career with the Tigers.

Unlike many players, Mike knew the history of the game and followed it very closely. He had a true appreciation of where he was and what he was doing.

Tom Gordon

He was called "Flash" Gordon, but Manager Jimy Williams always called him Thomas, so I did too. He was a quiet guy, but he had tremendous stuff. When he came up as a starter with the Royals in 1998 he had one of the best curveballs ever. The Red Sox converted him from a starter to a closer. In '98, he set the team record for most consecutive saves in a season (46). At the time, that was also the major league record. After stops with the Cubs, Astros, White Sox, Yankees, and Phillies, he finished his career with the Diamondbacks when he was 41 in 2009.

I talked with Gordon quite a bit about pitching and we became friends. We were both in the Stephen King novel *The Girl Who Loved Tom Gordon,* about a little girl who got lost in the Maine woods. The only thing she had with her was her radio, and she listened to me broadcasting Red Sox games. She longed for the time Tom Gordon would come in to save the game. That kept her going, despite meeting some monsters—real or imagined. The novel has a happy ending.

Stephen King tells me that eventually a movie will be made of *The Girl Who Loved Tom Gordon.* It's still in the works, but it hasn't happened yet. I asked King whether I could play myself—either that, or have Brad Pitt play me.

Jeff Gray

Jeff's career lasted only three seasons. He spent 1988 with the Reds, then 1990–91 with Boston. He was a set-up man with great command. He was very deliberate and took a long time between pitches. He really helped the Red Sox out of the bullpen.

Jeff had suffered a stroke when he was in college at Florida State University, where he roomed with future Red Sox second baseman Jody Reed. Jeff recovered from that and made it to the big leagues. But in '91, he had another stroke in the Red Sox clubhouse, which pretty much ended his career. He tried to come back, pitching in the minor leagues, but he could not throw as hard. He stayed in baseball as a minor league pitching coach. Jeff was a very serious guy, and was very serious about pitching. He got the most he could out of his tools.

Rich Hill

Rich joined the Red Sox midway through 2010. I knew Rich because he grew up in Milton, Massachusetts, and now lives in South Boston. Rich is related by marriage to my daughter-in-law Rachel. Rich is a classy lefty. He won 11 games for the Cubs in 2007. Then he went to the Orioles. He had labrum surgery in '09.

Rich is a product of the University of Michigan as is his wife, Caitlin.

In '09, when he was still with the Orioles organization, Rich took my class at Northeastern.

He pitched well at the end of the '10 season, including a game in Seattle in which he faced one batter. Then the Red Sox scored in the eighth inning, and Rich was out of the game, but he got the win.

In '11, he stayed near us in Ft. Myers. We got together often. Then, during the '11 season, he pitched well with very little run support. He set a Red Sox record for most appearances (15) and most innings pitched (12) without allowing a run.

Unfortunately, Rich then hurt his arm and had Tommy John surgery in June

Rich is a very bright, sensitive young man. His dad, Lloyd, was a high school principal. His dad also played football at Brown University, where he blocked for Joe Paterno. Lloyd also sparred with Rocky Marciano.

Rich is a very special guy and good friend. It was great to have him in my class.

Dennis Lamp

Dennis is one of the funniest guys I've ever been around. He does great impressions of people like Harry Caray and Jerry Howarth, the Blue Jays broadcaster. Dennis was a very good reliever for the Red Sox. He'd been a starter for the Cubs. Dennis also pitched for Toronto, where he was 11–0 in 1985. He had a great slider. He could throw it on the black outside corner. Dennis was a set-up man, but he wanted to be a broadcaster. That didn't quite work out. Today, he lives on the West Coast.

Jonathan Papelbon

Jonathan came up as a starter in 2005. I remember his first game on July 31 against the Twins, and his first win in September at Toronto.

He became a closer in '06. Jonathan has his own style. He's become a real character. I got to know Jonathan as a rookie. He has a great family. His dad, John, is a good friend. His mother, Sheila, a banker, is originally from Youngstown, Ohio, Jan's hometown, and played softball at Louisiana State. The Papelbons are our good friends. I was saddened to see Jonathan go to the Phillies after the 2011 season.

Paul Quantrill

Paul is one of the brightest guys, and one of the most mature athletes I've ever been around. A native of London, Ontario, he went to the University of Wisconsin. He came up to the Red Sox and pitched very well out of the bullpen. He later became a starter. He had several different roles on the mound. He had great command of his fastball. After his very brief stay in Boston, he went to the Phillies, Blue Jays, Dodgers, and then the Yankees, where he gave up the walk-off home run to Big Papi in Game 4 of the ALCS in 2004.

Paul would always take the ball. It seems he never got hurt. Later in his career, Paul pitched in 80 games a year five times. He had a great family and was a very solid citizen. He got as much as he could out of his talents. He retired after the '05 season, having pitched in 841 big league games.

Jeff Reardon

Jeff is a native of Pittsfield, Massachusetts, and went to the University of Massachusetts in Amherst. He's a member of the school's Athletic Hall of Fame. Reardon pitched in 880 games (at one time, he was first on the all-time saves list) but never started one. All of his appearances were in relief. He closed for the Red Sox from 1990 to '92. He was a very stoic guy who helped the Twins win the world championship in 1987. Jeff was very good to the Jimmy Fund. He was a humble man who had an excellent career. He was something of an underdog. Jeff was not drafted, and always felt he had to prove himself. He did. I considered Jeff a good friend.

John Trautwein

John Trautwein pitched in exactly nine games for the Red Sox, all in 1988, going 0–1 with an ERA of 9.00. As a Rule V pick from Montreal Expos, the Red Sox were required to keep him all season or Montreal could get him back for half of the waiver price.

What made Trautwein so memorable was his intellect. Trautwein was a chemistry major at Northwestern where his catcher was Joe Girardi. During that '88 season, my son Duke came to Fenway with a homework assignment in physics. He was trying to figure out how far a Bo Jackson home run off Oil Can Boyd would have travelled had it not hit the back wall in center field.

He asked Trautwein for help and they sat together in the Red Sox dugout with Duke's physics textbook, trying to figure it out. Trautwein was interested because he had just given up a monstrous home run to Mark McGwire which can still be seen on YouTube. We talked about Trautwein's physics formula on the air. Dan Shaughnessy wrote about it in the *Boston Globe* and Trautwein got several invitations to speak to physics classes in area high schools.

Trautwein left baseball after a few more years in the minor leagues and became a very successful chemical executive. Now he has his own computer repair company in Georgia. John has a wonderful family but experienced the ultimate tragedy on October 15, 2010, when one of his four children, 15-year-old Will, committed suicide at home. There were no warning signs. Will seemed happy and well-adjusted.

Now John and his wife, Susie, have created a fund called Will to Live to help raise awareness of teenage suicide. The Trautwein family has a remarkable attitude and resolve. They visited Fenway in July 2011 and we did a pregame show together.

Bob Stanley

Bob Stanley, known as "the Steamer," is one of the best players I've ever been associated with. A first-round pick by the Red Sox in 1974, Bob, who grew up in Kearney, New Jersey, spent his entire 13-year (1977–1989) career in Boston. He holds the team record for most appearances by a pitcher (637). Bob also holds the team record for most wins in relief (85). He held the record for most saves in a Red Sox career (132) until Jonathan Papelbon broke it in 2009.

Bob, his wife, Joanie, and their kids used to have two rooms at the motel in Winter Haven, Florida, during spring training, right down the hall from our room, so we saw them quite often.

Bob was a sensitive guy with a great sense of humor. I think he was misunderstood by the fans. They could be very rough on him, but I don't know why. He gave his all every time he pitched. Bob gave his heart and soul to the Red Sox. In a fair and perfect world, Bob Stanley would have closed the '86 World Series. In my opinion, he should have started the final inning instead of Calvin Schiraldi. The Red Sox had taken the lead and Bob was throwing great at the time.

Bob could be outspoken at times about issues and events on the ballclub, but he was a guy who wore his heart on his sleeve. He was an emotional guy who loved the Red Sox. Bob was a truly great pitcher in the '70s and '80s.

He retired after the '89 season. Shortly thereafter, his son, Kyle, was diagnosed with cancer—a facial tumor—so Bob's retirement came at a fortuitous time. Kyle was treated at the Jimmy Fund clinic and I am happy to say has made a complete recovery. Even before Kyle's diagnosis, Bob was a tireless worker for the Jimmy Fund.

Bob befriended a youngster who was being treated at the Jimmy Fund clinic. We found out later that after he passed away, he was buried in a Red Sox jersey that Bob had given him.

Bob and his family are some of my all-time favorite people. Bob Stanley, a true Red Sox Hall of Famer.

Coaches and Managers

Glenn Hoffman

Glenn, who grew up in Anaheim, managed the Dodgers and is now the third base coach for the Padres. He was the shortstop when I arrived in Boston in 1983. I knew him very well. Glen was very supportive of me. Sometimes, Glen's little brother would tag along. His little brother Trevor later became a relief pitcher and was the all-time leader in saves before Mariano Rivera passed him. Trevor is probably ticketed for Cooperstown.

Lynn Jones

Lynn is probably my best friend among Red Sox coaches. He was the first base, outfield, and baserunning coach in 2004 and '05. Lynn and I go way back. He's from Conneautville, Pennsylvania. When he was in high school, he used to watch me on television when I was working in Youngstown. His brother Darryl, who played briefly for the Yankees, is also a good friend. I worked with Lynn's brother Paul at WKYC-TV Channel 3 in Cleveland. Paul worked in the station's management.

Lynn was a very good defensive outfielder for the Tigers and Royals. He was a caddie for Lonnie Smith with the 1985 Royals. He hit a double and a triple in the '85 World Series. Lynn worked with his brother in the investment business after he retired from baseball. Lynn came back to baseball as a Red Sox coach.

Since leaving the Red Sox, Lynn has worked as a roving outfield and baserunning instructor for the Cincinnati Reds and the Atlanta Braves. Lynn and I have remained very close over the years.

Ron Jackson

Another coach who is a good friend is Ron "Papa Jack" Jackson, the Red Sox's hitting coach from 2003–06. Ron is from Birmingham, Alabama. He was a major–leaguer for 10 years. He's the guy who really turned David Ortiz into a home run–hitting superstar in '03. David used to have trouble hitting the inside fastball. Papa Jack got him to adjust, and he took off from that point. Jackson was an excellent hitting instructor. Ron was part of the '04 world championship team. Ron was a good friend who would come to our spring training parties every year, along with Lynn Jones and Joe Morgan.

Dick Berardino

Dick, a local guy from Watertown, Massachusetts, played football at Holy Cross where he once tackled Jim Brown. Dick played in the Yankee system making it as high as AAA. He was a solid teacher and a former manager in the low minors where he managed everyone from Wade Boggs to Dwight Evans to Jim Rice to Mike Greenwell before they were promoted to the big leagues. Dick was the Red Sox third-base coach under Joe Morgan (1989–1991). Like me, Dick is a member of the New England Chapter of the National Italian-American Sports Hall of Fame.

Al Bumbry

A member of the Baltimore Orioles Hall of Fame, Al was a Red Sox first-base coach (1988–1993). Al was a great guy who always had a smile. We socialized with Al and his friend Annette. Al once came to Jeffrey Lyons' softball game in New York's Central Park. Jeffrey was very grateful. After that, Al had Broadway theater tickets any time he wanted them.

Rich Stelmaszek

Rich has been a bullpen coach with the Minnesota Twins since 1982. 2011 was his 30th year—a long run. Rich is a great guy from the south side of Chicago. He was a catcher with the Washington Senators, the Texas Rangers, California Angels, and the Chicago Cubs.

He played for Ted Williams when Williams managed the Senators, who became the Rangers. Rich tells the funniest Ted Williams stories which can't be reprinted in a book for a family audience.

I see Rich during spring training in Ft. Myers, and when we visit Minnesota or the Twins come to Boston during the season.

Jeff Torborg

Jeff has been a special friend of mine for 35 years. He was the Cleveland manager when I started working with the Indians in 1979. I got to know Jeff when he was a coach. I did a story on his family when he managed in Cleveland. Jeff and his wife Suzie have three sons. We've stayed friends during his stints as the Yankees' bullpen coach, and during his other managerial stints with the Chicago White Sox, New York Mets, Montreal Expos, and Florida Marlins. We see Jeff and Suzie during spring training. They live in Sarasota, Florida. I often have Jeff sitting in with us on the air doing analysis. He was a great broadcaster for CBS Radio and Fox TV. Jeff is now retired.

Dave Garcia

Dave Garcia took over as manager of the Indians in July 1979, succeeding Jeff Torborg, who was fired after 95 games. Dave was a great storyteller. He frequently told wonderful stories about his career in the minor leagues. I learned a lot of baseball by listening to Dave. I also learned more about the art of storytelling because he was so enthralling. Dave, now 91, is still scouting in San Diego.

Ace Adams

Ace was the batting-practice pitcher for the Red Sox during the mid-1980s. Ace became a great friend. His father was a great recruiter for Colgate and a wonderful athlete there. Ace went to the University of Michigan and was later an assistant baseball coach there. He really ran the program when Bill Freehan, the great Tigers catcher, was the coach. When the Red Sox played in Detroit, we'd go out to Ann Arbor to see Ace. Ace coached in the Red Sox system, and is now coaching in rookie ball in the St. Louis Cardinals' system. Ace works very well with young pitchers. I sent Duke to him for pitching lessons. Ace has a language all his own.

Bill Fischer

Bill was a pitching coach (1985–1991) brought in by John McNamara and kept by Joe Morgan, with whom he became very close. Bill was a gruff guy who was a lot of fun to be with. Ken Coleman referred to Bill as the "burly Red Sox pitching coach." Bill worked very well with pitchers on their mechanics. Tom Seaver loved him when they were both with the Reds. Roger Clemens loved him when they were both with the Red Sox. Bill and his wife, Val, were very good friends of ours, and we still keep in touch at Christmastime.

Rich Gale

The 6'7" Rich was a pitcher whose best years were with the Royals. He was with the Red Sox in 1984 and returned in 1992–93 as Boston's pitching coach. He still works in the minor leagues. He is very thorough, hands on, and effective.

DeMarlo Hale

DeMarlo played in the Red Sox system in the 1980s, managed very well in the minors, and coached with Texas before becoming the Red Sox's third-base coach (2006–2009). He's been Boston's bench coach since 2010. He's an outstanding baseball guy with a great temperament. DeMarlo is an excellent developer and teacher of young talent. To me, DeMarlo, a great personal friend, is the next outstanding big-league manager.

Tommy Harper

I was with Tommy when he was a Red Sox coach in 1983 and '84 and again from 2000 to '02, when he was a baserunning and outfielder instructor. He held the Red Sox's single-season stolen-base record for 35 years—the longest of any Red Sox record—with 54 in 1973 until his protégé Jacoby Ellsbury broke it in '09 with 70. He will always hold the Seattle Pilots record, with 73, best in the AL in 1969.

Tommy is a man of great courage. When Tommy was a Red Sox minor league instructor in '85, he challenged a longtime policy of the Winter Haven Elks Club in spring training. For years, the Red Sox distributed cards to white players, front office, and media people inviting them to dine at the Elks Club in Winter Haven. Black players were not invited. Tommy stood up to this. (The policy had been in effect when he was a player and later when he coached.) At one point, it pretty much cost him his job. Like other members of the organization, I also received a card. Upon learning of the Elks Club exclusivity, I ripped up the card on principle—not that I would ever think of going to eat in a place that featured dead animals on the wall. Tommy sued the Red Sox and won. Several years later, he was brought back as a coach by Dan Duquette. Today, Tommy works as a special consultant to the club.

Tommy was inducted into the Red Sox Hall of Fame in 2010 as much if not more for his courage as for his accomplishments on the field as a player and a coach.

Wendell Kim

Wendell, about 5'3" tall, spent most of his career in the Giants' organization. He was the Red Sox's third-base coach—"Send 'em in Kim"—from 1997 to 2000. He loved to perform magic tricks. He was very good at it. Wendell stayed at our home twice and did magic tricks for Jan's third-grade class at South River School.

Brad Mills

Brad was Terry Francona's bench coach (2004–2009). In Game 2 of the '07 World Series, with the Red Sox leading 2–1 in the eighth inning and Jonathan Pabelbon on the mound, Brad called the pickoff move that got Matt Holliday picked off first base, the pivotal play of the Series. Brad is a very nice man and a classy gentleman.

John McClaren

John was the Red Sox's bullpen coach in 1991. Joe Morgan hired him and he remained loyal to Joe. John went on to manage the Mariners for parts of 2007 and '08. He has had a long career in baseball.

Johnny Pesky

Johnny was a coach with the Red Sox from 1975 to 1984. He'd managed the team from 1963 to '64. Johnny did it all for the Red Sox: a great player, coach, manager, advertising salesman, broadcaster, assistant to the general manager, and goodwill ambassador. Most of all, Johnny Pesky is Mr. Red Sox, beloved by fans throughout New England.

Mike Roarke

Mike, a native of West Warwick, Rhode Island, was the Red Sox's pitching coach in 1994. Mike and his wife, MerrySue, are both personal friends. Mike, who spent four years as a catcher with the Tigers, was considered one of the best pitching coaches of his era. Unfortunately, the '94 Red Sox team did not have a whole lot of talent and finished fourth. 1994 was also the strike year, so the team played only 115 games. In 2006, Bruce Sutter invited Mike to the Hall of Fame in Cooperstown when Bruce was inducted because Mike worked with him on his split-finger fastball.

Rac Slider

Rac managed for many years in the Red Sox's farm system and coached third base for Joe Morgan. He was the bullpen coach under John McNamara.

A native of Simms, Texas, Rac is the only guy with whom I've ever discussed the branding of a cow.

Lee Stange

"The Stinger." I was with Lee in 1983 and '84 when he was the Red Sox pitching coach. I still see Lee at Red Sox fantasy camps. A very nice man, Lee is very laid back. He let players work to their strengths and did not overcoach. Lee was very well liked.

Frank White

Frank played a stellar second base for the Kansas City Royals from 1973 to 1990. Frank's one of the best I've ever seen, and he's a member of the Royals' Hall of Fame. Frank was with the Red Sox (1994–96) as the first base coach. I really enjoyed talking baseball with Frank, especially about playing the middle infield.

Eddie Yost

Brooklyn-born Eddie Yost was known as "the Walking Man" because he led the AL in walks six times, and had more than 100 walks eight times.

I was with Eddie in 1983 and '84, when he was the Red Sox's third-base coach. Long before year-round conditioning became something that every player did—or tried to do—he remained in tremendous condition his entire life. He played in the majors for 18 years, mostly with the Washington Senators.

Eddie was a very strong baseball man who really knew the game inside and out. I loved to spend time with him. His hobby was fixing clocks, which he continued to do in his retirement.

Don Zimmer

Don Zimmer was the Red Sox's manager from 1976 to 1980, including the "Bucky Dent" game which ended the '78 season. Don was the Red Sox bench coach in 1992. I thought that Zim was a great baseball man. I loved hearing stories about the Brooklyn Dodgers from him. He's now a special coach with the Tampa Bay Rays, on the field and in uniform before games. I still talk with Zim when Boston plays Tampa Bay. He's a great storyteller. Don is the last Brooklyn Dodger still in uniform.

Jim Leyland

Jim is a great guy. I met him during the 1986 World Series party in New York, shortly after he was appointed as the new manager of the Pittsburgh Pirates. He led the Pirates to the NLCS for three years, then won a world championship with the Florida Marlins in 1997. He's been managing the Detroit Tigers since 2006.

I love to sit in his office during his news conferences before the game because I always learn something about the game, some nuance. Jim is a very good judge of people and he really knows the game inside out from all his years in the game, although I don't believe he ever played above AA.

Joe Maddon

Joe's been in baseball for more than 30 years as a coach and a manager, now with Tampa Bay. He's an erudite guy who went to Lafayette College, which is in the Patriot League like Colgate, my alma mater. We always talk about that. Joe could probably manage anywhere. He's great with the media. He's always interesting. We talk about bike trails because we both like biking and occasionally exchange wines. Joe has great people skills and that certainly goes for dealing with players as well. Tampa Bay gets the most out of its talent—and out of its budget.

CHAPTER 15

"Everybody Wants to Rule the World"

Managers, General Managers, and Front Office

DURING MY YEARS WITH THE RED SOX, I'VE WORKED WITH SOME VERY COLORFUL AND OUTSTANDING MANAGERS.

Ralph Houk (1983–84)

I was thrilled to be with Ralph because I had been a Yankee fan in 1961 when he first managed and won the AL pennant in his first three years. Ralph was very nice to me. I frequently sat with Ralph in the dugout before games. I loved to get him to tell old stories about Mickey Mantle, Roger Maris, Moose Skowron, Bobby Richardson, Tony Kubek, the stars of the '61 team. Ralph always rode the bus to the ballpark at five o'clock. He liked to kid around. I remember one time in '84 he was watching the College World Series on ESPN, pitting Cal-Fullerton against Texas. Ralph bet me on the game. Ralph knew that the game was on tape. I didn't. He got the biggest charge out of that.

We never saw Ralph on the road except on the bus or at the ballpark. He was never visible around the team hotel. But one time toward the end of the '83 season, my first year, I saw him toward the end of the season at the hotel pool in Baltimore. The Red Sox were headed for a sixth-place finish in the AL East. He said he was getting his skin ready for Florida. He lived in Florida. He asked me how it was going with me. I told him that I thought I might not be asked back for a second season with the Red Sox. Ralph scoffed and told me that the baseball people loved me. He said that they all thought I was doing a great job. He told me that I had nothing to worry about, I'd be back the following season and for as long as I wanted to be. Decisions about broadcasters were, of course, not part of his domain. But Ralph had a way of making you feel 10 feet tall. He did that with players too. That was a characteristic that made Ralph a very good manager.

Ralph had been a catcher on the Yankees (1947–1954). He had five seasons in which he played fewer than 10 games. Why? Because the Yankees had a catcher: future Hall of Famer Yogi Berra. Perhaps his own experiences being an "extra man" made it easier for Ralph to relate to all the extra men he managed. He called them the "extree men" in his Kansas accent.

As far as his Red Sox team goes, Ralph was in Boston during a period of transition. Houk was hired after Fred Lynn, Carlton Fisk, and Rick Burleson had left. He got the team to respectability despite the defections. Houk really emphasized pitching. He broke in Roger Clemens in '84 when he was just 21 and was very careful with him. The players loved Ralph as did most members of the media.

John McNamara (1985–88)

After Ralph came John McNamara. John emphasized pitching, and worked very well with the pitchers. John was very considerate of the broadcasters, but he did not want to do a pregame show. He didn't seem to enjoy mixing with the media. But I do recall when the Red Sox clinched the AL East title in 1986, we were in the clubhouse doing postgame interviews and McNamara said to me, "You and Ken Coleman are a part of this. So congratulations to you guys too—enjoy it." I thought that was a very gracious thing to say.

Poor Mac never recovered from losing the '86 World Series. There are all kinds of theories about whether Roger Clemens asked to be taken out of that game, or whether McNamara took him out. Only Bill Fischer, the pitching coach, knows, and he's not saying. But Clemens did come out of the game, the Red Sox lost Game 6, and lost the Series in Game 7.

Despite the loss, there was a parade in Boston two days after the Series. 500,000 people turned out to greet the AL champions. After it was over, I went to the manager's office and congratulated John on winning the pennant. The team had gone a long way and had had an excellent season. I'll never forget Mac's succinct response. "Why me? Why me? I go to church every Sunday. I live the right way. Why did this happen to me? Why did we have to lose this World Series? Why me?" I know John went to church, because I occasionally went with him. Mac was a very conflicted guy. I don't think he has ever recovered from losing that World Series. The loss has continued to haunt him.

Joseph Michael Morgan (1988–1991)

John McNamara was let go in 1988 and replaced by the third-base coach, Joseph Michael Morgan. Joe is probably my best friend in baseball, day in and day out. I got to know Joe in '85 when he became a major league coach after a long career as a minor league manager. He really wanted to manage in the big leagues, and when McNamara was fired at the All-Star break in '88, Morgan was hired. He was told, "You're interim. That might mean one day or one week." When the media asked him about it as his first press conference, he told the writers, "Interim, sir, is not in my vocabulary."

The team won 12 games in a row and 19 out of 20. It was a sensational run. Joe did not go by numbers. He had a tremendous sense and feel for the game and when he should make moves. A great manager, but an even better friend. We had so much in common, shared during baseball conversations and exchanging trivia and evaluations of players. Joe had been a scout after managing in the minors for two years. He scouted Roger Clemens and Greg Maddux. He watched Maddux pitch in Las Vegas, and taught him how to throw a changeup. I've shared many great memories with Joe. He has a language all his own.

My children love Joe and quote him all the time. One of his favorites was the night the 12 wins in a row streak ended in Texas. Tommy was with me. We had a pizza in Joe's hotel room, and when there was just one piece left, Joe said, "Always that last piece, always that last piece. Jump on it kid, with both hands!"

Joe Morgan's three and a half years as manager was probably the most fun I've ever had apart from winning world championships. Joe was the most honest manager the Red Sox have ever had, and the most honest man I've ever known. One of my favorite stories happened in '89 in a game against the Chicago White Sox in Comiskey Park. The Red Sox had been platooning catchers, with Rich Gedman batting lefty against righthanders, and Rick Cerone batting righty against lefties. I taped the pregame show with Joe Morgan. After I turned the tape recorder off I asked why Cerone was catching instead of Gedman with Shawn Hillegas on the mound for the White Sox. Joe said, "Because Hillegas is a left-hander." I said, "No, he's not, Joe. He's a righty." "Oh, I [screwed] up," said Joe. He didn't change the lineup. As it turned out, Rick Cerone hit a three-run homer off Hillegas to win the game for Boston. I knew that Cerone was in the lineup by accident, because Joe Morgan thought that Hillegas was a left-hander. But I didn't mention it on the air because Joe is my friend and the Red Sox won, so what's the difference?

Reporters asked whether he had had a hunch, like playing a horse. (Joe loved playing the horses.) They wanted to know whether that was why he had put Cerone in instead of Gedman. He could have said yes, and looked like a genius. Only he and I would have known. But Honest Joe Morgan, a man incapable of telling a lie, the original George Washington clone, said, "No, I screwed up. I thought Hillegas was a left-hander." A couple of the writers ripped him for it, but most appreciated his honesty.

In early August of the 1991 season, Joe was almost fired. The Red Sox were under .500 and trailing in the AL East. But the team got hot. The Sox were half a game from first place on September 22, before falling short of Toronto.

Two days after the end of the season, Joe went in to talk to the front office people about his coaches. He saw everybody sitting there: Haywood Sullivan, John Harrington, and general manager Lou Gorman. Joe realized that he was not there to talk about the coaches. Joe, always direct and to the point, asked, "Well, am I out of there?" He was told yes, he was out. Then Joe said, "I just want to say one thing. Your team is not as good as you think it is." And wow, was he ever right. In '92, the Red Sox finished in last place (23 games behind the Blue Jays) for the first time since 1932. He was prophetic.

After he was fired, Joe didn't want to go home right away because he wasn't ready to face the media. So he came to our house. I remember that I had gone out to get a lawn mower fixed. Jan heard about the firing while she was at the dentist. I heard about it when I got a call from a friend. Kate, then 12, had just come home from school and heard it on the news. Joe Morgan knocked on our door and asked, "Katie, did you hear?" She had, but she said no. "I'm out of there. I'm axed." said Joe. After that, Kate didn't really know what to say. Jan and I returned shortly thereafter. Jeffrey Lyons called. They had a nice conversation.

I think that the firing of Joe Morgan was a big mistake. He might have quit after '92, the last year on his contract, but he certainly deserved a better fate.

In my opinion, to this day, firing Joseph Michael Morgan is the single biggest mistake I've seen the Red Sox make.

Joe didn't come back to the ballpark for three or four years. Now, he does go to Fenway and occasionally does events for the team. He follows the ballclub day in and day out. He absolutely loves Dustin Pedroia.

Jan and I still socialize with Joe and Dot quite often. The Morgans go to their house in Naples, Florida, every winter, so we see them during spring training every winter. And during the season, we see the Morgans quite often.

Butch Hobson (1992–94)

Butch, a star quarterback at the University of Alabama—as his father, Clell, had been—was a power-hitting third baseman for the Red Sox and later the Angels and Yankees. Butch was a good baseball guy who could give a football coach's pregame pep talk to the team. But he inherited a bad team. During the off-season, shortly after Hobson took over, Jean Yawkey, the team's owner, died. She had been a great source of support for Butch. During spring training, Roger Clemens held out. I remember a TV shot of Clemens during spring training running around the track on the field. Butch was running with him, but Clemens was wearing headphones, and it looked as if he was ignoring Hobson. The image did not help Butch.

The team was slow, didn't hit much, and didn't have a whole lot of pitching. The Red Sox finished in last place in 1992 and fifth place in '93. Hobson was let go after the strike in '94.

Kevin Kennedy (1995–96)

Kevin was an excellent manager between the lines. He pretty much managed for the stars. He certainly favored José Canseco. Then he learned how important Mo Vaughn was to the team. Mo was really the go-to guy. The team won the AL East title in 1995.

In '96, the Red Sox looked like a slow-pitch softball team. Kevin Mitchell was probably the best outfielder, with Canseco and Dwayne Hosey, who didn't belong in the big leagues. The '96 Red Sox were a very limited club. They started 0–5 then went 3–15. They got into the race late and finished third. Kevin had some communication issues with Dan Duquette, the general manager, and was fired when the season ended.

Jimy Williams (1997–2001)

I probably did more pregame manager's shows with Jimy than with anybody. Jimy is another one of my favorites. Jimy took over the Red Sox in 1997. He managed the team until August 16, 2001. Jimy is a great instructor. He made Trot Nixon a hitter. He got him in the indoor batting cage and threw to him every day until he was drenched with sweat.

Jimy was also an excellent infield coach. He really worked very well with Nomar, getting him to make that wonderful turnaround jump throw from the third-base hole at short. Jimy got Nomar to stop throwing sinkers. Jimy hit thousands of ground balls to Nomar.

Jimy was a very principled guy even when it meant disagreeing with the general manager, Dan Duquette. He had Steve Avery, whom he had been with on the Atlanta Braves for a long time, as a coach. Williams didn't find out until the day before Avery's next start that there was a clause in Avery's contract providing that if Avery started a certain number of games in '98, his contract would kick in for '99 with big dollars. Avery already had 10 wins. Avery was due to pitch, and Jimy started him against the wishes of the front office. He said, "It's the right thing to do." Avery did start, and his big-money contract for the following year kicked in. But management held it against Jimy for the rest of his tenure. At the end of the '98 season Avery was gone. He signed with the Reds as a free agent.

I always thought that Jimy was an excellent game manager. He was a good communicator with most of the players and really knew the ins and outs of baseball. Jimy was also one of the best instructors I've ever been around.

Jimy was good with the beat reporters and columnists he saw every day, but he was a little suspicious of TV people and others he didn't see on a regular basis. Our families were close. His sons are good friends of mine. Sean, now in his twenties, has played in the independent leagues. His older son, Brady, is managing in the Tampa Bay system. Jimy worked spring training with the Braves, and later managed the Astros. Jimy Williams was a very solid baseball guy and a very loyal, honest man, just like Joe Morgan.

Joe Kerrigan (2001)

After Jimy Williams was fired, general manager Dan Duquette gave the managing job to pitching coach Joe Kerrigan. The best thing I can say about Joe Kerrigan as a manager is that he was a good pitching coach. Things fell apart and deteriorated into near anarchy on the team, especially after we came back from the break following the attacks of September 11. Pedro Martinez was very unhappy. The team tried to make him pitch when he was hurt. That didn't work. Carl Everett was very unhappy. Other players were very unhappy too. It was a very tough situation.

New owners took over. Kerrigan was still the manager when spring training started in 2002, but just a week or so into workouts, Kerrigan was replaced by Grady Little. Grady had been a Red Sox coach under Jimy Williams and was coaching with Cleveland. I spoke with Grady and asked, "Are you a candidate to manage?" He said, "I hope so."

Grady Little (2002–03)

The Red Sox brought Grady down to Ft. Myers from Winter Haven, where the Indians trained, and put him in a back room of the Red Sox clubhouse. When the new owners of the team announced that there would be a new manager, and brought out Grady to introduce him to the team, he received a standing ovation.

Grady did very well. In 2002, the Red Sox finished in second place in the AL East. In '03, the team made it to the final game of the ALCS. Grady's decision not to pull Pedro Martinez from that game in the eighth inning will probably be debated for many years. Some think that that decision cost him his job. Hideki Matsui and Jorge Posada hit run-scoring doubles and the Yankees rallied to tie the game, which they eventually won on Aaron Boone's walk-off homer in the 11th inning.

I understood why Little left Pedro in the game. Pedro Martinez was the Red Sox's best pitcher. Even though the Boston bullpen had done well earlier in the series, there was no true closer.

I'll never forget a chance encounter I had in the parking lot after a frustrating loss that season to the St. Louis Cardinals. A Red Sox executive said to Jerry Trupiano and me, "We don't know what's going on with Grady. We give him all these statistical breakdowns, but he manages anecdotally." Clearly, there was some unhappiness in the team's upper management at Little for not using the stats and other computer-generated information that was available to him. They thought Grady was managing by hunches. I still think that Grady was a good manager.

Terry Francona (2004–2011)

Terry Francona took over after the 2003 season. To me, Terry Francona and Joe Morgan are the best managers in Red Sox history. "Tito," as his friends call him (after his father, Tito, a major league outfielder), is a very good manager. He has excellent people skills. He knows how to deal with players, players who are stars and players who are not. Terry's strategy is outstanding, but most managers are okay with strategy. It's how Terry handles people that sets him apart. He knows how to use people in spots to succeed. He never asks anybody to play hurt. He has the ability to get the most out of all 25 players on the team, and that's what a good manager does.

Terry Francona had the second-longest tenure (eight years) of any Red Sox manager. (Joe Cronin managed the team for 13 years.) And, of course, he guided the team to two world championships.

I've also worked with a diverse cast of general managers.

Lou Gorman (1984–1993)

I've written about Lou Gorman in a number of parts of this book. Here's another. Lou was one of the warmest people in baseball, a wonderful guy who was beloved by everyone who knew him, even the secretaries in the office. When he'd send out for lunch, he'd buy lunch for everybody. Young people in the Red Sox office especially liked Lou. As general manager in 1986, Lou made some very good deals that helped the team. He acquired Dave Henderson and Spike Owen, and helped Boston get to Game 7 of the World Series. He was the general manager from '84 through the 1993 season, but he never had the ultimate power. Haywood Sullivan was the club president above him. I thought that Lou did a wonderful balancing act dealing with some of the club's problems and ownership camps, from Sullivan to Yawkey to John Harrington. When there was a dispute, Lou was always in the middle. He took a lot of bullets for the organization. When decisions were made by upper management, Lou was the guy who faced the media and the public. Lou was a great baseball guy and a great storyteller.

Lou loved baseball and loved the U.S. Navy, where he was a reserve officer for 30 years. He had been in the Navy before he got into college. He also loved Stonehill College.

One of his favorite stories was about the bakers in the Navy. He described the smell of fresh-baked pastries and bread wafting throughout the ship. He had us all salivating when he told the story.

After Lou's tenure as general manager, he remained with the club as a senior advisor. I saw him at the stadium in Ft. Myers and at Fenway Park almost every day, and he and I spoke all the time. During the regular season, he maintained an office at Fenway, where he held court and continued to tell great stories. He also picked the menu for the owners' box daily.

In March 2011, I did a speech for Lou at a senior citizens men's group on the island of Boca Grande off the West Coast of Florida. Lou was ill and asked me to fill in for him. The next day, he called to thank me. He was very complimentary. That was the last time I spoke with Lou. Fittingly enough, he passed away on Opening Day '11.

Dan Duquette (1994–2002)

Dan was a very smart guy whom I first met when I was with the Milwaukee Brewers. He was in his second year in the Brewers' scouting and farm department. Harry Dalton, like Dan an Amherst graduate, was the general manager. Dan was a catcher on his college team who loved baseball. I thought that Dan had a good sense of baseball talent. He made one tremendous trade in particular, obtaining Jason Varitek and Derek Lowe from Seattle for Heathcliff Slocumb. After the 1996 season, Dan let 34-year-old Roger Clemens leave for Toronto as a free agent. In Toronto, Clemens won back-to-back Cy Young Awards in '97 and '98, as well as the mythical Triple Crown of pitching in both years, plus additional Cy Young Awards in New York (2001) and Houston ('04). He was selected for the All-Star team six more times and won 20 games three times.

Dan took a lot of heat for that decision. But with the allegations against Roger, in the final analysis, who knows what the case really is?

I also thought that there was a mistake made when Mo Vaughn was not given a decent offer and was in effect driven out of town after the '98 season. In my opinion, letting Mo get away and firing Joe Morgan are the two biggest mistakes the Red Sox have made over the last 30 years.

Mike Port (2002)

Dan was the Red Sox's general manager during a tough era. Team ownership changed. He was out in 2002. Then Mike Port took over on an interim basis.

Mike is a really wonderful baseball guy with a dry sense of humor. He had been the general manager of the Angels. Mike was liked and respected by all. He was extremely competent and was very much a gentleman. I thought he did a very good job in '02 after the turmoil with the change of managers and general managers. Mike went on to have an excellent career in the baseball commissioner's office as vice president in charge of umpires. They had tremendous respect for Mike as well.

Mike Dee (2002–2009)

One of the best executives I have ever encountered in baseball is Mike Dee, former chief operating officer of the Red Sox. Mike, a Baltimore native, came to Boston from the San Diego Padres. He gave the Red Sox a touch of class and social grace, reminiscent of our former traveling secretary, the late Jack Rogers. Mike also brought a wealth of innovative business ideas to the club and is largely responsible for the Red Sox' new spring training facility, Jet Blue Stadium. Mike comes by his friendly nature and class naturally. His parents, Jim and Ruth Dee, our dear friends and neighbors in Ft. Myers, have to be the most contemporary octogenarians we know. Mike left the Red Sox in 2009 to become the CEO of the Miami Dolphins. Baseball's loss is football's gain.

John Henry, Tom Werner, and Larry Lucchino; Theo Epstein (2002–2011)

When he was hired, Theo Epstein was just 28, the youngest general manager in the game. I always found him a personable and very bright guy. Theo was also very thorough. He knows talent and knows how to talk to players, and how to get along with players. Of course, not every free agent works out, but I think Theo has done a very good job of building the Red Sox farm system. We see much better athletes in the farm system, guys coming up who are more athletic and better conditioned with greater speed.

In his first year as general manager, Theo's team went to the seventh game of the ALCS. He won the World Series in 2004, his second year, and again in '07. Of course, he has had great support from the team's owners to spend the dollars that it takes and that's certainly another credit to the owners.

Shortly after the very disappointing end of the 2011 season, Theo left Boston to become president of baseball operations for the Chicago Cubs. For three years, Theo and I did a pregame show every day. And in later years he was available when we needed his perspective. Theo left a wonderful legacy and I will miss his friendship.

Haywood Sullivan, Jean Yawkey, and John Harrington did a good job as owners. The team was run by the Yawkey Trust. Profitmaking didn't seem essential.

They did spend to win. At times, perhaps they tried to win too quickly, such as in the early 1990s, when they signed some free agents in an effort to win one for Jean Yawkey before she passed away. That didn't work out. There didn't seem to be a great concern that they maxed out financially.

The ownership group of principal owner John Henry, chairman Tom Werner, and Larry Lucchino, the president and CEO has made winning a top priority. Henry is the best type of owner a team could have: positive, generous, and innovative. He lets people do the jobs they were hired to do.

Around the time that John Henry, Tom Werner, and Larry Lucchino bought the team in '01, there was much speculation that the Red Sox would build a brand-new stadium. The previous owners had models and plans for a "new Fenway," with more seats and more luxury boxes but retaining the ballpark's quirky dimensions. With only 33,000 seats, Fenway had the smallest seating capacity in the majors. But the new owners decided that the Red Sox would continue to play at Fenway Park, which turns 100 years old in 2012.

In addition to routine maintenance, the new owners have spent millions of dollars to make many outright improvements to the park, such as the new seats above the Green Monster. These seats have become extremely popular. A "Monster seat" now sells for about $200. Fenway Park now holds about 38,500 fans.

They also added numerous player amenities, such as refurbished clubhouses, new batting cages, and a new weight room.

Money has never been a stumbling block when it comes to signing talent. The triumvirate has worked very well. Larry Lucchino virtually rebuilt Fenway while maintaining its nearly 100-year-old charm. He needed to get involved civically and politically with Boston city government to get things done. Tom Werner has dealt very successfully with the New England Sports Network, which is part of their purchase of the team.

This group has worked very well over its decade of ownership. The team has been competitive during every year of their stewardship. The owners provided former-GM Theo Epstein, former-manager Terry Francona, and the coaches with the wherewithal to win. They have also been very supportive of us as broadcasters. They have never told us what to say or what not to say. That goes for the previous ownership group, general managers, and managers. They trust our journalistic judgment and our honesty and integrity. We are very thankful for that and recognize that it's not like that everywhere.

Chapter 16

"These Eyes"
Umpires

I'VE ALWAYS HAD A LOT OF RESPECT FOR UMPIRES. They have a very difficult job. Some of them are very good. I think there was a time when umpires were like Supreme Court justices; they couldn't be touched. Some got complacent, some got out of shape, some got arrogant. But I think that baseball reeled it in after the umpires' disastrous resignation in 1999, part of an ill-advised union tactic that backfired when major league baseball accepted the resignations. The umpires' union was dissolved and they formed a new union with new leadership. Baseball regained control of the umpires. Since then, we've seen a much better product by the umpires. Now, they are graded and although it doesn't happen very often, they can be replaced if they are incompetent. They hustle, they work hard, and they try to stay in shape.

In my opinion, the best umpires working today are Tim Tschida and John Hirschbeck. Both are friends of mine, so there is a little personal feeling involved.

Tim Tschida is a native of St. Paul, Minnesota, and went to Cretin-Derham Hall, the same high school as Joe Mauer and Hall of Famer Paul Molitor. Tim's very close with a number of hockey officials, and actually officiated high school and college hockey games. He's in excellent shape. Tim lives in the same complex as Jan and I in Ft. Myers. We always see him out rollerblading, riding his bike, or working out in the gym. For umpires, as for players, staying in shape is a year-round job. Tim works hard at his trade. He's been a big-league umpire since 1986. If he works to retirement age, Tim will have worked more years than anybody, but he won't necessarily have umpired the most games, because major league umpires now have mid-season vacations. I think Tim has earned enshrinement in the Hall of Fame.

The same goes for John Hirschbeck, who has been in the majors since '84. His brother Mark was a major league umpire for 15 seasons. John, from Stratford, Connecticut—not far from my hometown of Hamden—has been a friend for many years. He lives in Poland, Ohio, not far from Youngstown, so we have a common bond. John was stricken with testicular cancer when he was in his fifties. He also underwent vertebrae fusion surgery on his neck. Many umpires have problems with their vertebrae and necks because of getting hit by foul tips.

John is in great shape and hustles. He bears down on every play and on every pitch when he's behind the plate. He's had a lot of setbacks to deal with, including his children's illnesses. His oldest son, John, passed away at the age of eight from an extremely rare disease called Adrenoleukodystrophy, a degenerative nervous system disorder. His other son, Michael, who also has Adrenoleukodystrophy, is now 23. John's two daughters are healthy. Although he still suffers many seizures, Michael often makes trips with his dad and sometimes works as a batboy. Former Red Sox manager Terry Francona is very fond of him and the two are very close.

John was the umpire whom future Hall of Famer Roberto Alomar spat at in '96 during an in-game confrontation, but in the intervening years, the two have become quite close. Roberto donated $50,000 himself and helps raise funds for Hirschbeck's charity, ALD Research at the Kennedy Krieger Institute in Baltimore. While he has been regarded as a pitcher's umpire, John is an excellent balls-and-strikes umpire. He runs a good game, he's in charge.

Steve Palermo was a great umpire with great instincts and a great joy for the game. Steve always had a bounce to his step and was very highly regarded. But his career ended in '91 in the parking lot of a Dallas restaurant when he came to the aid of some waitresses who were being robbed. Steve was shot and suffered a spinal injury. Through hard work and intensive rehabilitation, Steve is now able to walk with just the use of a cane, but his umpiring career was over. He's been a supervisor of umpires for many years. He always comes to see us when he's at Fenway Park, or in Kansas City where he lives with his wonderful wife, Debbie, who has done great things with Steve and his foundation to assist others with spinal injuries. Steve Palermo was the best umpire of his time, and would have gone to Cooperstown had he not been shot and unable to work again.

The umpire working now who reminds me of Steve in his umpiring style is Lazaro Diaz, an excellent, hustling young umpire.

I learned about dealing with umpires—as with so many other things—from Ernie Harwell. Ernie would visit with the umpires in the umpires' room at the ballpark, and I try to do that too. I've gotten to know some of the members of Tim Tschida's and John Hirschbeck's umpiring crews.

I think going to see the umpires before the game is important. Sometimes, it's instructive to try to see things from the umpires' point of view. They need friends too.

Jeff Nelson, a cancer survivor from the Twin Cities, is another umpire I really respect. Jeff has been on our Jimmy Fund telethon/radiothons.

Rick Reed is another umpire I really respected during his 28 years in the big leagues. He suffered a stroke two years ago and came back to work, although Major League Baseball was a little uncomfortable with that. He finished that season and retired to become an umpire "observer" in Detroit, where he lives.

I thought that Rich Garcia was a very good umpire despite making the infamous home run call in the Jeffrey Maier incident during Game 1 of the '96 ALCS. Rich always hustled and bore down, ignoring all distractions, and concentrating on the play in front of him. Rich was later a supervisor of umpires until 2010.

Of course, we do point out when an umpire blows a call, especially when an umpire tries to call attention to himself. There are a few who do not realize that the fans do not come to the ballpark to see them work.

CHAPTER 17

"What a Fool Believes"

What it Takes to be a Major League Broadcaster

HOW DO YOU PREPARE TO BE A BROADCASTER IN BASEBALL? It takes a lifetime. Baseball is the hardest game to broadcast because of the non-action. That little white sphere with the 108 red stitches, weighing just 5½ ounces, is only in play about eight minutes during a typical three-hour game. The rest of the time, it's being held, somebody is scratching something, somebody is spitting, somebody is talking or arguing, or gesticulating, but the ball is not moving. What you really need is to know the game of baseball. Basketball carries itself. The only time the action stops is when there is a foul shot or a timeout. When there's a foul shot, the analyst talks. When there's a timeout, you go to commercial.

Hockey is very similar in this respect to basketball, the action of the puck on the ice carries itself. But with the clock running virtually all the time in hockey, there is even less time for the analyst to explain what just happened, or what might happen next. Sure, the action comes to a halt occasionally—when there is a faceoff, or after a goal—but those breaks are rather short.

Football is similar. The split between the play-by-play caller and the analyst is very distinct. When they break the huddle, the play-by-play announcer sets the tone. After the play, the analyst explains what went right, or what went wrong and why it happened.

In baseball what happens between pitches is really what makes or breaks the announcer. First, you have to be ready to capitalize on the action and be ready for it. But you have to be ready to fill the time between pitches or you'll lose your audience because there is so much time between pitches. There is a 12-second rule for pitchers, very seldom enforced with nobody on base. With runners on base, it can take longer than that. There is plenty of time to discuss strategy as moves are being made.

That's why I think calling a baseball game is more difficult than basketball, football, or hockey. It takes more knowledge not only of the game in front of you, but you have to know the history of the game—what came before. I think it starts when a kid is old enough to start collecting baseball cards, or to root for one team, or to have a favorite player, or to have a catch in the back yard or at the ballfield.

You can't be ambivalent or neutral about baseball. You have to love it because the games are long, the season is long, and not every game is a great game. You have to be a true baseball fan, with a real love of the game to be able to broadcast it.

I always preach that youngsters should play the game as long as they can, but play it like a thinking man: think about why you're throwing to a certain base. Think about why the ball reacts the way it does when you spin it for a curve ball, or throw across the seams. Learn the game. You will find that not everybody has the same skill level. Most of us broadcasters who are not retired ballplayers wanted to be major league baseball players. And most of us did not become ballplayers because we didn't have the ability. But we loved the game, and wanted to stay around it, so we picked the next best thing: broadcasting.

So, I suggest playing the game as long as you can. Collect baseball cards, and learn about the different teams and players. That's how I learned. I didn't just collect the cards; I read the backs of the cards. I learned about the players, their backgrounds, and their different talents. I was also a pretty good card flipper. All of this added to my knowledge of the game.

Baseball is also a game to be researched and studied. It's important to read biographies of the greats of the game, and to read the history of the game. Everything that happens in baseball relates somehow to yesterday's game, or last week's game, or a game last year, or ten years ago, or even fifty years ago. You saw a triple play today? When was the last one? Did it happen the same way? Which players were involved? A no-hitter? By whom? Against whom? Baseball is built on what happened in the past.

In football, the players are so much bigger and the games last so much longer now than years ago. There are more plays now because the clock stops so often.

Basketball is a totally different game than it was years ago because of the pace, the size of the players, the shot clock, and the evolution of the game.

Sure baseball players are bigger and faster and stronger now than they used to be. But baseball is really the only sport where you can compare statistics from the past to today because, except for a little tinkering like the designated hitter in the AL, longer schedules, bigger gloves, night games, and batting helmets, baseball is virtually unchanged since 1893 when the pitcher's mound was moved back to 60'6" from home plate. The bases are still 90 feet apart. It's still three strikes and you're out.

I think it's important to read about the history of the game, and its stars: the Dead-ball Era, the Steroid era, what happened to baseball during the Depression, the Year of the Hitter, the Year of the Pitcher, World War II's effect on the game, and the expansion era.

Baseball has reflected other changes and trends in American history, too, including the influx of different ethnicities in the game: the Irish and German immigrants after the turn of the 20th century, the Italians in the 1930s and '40s, then the coming of Jackie Robinson and other black ballplayers. In the '60s and through today, the increasing number of Hispanic ballplayers from Latin America and the Caribbean. In the '90s and 2000s, the increase in the number of Asian players, mostly from Japan. The history of the labor movement in America is also reflected in baseball.

The game of baseball is a microcosm of American history, and I think that a good sense of history is essential for a good baseball broadcaster. As I said, everything that happened in last night's game was influenced by what happened last week, last month, last year, and 50 or 100 years ago.

I think the young fan who aspires to a career behind the microphone should learn how to keep score in a baseball game. It's very simple. Here again, past is prologue: what happened in the second inning is built on what happened in the first inning. And what happened in the ninth inning is predicated on what went before. If you keep score, you can see what happened before. I have kept all my old scorebooks since '79. I have them in my attic and refer to them when I have to look up something.

Baseball is also a great game of anecdotes. You can read them in books or in magazines, or more recently online. But I always thought that the best stories come from face-to-face conversations with players.

Baseball has more memorable moments than any other game—moments besides who won, who lost, and who hit a home run or scored.

When I started out as a broadcaster, I had to overcome the trepidations about asking big-name athletes for an interview. I remember as a young broadcaster in Youngstown, Ohio, going to Cleveland Stadium on a very cold Saturday afternoon in April. I wanted to interview Ted Williams, then the manager of the Washington Senators. I had all kinds of fears about Ted. I knew what he thought about the media, and I knew he didn't really like reporters. But I sat in the dugout before the game and listened to him tell stories and talk about hitting—his favorite topic. Ted had an unusual way of talking: profane. It broke the ice and gave me the courage to go up to him and ask for an interview, which I did. He agreed, and we talked about some of his players, including Jim French, a young catcher from Andover, Ohio, not far from Youngstown. Williams called him "Frenchy," and he loved him. Of course, Ted liked just about every player. We did the interview, and what I remember most is that Williams never took his eyes off the hitter in the batting cage. He talked, he answered my questions, but he never looked at me. He kept studying the hitter in the batting cage.

That's Ted Williams, all about hitting. That was a breakthrough for me that gave me the courage to talk with a player of that stature. I still have a blown-up photograph of that encounter.

One day years later, Ted Williams tried to sell my dad, Dr. Frank, and me some real estate in Citrus Hills, Florida, where he lived and worked as a spokesman for a developer. As usual, Ted was very convincing about his land, 100 miles north of Tampa on the Crystal River. But I had kids in college, and my dad had a dermatology practice in Hamden, Connecticut. We declined to buy the land, but it was fun to hear Ted's strong sales pitch.

In '72, I was alone with Roberto Clemente in the Pirates' clubhouse in Pittsburgh. I did not have a tape recorder with me that day. And if I had been recording, Clemente probably would not have been as open with me.

He spoke about all the responsibilities he had in Pittsburgh with so many people wanting his time to do charity work or make appearances and that the pressure increased a hundred fold when he went back to his native Puerto Rico.

That conversation gave me a better understanding of Clemente. Later that year, on New Year's Eve, '72, I was working the night shift as a DJ at WJW radio and I saw a story on the newswire that Clemente's plane had crashed on a mercy mission to earthquake-ravaged Managua, Nicaragua.

Another necessary skill for the aspiring broadcaster is the social skill to be able to talk with a ballplayer about things besides baseball. That's where you get the great stories, the great anecdotes beyond runs, hits, and errors. Baseball is a great talking game, and it's also a great listening game. During a game, you have about three hours to talk, but I think the best advice I can give is to be a good listener.

As I mentioned, the preparation is your lifetime. You read the sports pages of the newspaper every day. In my case, I read the *Boston Globe* and *Boston Herald* every day at home. When I'm on the road, I read them online. The Internet has really expanded the information available to you. You have to be a good editor, have to know what you should leave out. But in baseball you have to stay current and know what happened yesterday with your team and your league and in the other league.

I believe that a problem many retired players trying to make it in broadcasting have is that because they just came off the field, they think they know everything there is to know about the game. What some fail to realize is that there is a 25- to 30-percent turnover in players each year. You have to stay current. You have to read the papers and check the Internet every day and not only for historical background: you also have to keep current. Those who know how to prepare do well. Name value might get a former player a job, but consistency keeps him there.

You prepare all day for a game—all week, all year, your whole life.

I keep file cards on every player in the AL. I don't do it for NL teams, because even with interleague play, we don't see the NL teams very often. The file cards are invaluable. I read each team's media guides, and make notes about the player's birthplace, residence, and occasionally his family. If he is one of 10 children, or if he is the father of triplets, I might put that on my card. I'll also add information that I've read, or learned about him in the papers, online, or in discussion with the player himself, the manager, the general manager, or teammates and other media people.

I write my index cards in longhand. It would be faster to do them on the computer and just update them, but in this case, the longhand helps me remember. I don't know whether that works for everybody, but it works for me.

In a typical game, the first time a batter steps up to the plate, I give his key statistics—batting average, home runs, hitting streaks—and what he's done against this pitcher before. In later at-bats, I recap what the hitter has done in previous at-bats during that day's game.

I also do a brief rundown on the pitchers: what pitches they throw, how they did in their last start, wins and losses, strikeouts, walks, innings pitched, hits surrendered, and ERA.

Much of our work is done before the home plate umpire says, "Play ball!" I usually try to get to the ballpark early, about three and a half hours before the first pitch. We have pregame shows to record, a manager's show, and player interviews. I talk to players and coaches from both teams behind the batting cage. We pre-record some commercials and station promotions. I also try to leave time to have dinner, usually in the media dining room where I pick up a lot of valuable information from other broadcasters, front office people, reporters, and scouts.

The games we broadcast today are roughly an hour longer than those called by Mel Allen and Red Barber in the 1950s and '60s. The reasons are many, but as a result, there is a need for more conversation.

Because of baseball's reliance on revenue from TV and radio advertising, the breaks between innings are somewhat longer than they used to be, in order to squeeze in more commercials. Another reason games are longer in the last 25 years or so is the emergence of the relief pitchers/specialists—not only closers, but lefthanders to face lefty batters, righties to face righties and eighth-inning specialists.

There are more conferences on the mound and more pitching changes and batters stepping out of the box and such. When I started listening to games on the radio and watching them on TV, while the new pitcher was walking in (or sometimes being driven in) and then warming up, the broadcasters would set the stage: Who's on base? How many outs? What's the count? Who is scheduled to bat next? Who might pinch-hit? What does the new pitcher throw? How has he done so far this season? How has he done against the next batter?

Bringing in a relief pitcher is one of the most important decisions a manager can make, and it leads to one of the most dramatic moments in the game. But today, as soon as the manager walks out to the mound and touches his arm—to signal either for a righty or a lefty—there's a commercial break. I'm not knocking commercials—they pay the bills—I'm trying to explain one of the differences in how the game is played between today and when I was a kid. Consequently, today's broadcasters need more information and more preparation than our predecessors because of the increased length of the games, and longer pre- and postgame shows as well.

Broadcasting a baseball game on radio is completely different from broadcasting a game on television. There are some markets where the broadcasters go back and forth to do baseball on both radio and TV, but the majority now split it. One set of broadcasters do only radio and others do only TV.

Radio is an announcer's medium. Television is a director's medium and an analyst's medium.

I think Ken Coleman put it best when he said that on television, the play-by-play broadcaster puts captions under pictures. He also draws out the analyst and reacts to the video. There are times as a TV broadcaster when you want a particular camera shot and you let the director or the producer know. But most of the time, you are reacting to the shot on the screen that has been selected for you by others. The actual play-by-play call on TV is minimal. We can all see it's a ground ball to shortstop. "Lowrie to Gonzalez—one out." The radio call of the same play: "Hard ground ball hit to the shortstop. He's up with it. He throws. Got him!"

As I said, radio is an announcer's medium. As Ernie Harwell said, "Nothing happens until I say it does." Obviously, the radio audience can't see the action. The radio broadcaster is given a blank canvas, and it's up to us to paint a word picture. There are so many things to talk about. Tell me what you see at that moment. What's going on?

On the Red Sox radio broadcasts we believe in a conversational broadcast. In this way, it is more similar to television than it is to the old-fashioned way of doing radio, where I did my innings, you did your innings, and you were silent the rest of the time. Baseball is a conversational game. What do you do when you go to a ballgame? You talk to the people sitting next to you or around you. It might be about baseball, or about food, or—as in our case—rock 'n' roll. It might be about what you did earlier in the day, or the previous night. There are many different ways to go and you're free to do that as long as you are ready to capture the action on the field when it happens. That's why nothing happens until we say it does. This is similar to an umpire's take on close plays. As Hall of Fame umpire Bill Klem said, "It ain't nothing until I call it!"

Major league broadcasting jobs do not open up very often. And when they do there are hundreds of applicants, from minor league baseball broadcasters to former athletes to sports reporters—like I was—who always wanted to do baseball but had little experience. Former players often have the inside track, especially if they apply to broadcast in the city where they played. However, the pool of ex-players who want to broadcast is large and they cannot survive on name value alone. The best of the ex-players know how to prepare and stay current and that goes for baseball analysts on TV and radio as well.

So, if you're planning a career in baseball broadcasting, you'll want to 1) play the game as long as you can, 2) read all you can about the history of the game—which takes a lifetime, as new books come out every year, 3) stay current through newspapers and the Internet, 4) and talk about the game with players, scouts, umpires, coaches—anybody you can find to talk baseball with. I am always learning more about the sport. I've learned things this year that I never knew before—for example about arm slots on cut fastballs. How can Mariano Rivera throw cut fastball after cut fastball, year after year, all virtually the same, yet another pitcher struggles to master this pitch? Is his arm slot different? What's comfortable for him?

There are all kinds of little things you can learn, not only about individual players, but about the history of the game. That's why it's so important to be a good listener. When you broadcast a baseball game, you have three hours to talk. Listen before the event.

CHAPTER 18

"Get Ready"

Preparing to Broadcast a Game

I UPDATE MY FILE CARDS WITH NEW STORIES, NEW STATS, NEW FACTS AND HAPPENINGS ABOUT EACH PLAYER. I make up new cards before our first series with each team once each year. As the teams change rosters through call-ups, free agent signings, and trades, I update my cards. I am fortunate that I have been blessed with excellent recall, and I don't have to constantly consult my notes. Recall is a God-given talent, but you can improve it with various techniques. As I mentioned, one that works for me, is writing something out by hand.

Let's assume you have done a lifetime worth of prep work. You've read the newspapers, checked the Internet, looked at the media guides, reviewed your cards, you know who's hot and who's not. You get the ballpark three or four hours before the first pitch. I do this for several reasons.

The pregame show is part of the preparation. Then I go over the notes. Each team hands you a packet full of statistics and game notes before each game, even in spring training. When I started with the Indians, and even later with the Red Sox, the game notes all fit on just one page. Today, they are seven or eight pages. The philosophy years ago was that if it didn't fit on one page, it was information you don't need.

Today, there is a hitters' page, a starting pitchers' page, a relief pitchers' page, a promotional page, and a historical page. Also included are injury and transaction updates.

I highlight some of the items I might want to refer to during the broadcast. For example, the game notes provide up-to-date hitter-pitcher matchups. When a particular player comes to bat, you may want to look up how he's done before against this pitcher.

This is all part of the pregame prep. I have my own scorecard, which I have printed every year. I modeled my scorecard after the Herb Score card. Score had been an excellent left-handed pitcher, and we worked at the same time in Cleveland, when he did radio and I did TV in 1979.

Herb's scorecard had diamonds for defensive charts, and places to record wins, losses, weather, attendance, umpires, winning record, losing record, plus the lineups. But this scorecard is designed with room for lots more specific information: home runs, RBIs, batting average, and notes for each hitter. I fill out my scorecard from the manager's lineup card posted in the clubhouse well before the game starts. I always carry a bottle of Wite-Out in case there is a late change in the lineup as I've written it down. I keep my scorebook in pen, but Jon Rish keeps score on his laptop computer. He has a program that does it all. I don't want to worry about something technical when I have a game to call. I don't want to be distracted. But it works for him. I have my laptop in front of me during the games, but that's just for research and news stories. I don't want to get bogged down with technical minutia that might distract me from watching and reporting what's happening on the field.

Keeping score, of course, is essential. Putting that scorecard together is what you do to get ready for a game.

You've read the notes, you've done the scorecards, you've interviewed the manager for the pregame show—Dave O'Brien and I now alternate that duty—and any player interviews we might want to tape to be ready for the sound of "Play ball!" at 7:05 PM. Then comes the dinner hour. Each major league ballpark has a media dining room. Some are better than others. They all used to be free of charge for the media, except for a tip. When Charlie Finley owned the Oakland A's, he figured out a way to save money in the media dining room. He always served the same thing: Kentucky Fried Chicken.

Now, everyone charges between $7–10. (Frankly, the food was probably better in most media dining rooms before they started charging.) We don't pay at home because the radio station pays the team millions of dollars each season for the rights, and that is included in the fee.

But the food is not the main reason I like to eat dinner in the media dining room. It's the chance to see other people: beat reporters for both teams, columnists, broadcasters, broadcast engineers, some front-office people, and scouts. I like to spend my time sitting and eating dinner with scouts. It's sort of a mutual pick-your-brain relationship. Many scouts are friends, some very good friends. All the information we get from a scout is not about his own team because if he's on the road, he probably doesn't get to see his own team very much. But he may know something about a team he's scouting (in advance of his team playing them), that we've played before. In my experience, speaking with scouts is a great way to learn about players: their characters, their ability to play with nagging injuries, how a player runs, who has a strong arm, etc.

Scouting is a very lonely lifestyle on the road, so many scouts are glad to have somebody to talk with. But it's not a one-way street. They learn about players I've seen or spoken to, on the Red Sox and opponents: who's on a hot streak, who's hurt, who's about to be called up to the big club. There are really no trade secrets in baseball. In my experience, scouts are trustworthy. They have the eyes to be able to discern skills. There is a debate about relying on computerized stats or the eyes and judgment of scouts. But to me, it's no dichotomy at all. You use both. The stats do tell a story, but only so much. They can't tell you if a pitcher has a bad delivery, or the way he might leave himself susceptible to an injury. Statistics can't tell you about heart, a very important factor in the game. Statistics can't tell you who can go to the post when he might be ailing, or whom you might want coming to bat with the game on the line.

Scouts can tell you about a player's skills and shortcomings. Statistics reveal a great deal, but they can never answer these questions. Frequently, the scouts can provide an insight, a sidelight, or sometimes even just an anecdote that will give you a new perspective on a player that you just can't get from any other source.

Most scouts travel alone. That is, it's rare for two scouts from the same team to travel together. So while there may be a number of scouts having dinner in the media dining room, chances are they are all from different teams. They may get together with scouts from other teams, or stay at the same hotel, or occasionally share rides. But generally each scout travels and works alone, not with a group of about 60, as we do with the Red Sox traveling party. So scouts might well be looking for some company, some camaraderie in the media dining room. I enjoy their company.

As you approach game time, there are probably some commercials to record. By the time the umpire says "Play ball!" a large part of your job has already been done. Then comes the performance part. You've done your prep, now you perform. By perform, I mean reacting and being on top of the plays. You have to be able to fill between the pitches—that's where the prep work comes in. You have to have stories, you have to have information. In my view, it's always better to use an anecdote instead of a statistic. That's what people enjoy. Any number or stat you use should tell a story. If you say that a batter has hit in seven or his last ten games, and is hitting .285, that doesn't tell you much. But if you say that this hitter has nine hits in 21 at-bats and three home runs against this pitcher, that's a stat that tells you a story: that this batter may have success against this pitcher. You want the numbers to amplify a story you are trying to tell you audience.

When the ball is put in play, you have to be ready to capitalize on the action. As I said, the little white ball is only in play for about eight minutes during a three-hour ballgame, but you better be ready during those eight minutes. You have to tell the audience where the ball is, where the runner is, who is fielding the ball, and what does he do with it. Don't get caught in the middle of a story or the middle of a sentence by the pitcher delivering the pitch. Any comment you're making should stop when the pitch is made. Ultimately, that's how you are judged: by how you describe the action. And once that ball is pitched, there's a lot of action. Even if you've only seen one inning of baseball in your life, you know that lots of things happen at the same time when the ball is hit. The batter takes off for first base, the fielders react. What are the baserunners (if any) doing? Running or holding up? What is the third base coach doing? Sending the runners or holding them up? What about the fielders? Where's the cutoff man? Is there going to be a play at a base, or at the plate?

When you sit down to write that paragraph, you have to write the sentences one at a time. But all the action on the field happens at the same time. You have to be prepared to describe it all. On television, assuming adequate camera work, the viewer can see what happens. But on the radio, *nothing happens until you describe it.* It takes less than one second for the ball to leave the pitcher's hand and get to home plate. Be ready for the ball to be put in play.

When you watch or listen to baseball highlights on a sports wrap-up show, all you hear are the action calls, not the between-pitches commentary. While it takes a well-rounded broadcaster to fill the time between pitches, it also takes a prepared broadcaster to describe and explain the action when the ball is pitched.

I believe in describing everything as vividly as possible on radio. I once read a line by Jack Craig, the first radio and TV sports columnist for the *Boston Globe.* He said that no two ground balls to the shortstop are alike. And I subscribe to that theory. Is it a slow roller that the shortstop has to charge? Is it a hot shot right at him? Is it hit in the hole, so he has to field the ball off-balance? Is the ball hit over second base, so he has to field the ball, turn his body, and throw to first? Always remember: no two ground balls to the shortstop are alike.

A drive is hit to the outfield. Is it deep? Is it a medium fly ball? Is it shallow? Back by the warning track? You really don't know. Follow the flight of the ball until it lands: either inside the park, in a fielder's glove, or out of the ballpark for a home run. Don't anticipate. It's better to wait and get it right.

Ken Coleman warned me about that in doing games at Fenway. The Green Monster in left field is 37 feet tall and very close. The ball might hit the wall, and not go out of the park into the Monster seats, or in the old days, into the screen that used to hang there. You can easily be fooled. Is the ball going to hit the wall or go over it? Don't call it prematurely. If you wait a second or two to make the right call, you really haven't lost anything. And you have gained something valuable: correctness and credibility. You made the right call. We have all heard broadcasters go into their home run calls on a ball which eventually hits the outfield wall, or is simply caught.

I believe in building up the drama. "There's a drive to deep left field, there goes the left fielder toward the wall. He looks up…it is gone!" The worst thing you can do, especially on a ball hit by your home team, is say "There's a drive to left, I think it's gone…No, it's caught at the warning track for an out." That just disappoints your audience. I think it's better to build excitement by the tone of your voice. Let the audience hear the way you describe it. "This ball is pretty well hit." You usually don't have time to say, "It has a chance to leave the park." But the audience can tell by the tone of the broadcaster's voice. If a home-team home run ball leaves the ballpark, there's elation in the stands, and in your voice, even if you're not a homer. Even though I've broadcast Red Sox games for 30 years, I don't think of myself as a homer. I think of myself as a reporter. But of course, I'm glad when the Red Sox win. It's good for the team, good for the fans, and ultimately, good for me. If that ball that you've hyped up doesn't go into the stands for a home run, the listeners are mad at the broadcaster for leading them on and disappointing them.

As for home run calls, as my old partner Bob Starr said, "I don't have one a standard home run call because all the good ones are taken." Also, no two home runs are alike. I believe a broadcaster should call each home run individually.

I do not root openly for the Red Sox. I am not on the Red Sox's payroll. I don't play the game. I do not refer to the Red Sox as "we." But people can tell from the sound of my voice when good things are happening for the Red Sox.

My advice: follow the ball until it lands, don't anticipate—unless you are 100 percent sure—because it may not be gone.

Of course, if the opposing team hits a home run, that's completely different. I've been told that listeners can tell by the tone of my voice if the Sox are winning or losing. When I call a home run for the other team, sometimes my voice expresses pain or disappointment.

I believe that a broadcaster should give the score as often as possible. Red Barber used to use a three-minute egg timer. When the sand ran out, he'd give the score, and flip it over. I tried that once, but it didn't work because I didn't remember to turn it over. When in doubt, give the score. If you have nothing to say, give the score. You cannot give it too often. Of course, if your team is losing 12–2 you might not give the score quite as often, because you don't want the listeners to tune out. But as an honest reporter, you still have to give the score often, so your audience knows that your team is getting blown away.

I try to recap the scoring in the game as often as I can, especially in a low-scoring game. I also review the highlights of the game—who hit a grand slam or a three-run homer. Those are the bits of information that I try to stress during the course of the three-hour broadcast. But again, with all the stats you give and anecdotes that you tell during the game, you have to be ready when there is action on the field.

After the game, as I'm driving home, I like to listen to other games on the radio. I have an XM-radio in my car, so I can listen to every other game during the 50-minute drive. XM carries the home team broadcasts of 14 other games.

Listening to other broadcasters talk between pitches in the games they are broadcasting is another source of information for me: who has an injury, who's changed his batting stance, who was just called up, which pitcher has a new pitch, who's in a slump.

The next day, it starts all over again. I read the papers and check the Internet. If I'm out of town I read the local newspapers as I ride the exercise bike. Then I get ready to go to the ballpark to continue my prep work before the game, and, I hope, broadcast another Red Sox win.

CHAPTER 19

"Jimmy Mack"
The Jimmy Fund

THE JIMMY FUND AND RED SOX RADIO HAVE GONE HAND IN HAND SINCE IT BECAME THE OFFICIAL CHARITY OF THE TEAM IN 1953. The Jimmy Fund was founded in 1948 and was named for a boy called "Jimmy," whose true identity wasn't revealed until about 50 years later. Jimmy was at Children's Hospital in Boston, suffering from non-Hodgkin's lymphoma, which at the time was almost always fatal. On May 22, 1948, Ralph Edwards did his radio show, *Truth or Consequences*, from "Jimmy's" bedside. "Jimmy" was a Boston Braves fan. Warren Spahn, Bob Elliott, and other members of the team were there. The show was a fund-raiser to buy a TV set for the boy so that he could watch the Braves while he was in the hospital. The call went out for at least $20,000 in donations. The Braves went on to win the pennant that year, but their biggest triumph was that the show had a tremendous response and raised more than $230,000. They bought the TV set, and with the excess funds which came in, the Braves started the Jimmy Fund, headed by Dr. Sidney Farber, the father of modern chemotherapy, who was "Jimmy's" doctor at Children's Hospital. (The Dana-Farber Cancer Institute is partially named for Dr. Farber.) Dr. Farber tried to protect the privacy of his young patients, so "Jimmy's" real name was never used. The association of the Jimmy Fund with the Boston Braves continued.

Lou Perini, the owner of the Braves, and public relations director Billy Sullivan, who later owned the Boston and then New England Patriots, were the executives who cemented the relationship between Dr. Farber and the Braves. In '53, when

213

the Braves left Boston to move to Milwaukee, the Red Sox picked up the mantle and the Jimmy Fund has been the official charity of the team ever since.

As for "Jimmy" himself, most people thought that he had passed away. Cancer was a word that was avoided. Many patients were simply not told that they had it. Everything was hush-hush. Some believed that "Jimmy" was the son of a dairy farmer in Connecticut, but no one really knew until years later when his sister, Phyllis Clauson, came forward with documentation that the real "Jimmy" was alive and working in Maine. His name was Carl Einar Gustafson but he went by Einar. He was a tractor-trailer driver and a wonderful gentleman. Einar was the perfect model for "Jimmy," who has helped raise many millions of dollars in the fight against cancer.

Einar came to Fenway Park where he interacted with patients, including Uri Berenguer. More on Uri below. Einar spoke with many patients at the Children's Hospital.

Einar passed away from a stroke in 2001 in Caribou, Maine, at the age of 65. But finding Einar Gustafson was one of the true miracles of the Jimmy Fund.

Curt Gowdy, then the Red Sox radio broadcaster, did a lot for the Jimmy Fund after the Red Sox adopted it because of his closeness with Ted Williams, one of the Fund's biggest supporters. Carl Yastrzemski, whose mother died of cancer after having been treated at Dana-Farber, was a major fund-raiser for The Jimmy Fund.

Mike Andrews, who played second base for the Red Sox on the "Impossible Dream" team in 1967, went on to become chairman of the Jimmy Fund for many years. Mike likes to tell the story of being asked to visit with a little boy behind the batting cage after batting practice. Although not convinced that this was what he really wanted to do, he nevertheless met the young man. After he left, he was informed by a Jimmy Fund official that the young man had a terminal illness and had only a short time to live. That really hit Mike hard. He proceeded to volunteer for the Jimmy Fund. Then he worked in the office and eventually was named chairman of the Jimmy Fund, succeeding Ken Coleman. Ken succeeded Curt Gowdy as the voice of the Red Sox and became chairman of the Jimmy Fund when Bill Koster retired. He combined his baseball broadcasting—for the Red Sox, and during the four years he broadcast Cincinnati Reds games on TV—with his work for The Jimmy Fund. Ken was extremely dedicated. He said baseball was his love, but the Jimmy Fund was his passion. Ken Coleman dedicated much of his energy and his life to the battle against childhood cancer, the care of children with cancer, and cancer research.

Ken used to visit many of the Red Sox radio affiliates in places like Berlin, New Hampshire, and Calais, Maine, to do his own local radio-telethons with the local broadcasters all day long to raise money—not large amounts—at each station. I accompanied Ken on some to some of these fund-raisers to Bangor and Calais; Johnston, Rhode Island; and Pawcatuck, Connecticut. We'd do events for the Jimmy Fund and pick up checks. Some of these events continue, but most of our efforts are now on a larger scale.

Ken brought me into the Jimmy Fund. I had heard Curt Gowdy talk about it on the air when I was a kid. He spoke about the wonderful work that the Jimmy Fund did, and its fundraising efforts. I got an even closer view through Ken Coleman when I came to the Red Sox in 1983. Ken, without really asking me, learned of my willingness to volunteer on behalf of the Fund. I went to several events with Ken in the off-season—events at Fenway Park, golf tournaments, fund-raisers, and banquets. This continued during the seven years I worked with Ken. When Ken retired from broadcasting, he continued his work for the Jimmy Fund.

In 1990, Mike Andrews, the Chairman of the Jimmy Fund asked me if I'd like to be their Red Sox representative at Fenway Park, a paying position. I'd be the master of ceremonies at ballpark events, and I'd speak at fund-raisers at Fenway, introducing players, picking up checks, and performing other duties on behalf of the fund. I was glad to do so. I continue to speak at the ballpark at Jimmy Fund events—the Red Sox graciously donate a room at Fenway for meetings several times a season—and do whatever they ask.

I still participate in local radio fund-raisers by phone, such as those of WZON, a Red Sox affiliate in Bangor, and WTIC in Hartford.

Each August for the last 10 years there's been a Jimmy Fund radio-telethon. The first year, we raised about $300,000. Last year, the event raised a little more than $3 million. This is a two-day event on our flagship station, WEEI, and simulcast on TV by NESN. It's also carried throughout the Red Sox radio network, which reaches all over New England. Our record was set in 2009 when we raised $4 million. We didn't quite match that in 2010 because of the economy, but we still did very well. In 2011, the radio/telethon brought in about $3.3 million.

While we're broadcasting the game, visitors come into the broadcast booth and tell about their experiences with The Jimmy Fund. Some are kids who have been successfully treated at Dana-Farber. Representatives of a number of our big Red Sox broadcast sponsors come on to say that on behalf of their dealers, they are proud to donate $10,000 or $25,000. I'll never forget the day in '05 when Donald Trump came into the booth. We told him that we were just $65,000 short of our fund-raising goal. My partner Jerry Trupiano asked The Donald if he knew anybody who could help us go over the top. Trump pledged $65,000 right there for the Jimmy Fund.

My other duties include going to the Jimmy Fund clinic with players, and seeing them interact with kids. Every year, Lisa Scherber, a nurse at Dana-Farber, brings a group of about 50 teenagers from the clinic on two road trips—one to spring training in Ft. Myers, Florida, and one during the season to a Red Sox away game. They've been to Baltimore, Atlanta, and Pittsburgh. The trips are privately funded by generous donors who pay for the transportation, hotel, and meals. The kids have an unforgettable experience. The go on the field, meet the players, have autograph sessions, and have their pictures taken with the players. I'm very glad to participate with them.

Seth Ketchum

Seth was an 11-year-old Red Sox fan from Pittsfield, Massachusetts, about two hours west of Boston. He was being treated at the Jimmy Fund clinic for terminal cancer. Seth had become withdrawn. He didn't speak to his mother or grandmother. Jimmy Fund chairman Mike Andrews asked me if I could get Seth's favorite players to call him and sign some bats and balls for him. We were in Oakland when I got the call. Mike said that Seth's favorites were Jody Reed, Jeff Reardon, and Roger Clemens. I got them all on the phone to speak with Seth, and to wish him well. That night, Roger Clemens won the game, Jody Reed drove in the winning run, and Jeff Reardon got the save. This helped bring Seth out of his shell. He started to communicate with his mother and his grandmother again. The Jimmy Fund got him tickets to a Red Sox game at Fenway Park. We had Seth up in the broadcast booth and on the field where he met his three heroes. Jeff Reardon was particularly close with Seth because he's from Pittsfield. Seth had a wonderful visit with autographs and souvenirs. We were informed that after the visit, Seth did much better socially, but a few months later we learned that he had passed away. Shortly thereafter I got a wonderful letter from Seth's mother, Lucy:

"Being at Fenway Park was truly a dream come true for Seth. He had lived and breathed the Red Sox...and during his last few weeks it was a major part of what helped him to get through each day. His meeting with you and with the players he so greatly admired was such a positive experience for him in the midst of some tough and frightening times…Your phone call from Oakland did so much to lift his spirits on a day I remember as being an especially difficult one and your tribute on the pregame show the Saturday after his death was beautifully done and shared by all of his family and friends gathered together at the house.

"Seth said on our return from the game that night, 'Mom, there's something I forgot to tell them. I think the Jimmy Fund is the best charity they could ever have.' I am aching and empty without my son, but I pray that through the continued support that the Red Sox provide, the Jimmy Fund will one day play a part in eliminating such a tragedy from the lives of other children."

Jason Leader

One day in 1993, I got a call from Mike Andrews about a youngster from Niverville, New York, near Albany. Jason Leader, the oldest of several children, was coming to the Jimmy Fund clinic for the treatment of several tumors. He was not doing well. Mike asked me whether I could get Jason's favorite player, Mo Vaughn, to call Jason on his 10th birthday. We were at Anaheim Stadium and had to go to an equipment room to find a telephone. (This was before cell phones.) I called Jason at Children's Hospital, and I told him that somebody wanted to wish him a happy birthday. Then I put Mo on the phone. He told Jason to keep plugging away. Mo said he'd try to hit a home run for him that night. Mo closed by saying he hoped he saw Jason when the team returned to Fenway. Then he repeated that he would try to hit a home run for Jason. It was like the Babe Ruth–Johnny Sylvester story. In the seventh inning of the Saturday night game, Jerry Trupiano was doing the play-by-play. Mo Vaughn came up with the bases empty, and the Red Sox losing 5–3. Mo hit a bomb over the left-center field wall that made the score 5–4. I went on the air and told the story about Mo Vaughn promising Jason Leader, the young cancer patient, that he would try to hit a home run for him.

Because Jerry was doing the play-by-play, I had a few minutes to go down to the press box to tell the Boston writers what had just happened. They took it from there. By that time, it was about midnight in Boston. But the story made some of the Sunday papers. Others picked it up on Monday. The story was well-received. The team was off on Monday, but on Tuesday, back in Boston, when I went to the ballpark, all kinds of media were there—national media, magazine shows, global media—everybody wanted to hear about the Mo Vaughn–Jason Leader story.

We had Jason visit at Fenway a few times. His first time there, he went onto the field. Mo was 6'1" and weighed 225 pounds. Jason was a tiny kid. They made a great photograph. On subsequent visits, Mo would bring Jason into the clubhouse, and they had some private time together. They formed a wonderful bond. During this time, Mo's parents, Leroy and Shirley, became very close with Jason's parents, Phil and Sue. A year later, on Jason's birthday, he got a large package from Mo: balloons, baseball cards, and lots of Red Sox items.

Around the time of the baseball strike in August '94 we got word that Jason was not doing well. Shortly after the strike started, we got word that Jason had passed away. I made the drive with Mark Cummings and Suzanne Fountain, Jimmy Fund executives, to the funeral in Niverville. The funeral was held in a tiny wooden church that looked like something from *Little House on the Prairie*.

It was filled with children, and of course, Jason's parents and family. It was an overflow crowd, and we stood in the back. Just as the service was about to begin, a car drove up and Mo Vaughn stepped out. He had driven himself for three and a half hours from Boston to attend Jason's funeral. He went in and sat close to the family. He walked out with Phil and Sue Leader, had a private conversation with them, embraced them, and spoke with Jason's younger brothers and sisters. And left. He didn't want any publicity, although there were camera crews there. We stayed a little while after the ceremony.

The relationship between the Vaughns and the Leaders did not end with Jason's tragic passing. They remained very close. For many years, Sue Leader would walk in the Jimmy Fund/Boston Marathon Walk, on the same team with Shirley and Leroy Vaughn. Sue sometimes goes on vacation with the Vaughns when she can get away from her job working for the State of New York. When Mo was inducted into the Red Sox Hall of Fame in 2008—he had not been back to Fenway since he was signed by the Angels as a free agent for the '99 season—he was there with his parents. Their guest was Sue Leader.

2011 was the 10th anniversary of the Jimmy Fund radio/telethon. Mo Vaughn and his parents came back to Fenway for the occasion. We arranged a reunion with the Vaughns and Jason Leader's mother, Sue, and her four surviving children, now in their twenties. Mo and Sue were on the air together and it was very moving as they reminisced about the great friendship Mo had with Jason. Their appearance resulted in countless pledges as we totaled nearly $3.5 million.

And Mo's Mom, Shirley, added a postscript to the story we had never known before. When Jason was dying in '94, he visited Fenway one last time and Mo gave him a uniform jersey. Mo took Jason into the clubhouse and Jason's parting words to his hero were, "Mo, stay strong," the same words Mo had written on the home run ball he had given to Jason the year before. Shirley said Mo broke down. That strong bond is still there years after Jason's death.

The story of Mo Vaughn and Jason Leader is one of my all-time favorites. I felt that I was placed in a position to bring Mo and his family together with Jason and his family, to bring some joy to these tragic times. Mo's relationship with Jason and the Leader family was something he was very proud of and happy to do.

Uri Berenguer

Shortly before the baseball strike of 1994, we went on a player visit to the Jimmy Fund Clinic, as we so often did. I met a 12-year-old boy with big eyes. He was being treated for histiocytosis, a rare form of bone cancer. I was introduced to him and was told that his name was Uri Berenguer. I instantly asked whether he was related to Juan Berenguer, also known as "Señor Smoke," a hard-throwing right hander who had pitched in the major leagues for 15 years. (Former Red Sox manager Joe Morgan said that Juan Berenguer was the fastest minor league pitcher he ever saw. Joe thought he threw the ball about 108 miles per hour when he pitched for the Tidewater Tides in the New York Mets system. But he was very wild then, which also made him the scariest pitcher ever. Later, he harnessed his control and became a top relief pitcher for the Mets, Tigers, Giants, Royals, Blue Jays, Twins, and Braves.) Uri said yes, Juan Berenguer was his uncle. Uri came to Boston from Panama with his mother when he was just three.

The doctors in Panama wanted to amputate Uri's leg. But his parents thought that American doctors might be able to save his leg, so Uri and his mother flew to Boston to be seen by doctors at Children's Hospital. They stayed at the Howard Johnson's motel right down the street from Fenway. Once he was diagnosed at the Dana-Farber Cancer Institute he was told that he had to undergo surgery. His mother didn't know whether the surgeons were going to amputate his leg.

When he woke up in the recovery room, he asked his mother whether his leg was still there. She told him yes, but she really didn't know until she lifted up the sheet on his hospital bed and saw for herself. The doctors had been able to save his leg and his life. Uri and his mother remained here and were soon joined by his older sister while Uri's father remained in Panama, where he worked for a pharmaceutical company.

Over the next 16 years, Uri had seven relapses and underwent seven surgeries on his leg at a great financial strain on his family, because they had no health insurance. Uri, his mother, and his sister lived first in Boston and then in Brockton. Eventually, Uri's father came to Boston, too. At times, Uri was confined to a wheelchair. When I met him, I learned of Uri's interest in baseball. We brought him to the booth at Fenway Park and made Uri an intern. He counted pitches, got us coffee, and gave us drop-in commercials. He loved doing this. Meanwhile, he continued to get healthier. He went to high school at Boston Latin Academy. Uri played baseball. One year he stole 26 bases. He also played football. I watched one of his high school football games when he was a defensive back. In that game, Uri was called for unnecessary roughness, even though he was smaller than everybody else on the team.

After high school, we helped Uri get a partial scholarship to Northeastern University. Professor Roger Giese helped sponsor Uri by paying part of his tuition. He showed great faith in Uri.

The Red Sox Spanish network was looking for a helping hand. Uri, with his bilingual skills, was an obvious candidate. First, he entered the booth as an assistant producer. Then he learned the engineering side of broadcasting. Pretty soon, he was filling in by doing some of the play-by-play and analysis. In 2000, he was doing the pregame show. Then in '01, at age 19, Uri became the youngest full-time professional broadcaster in major league history, doing the Spanish play-by-play for the Boston Red Sox.

Unlike many of the Spanish broadcasters around the country, Uri is bilingual. Many of them are not. After nine years of play-by-play, Uri was hired by NESN as a studio host. Uri continues to do the Spanish language radio broadcasts for the Red Sox, and occasionally works as a TV reporter for NESN, where he covers baseball. For three years Uri had his own nationally broadcast talk show on XM Radio, until XM merged with Sirius, who dropped the Spanish programming.

Uri is now a veteran radio broadcaster. He's 28 and has a son named Logan. He's had a marvelous career. More important, his doctor, Lindsay Fraser, told him when he was about 21 that he was cured of cancer. Uri still visits the Jimmy Fund clinic, where he plays Chutes and Ladders with the young patients. He ran the Boston Marathon on behalf of the Jimmy Fund, and he's walked the Jimmy Fund Walk.

Kate Shaughnessy

Kate Shaughnessy is the daughter of *Boston Globe* sports columnist Dan Shaughnessy. In the mid-1990s, when Kate was about 10, she was diagnosed with leukemia and was treated at the Jimmy Fund clinic. Roger Clemens sent her a big stuffed animal. She got a phone call from a really loud guy who told her, "Don't worry, you're really going to get better." She told her father that a really loud guy had called her on the phone to say that she's really going to get better, just fight it out. She told her father that the guy on the phone said that his name was Ted Williams.

On December 15, 1995, we had a Jimmy Fund banquet at the Park Plaza Hotel. Kate spoke about Ted Williams. She read a poem she had written. Here's the poem:

> Ted Williams is a really, really great guy.
> He really likes kids, but he hates wearing ties;
> He won two Triple Crowns and was the MVP twice,
> He feuded with sportswriters, but to kids he was nice.
> 521 homers, he's in the Hall of Fame.
> He's the Kid, The Thumper, and Teddy Ballgame.
> He would do anything for the Jimmy Fund.
> And I'd like to say thank you, for all that he's done.

Kate was cured. She went on to graduate from Boston University where she played softball. Today, she is coaching high school sports in Newton, Massachusetts.

The Jimmy Fund has changed somewhat over the years. It's no longer so much about going to restaurants and bars to pick up checks. Today, it's more about much larger events, such as the radio-telethon, the Jimmy Fund Marathon Walk, and the Pan-Mass Challenge Bike Race.

There are a number of other events, including more than 100 golf tournaments each year. My work for the Jimmy Fund has given me great satisfaction over the years.

CHAPTER 20

"Working My Way Back To You"

Everything Comes Back To The Red Sox

FOR SOME YEARS, I HAVE BEEN ONE OF 14 VOTING MEMBERS OF THE RED SOX HALL OF FAME COMMITTEE. Induction ceremonies are held every other year, usually in the off-season at a hotel, followed by a brief ceremony on the field at Fenway before a game. I have been honored to serve as co–master of ceremonies at several.

Red Sox Fantasy Camp started in the 1980s. Many other ballclubs have followed it. People over the age of 30—mostly, but not exclusively, men—pay $3,000–$5,000 to play ball for a week, usually Sunday through Saturday. That fee includes a Red Sox uniform—a lifelong dream for some. Participants dress and play at the team's spring training headquarters in Ft. Myers (previously in Winter Haven). They stay in hotels, but transportation and meals are provided. They play a game in the morning and another in the afternoon with professional ballplayers serving as managers and coaches. There's a lot of togetherness. It's like a male Disneyland with a lot of bonding. Many friendships and business relationships have been forged at Fantasy Camp. Many campers go back year after year. Several campers have come for 20 years. As they get a little older, the skills diminish a little more. Some were good players in their day—high school or college. Some never played at all. It's very important that the professionals who work at the camp are good socially, because that's what it's all about.

There are now two Red Sox Fantasy Camps. One is the "official" one, run by the club. The other was the first camp, run by Larry Marino. They have been using the Twins' facility in Ft. Myers, while the "official" camp uses the Red Sox's minor league facilities. I work at both of them, with most of my efforts devoted to the official one (they're only a few miles apart). Umpires are campers, too.

For several years starting in 1993, I played, too. Former big leaguer Mike Stenhouse ran the camp that year. I got a couple of hits and won the MVP game award. But after four or five years, I realized that I was taking at-bats away from people who were paying big bucks to play. So I retired with my .400 batting average.

There have been some injuries, a few broken legs and pulled muscles. So far, no fatalities. Many campers spend time in the mile-long trainer's room, having their hamstrings and quads looked at. I pride myself on never having gone into the trainers' room for treatment.

Now I emcee the opening cocktail party and closing banquet, and I do the public address announcing for the games. The week culminates in a game against former big leaguers. Campers bat against pitchers like Bill Lee, Bob Stanley, and Oil Can Boyd. Other former players who have participated include Johnny Pesky, Frank Malzone, Jim Rice, Bob Montgomery, Rich Gedman, Dwight Evans, and Mike Easler.

The Larry Marino camp usually draws 75–100 campers, with 100–120 at the Red Sox camp, depending on the economy. In 2012, Red Sox Fantasy Camp will open the Red Sox's new spring training ballpark in Ft. Myers. They're going to let the campers work the bugs out before the pros get there.

Dan Shaughnessy, the great sports columnist for the *Boston Globe* has said and written with only the smallest amount of hyperbole, "Everything comes back to the Red Sox." And in the case of my family and me, I think it's true.

The Red Sox are the reason I work for the Jimmy Fund. Without the Red Sox and their affiliation with the Jimmy Fund, I wouldn't have any qualifications except volunteering. The Red Sox are also responsible for my teaching career. Without my platform with the team, there's no way I would have been hired to teach at either Northeastern or Franklin Pierce.

And this is also reflected in the lives of my children. My son Duke went to Stonehill College because of his relationship with Red Sox general manager Lou Gorman. Duke went to Marshfield High, then spent a year at prep school at Loomis Chaffee, where he played on an outstanding championship baseball team in the New England Prep League. Duke was accepted at Ithaca College, an NCAA Division III baseball power, and a great school for broadcasting. He made the junior varsity team in his freshman year, but he didn't like Ithaca. It was too far from home and Duke didn't like the gray, horrible weather either. I could identify with that because I had gone to Colgate, just 60 miles from Ithaca.

Duke said that one night he had a dream that Lou Gorman—"Uncle Lou" to my kids—had told him about Stonehill College, his alma mater. Lou was in the second class at Stonehill, graduating in 1948. Lou had always preached Stonehill to Duke. When he awoke, Duke made the arrangements necessary to transfer, and after his first semester at Ithaca, he made the switch. Stonehill is a Catholic school in Easton, Massachusetts, run by the Holy Cross Fathers, the same order that runs the University of Notre Dame in South Bend, Indiana.

As a communications major, Duke had to pass a course in statistics in order to graduate. He was having a tough time in statistics, and mentioned this to Uncle Lou. The statistics professor got a call from Lou, and soon thereafter was seen in a box seat at Fenway Park. Duke passed the course. Duke likes to say that Uncle Lou got him into Stonehill, and got him out of it, too.

In the case of my son Tommy, he applied to the College of the Holy Cross in Worcester, Massachusetts. He had a very nice letter of recommendation from John Donovan. John started with the Red Sox as a batboy after World War II. He was a lawyer who later became a Vice President of the Red Sox. In the spring of '93, John, who was dying of cancer at the time, called to tell us that Tommy had been accepted at Holy Cross. He was very happy to tell us that good news. John passed away a few months later.

After graduating from Holy Cross and then working in medical research and studying science for two years, Tom was accepted at the School of Medicine at the University of Massachusetts, which was also in Worcester. Again, the Red Sox were involved.

Dr. Mike Foley, a member of the board of trustees of the University of Massachusetts, took a special interest in Tom, as did Dr. Arthur Pappas, who headed the orthopedics department at the University of Massachusetts. Dr. Pappas was a part owner of the Red Sox, and the team's orthopedic surgeon. Dr. Foley was the team's specialist in internal medicine, and also ran the first aid room at Fenway Park. Both were very influential on Tom. As an undergraduate, Tom studied hard and worked hard. Both were a factor in Tom's being accepted at U Mass. Medical School, which had only 100 or so spaces in its incoming class. It turned out to be a wonderful situation for Tom; and because it was a state school, he didn't have to take out any loans.

In the case of my daughter, Kate, she had applied to a number of colleges, including Boston College. She was recommended by John Harrington, at the time the chief operating officer and chief executive officer of the Red Sox. Kate was put on the waiting list, but he told her not to worry, just to sit tight. Shortly thereafter, she was accepted at Boston College, and had a wonderful time there.

All three of my children worked at Fenway Park. When he was 10, Duke worked in the visiting clubhouse as a gofer. He said he got to serve Billy Martin his postgame meal and drink. Duke loved it when Robin Yount sent him to the Boston Garden to buy tickets for a wrestling show and when George Brett stuffed him in a trash can. Later, Duke was a vendor and still later a security guard. I know that there were times he signed in to work as a vendor and then took off to do his own thing. He was more assiduous as a security guard.

Tom also worked as a vendor selling Coca-Cola. He did very well. Kate worked at one of the concession stands selling ice cream. Later, she worked in the media relations department and the alumni relations department under Dick Bresciani. They all had good experiences working for the Red Sox.

Chapter Twenty-One

"The Man From Galilee"
Faith

My professional life is a dream come true. I've often wondered why I have been so blessed. I have been given the opportunity to do what I always dreamed of doing for a living. How did it happen that I have been able to spend more than 30 years broadcasting major league baseball? I think there is only one conclusion: that it was God's plan for me. So many things broke right. I was in the right place at the right time.

But it's more than mere good fortune. I believe that I was placed in this situation. I think of my job as a vocation—a calling (no pun intended).

That was driven home to me by a priest, Msgr. John Dillon Day. For many years, I attended the Lions' Club Baseball Banquet in the Hyde Park section of Boston. It was a great event that kids could attend with their families for about $20. They could come for an evening of baseball celebrities and autographs and get a great dinner. Even into the late 1990s, that was still the price. Joe Morgan was instrumental in getting major league players to come. Msgr. Day was always on the podium. He was a great baseball fan and a great baseball historian. He quoted a poem—which he wrote—about the Braves and the Red Sox of the 1920s and '30s being in last place. He was also a student of Boston College sports. One day, Msgr. Day said to me, "Did you know that what you have is an apostolate [the mission of an apostle]?" I thought about it, but I was not quite sure what he meant. He went on to explain, "Your apostolate is that you get to bring joy, companionship, and fellowship to the shut-ins, the elderly, and the ill—the forgotten people of our society." His explanation really overwhelmed me. I'd always thought of my job as basically fun and games—I go to the ballpark, sit in the best seat in the house, describe the game I love, meet wonderful, colorful people, and travel first class all over the country on the company tab. But Msgr. Day's analysis really brought what I do into focus, and gave it added purpose.

When ratings are taken and when sponsorships are sold, advertising agencies and account executives look at the 18–49 age group. The elderly and shut-ins are not part of the equation. But they are to me. Many of the letters I get come from elderly and shut-ins, and people who have very little joy in their lives except for baseball. Via the Internet, our games are also heard by servicemen and women serving in all parts of the world. I should also include prisoners. I've had many letters from prisoners over the years. For these people, their joy is following the Red Sox on the radio. What Msgr. Day told me also brought me great joy, because it makes what I do so much more purposeful. I hope I never lose sight of that.

My spiritual life has been influenced by many people over the years. I think the greatest spiritual influence besides by wife, Jan, has been my dear friend Andre Thornton. I became friends with Andre in 1977 when he was with the Cleveland Indians. Andre was born in Tuskegee, Alabama, and grew up in Phoenixville, Pennsylvania—the same town where Mike Piazza grew up—about 30 miles from Philadelphia. After high school, he signed a non-drafted free-agent contract with the Philadelphia Phillies, and progressed through their system. He played in Huron, South Dakota; Eugene, Oregon; Spartanburg, South Carolina; Hampton, Virginia; Reading, Pennsylvania; and then, after being acquired by the Atlanta Braves, he went to AAA as a power-hitting outfielder, first baseman, and third baseman in Richmond, Virginia. Andre became very close with Hank Aaron in spring training with the Braves, and was about to be promoted to the big club when he hurt his leg sliding.

In '73 he was traded to the Cubs and made his major league debut that year with Chicago at the age of 23. In '76, he went to the Montreal Expos. Before the '77 season the Cleveland Indians acquired him from the Expos in a trade for a curve-balling right hander named Jackie Brown, one of the best trades Cleveland general manager Phil Seghi ever made. Andre had a terrific season in '77, smacking 28 home runs. I interviewed him a few times, and a strong bond—a professional bond—developed between us. I'm only two years older than Andre.

In October of '77—I'll never forget it—I was driving in to work at Channel 3 in Cleveland, and as I pulled into the garage, I heard a news report that there had been a tragic accident on the Pennsylvania Turnpike. Andre Thornton's van had overturned as he was driving from Cleveland to Phoenixville to see his family. His wife, Gertrude, and his young daughter, Theresa, were killed. Andre and his son, Andy, survived.

Andre lived in Bainbridge, Ohio, about five miles from my home in Solon. Shortly after the tragic accident, Jan made lasagna and I drove it over. Andre was very welcoming. His son was four or five, about the same age as my son Duke. I had gone to try to raise Andre's spirits, but he lifted mine with his great faith in our Lord and Savior Jesus Christ.

I came away from that visit immensely moved, that someone who had just undergone such a tragic loss would still have such faith. Andre became a great model for me. He introduced me to Baseball Chapel, a nondenominational service held in ballparks in a room off the clubhouse. In Tiger Stadium, it was held in the visitors' showers, because there was no other room large enough. There is one meeting for the home team, and one for visitors. In the late '70s, there was some antagonism toward Baseball Chapel by some who felt that the ballpark was not the place for an organized prayer service. They felt that if players wanted to go to church, they could, but not at the ballpark where they worked. But because of conflicting schedules, getting to church for scheduled services was often impossible.

Andre was our Chapel leader in Cleveland, and more and more people attended. Baseball Chapel grew to become very dear to me. It became part of my weekly routine on the road and at home when my pregame schedule permits and it remains so to this day. We've had some wonderful speakers over the years.

One of my favorite speakers is the Rev. Bob Gray, who spoke at the Red Sox Baseball Chapel meetings for many years. Bob was a former parole officer, a very difficult job in the Boston system. Then he went to divinity school and became an ordained preacher. Today he is the pastor of the Bethel AME church in Jamaica Plain. He is also the chaplain for the Boston Celtics, where he conducts a service before every home game. Bob brings so much joy and faith to all of us. He's very inspiring. I occasionally receive spiritual text messages from him.

When I got to Boston, our Chapel leader was Stan Babcock. Stan worked in the auto parts business and was a man of great faith. He brought me to Red Sox Chapel when I started in Boston. In the mid-'80s, the Red Sox Chapel was very small. It included people like Rick Miller, Reid Nichols, and Mike Easler. But as Baseball Chapel continued to grow in the minor leagues, players would continue to attend when they got to the majors. Stan was succeeded by Walt Day, a chaplain who was always very welcoming. Baseball Chapel continues to grow and thrive today.

A great influence on me has been Msgr. William Glynn, of Holy Family Church in Duxbury, Massachusetts. He's a great baseball fan, and is a great Red Sox fan. He goes to many games. In the fall of '94, I had spoken at his church when baseball was on strike—a very depressing time. Msgr. Glynn invited me to play golf with him, something I hadn't done in a very long time. On his 80th birthday his parishioners asked me to do a fantasy tape for him. I had Msgr. Glynn hitting a game-winning home run off Mariano Rivera of the Yankees.

His parish had about 10,000 people whom he pastored well into his eighties before he retired. He still goes to some Red Sox games. Msgr. Glynn baptized our grandchildren and he's been a tremendous influence on my entire family. He always preaches the theme of forgiveness in life, a key to Christianity. Msgr. Glynn is someone I'm very thankful for having met.

As a practicing Roman Catholic I go to Mass regularly, at home and on the road. On the road we go to the church that is closest either to the ballpark or to the hotel, depending on Mass schedule. Usually, I go to the same church in each city. My favorite church was St. Leo's in Baltimore, in the Italian neighborhood that reminded me of St. Donato's in New Haven where my nonna and Aunt Mary took me as a child, and where I was baptized.

The pastor, Father Mike Salerno, the son of a longshoreman, was from Brooklyn and was a real show unto himself, an emotional, effective preacher with a Brooklyn accent and a warm personality.

One time, after Mass, Jan and I went to the rectory to buy a St. Leo's raffle ticket for a new car. The secretary asked if we came to St. Leo's often. I said, "We're with the Red Sox, and come to hear Father Mike when we are in town."

She said, "Oh, you come for the show," meaning Fr. Mike's homilies. We had to admit we loved Father Mike and his colorful sermons.

Fr. Mike has since been transferred back to Brooklyn, so we now attend a Mass that is held at the Camden Yards warehouse each week.

Another memorable Mass was in Houston, across the street from Minute Maid Park. Mike Lowell, Sean Casey, and I were leaving the hotel to go to the church when we saw Justin Masterson, a young 6'6" pitcher, the son of a missionary and a joyous Christian who is Protestant. We asked Justin if he wanted to go to Mass with us. Not only did he attend, but Justin really got involved in the Mass and sang all the hymns with great passion and joy! Justin, born in Jamaica, where his dad was working as a missionary, was beloved by his fellow relief pitchers. In the bullpen, he would teach English to Ramon Ramirez and attempt to teach it to Hideki Okajima. He would try to learn their languages, too. When Masterson was traded to Cleveland on July 31, 2009, we were in Baltimore. A couple of his buddies, Manny Delcarmen and Ramon Ramirez, were actually moved to tears when the announcement was made—that's how much they thought of Masterson.

Another great influence has been Mike Lowell. Mike, Sean Casey, and I would go to Mass together every Sunday on the road. It was a tradition for us. I would get the Mass schedule and Mike would decide what time to go.

Once, we were in Anaheim in a rental car at 8:00 AM, on our way to an 8:30 Mass. Jan, Mike, Sean, and I were all going together, but Sean was late. Finally, we called him and he came down at about 8:23. Mike Lowell had a great line. He asked, "Where were you?" Sean replied that he thought the Mass was at 9:00. Mike said, "What time does this 8:38 Mass start?" Sean got a big kick out of that.

Later, in '08, Sean was very influential in getting a Mass said at Fenway Park through his friend Father Paul O'Brien, a Harvard grad, who is a pastor in Lawrence, Massachusetts, an impoverished area. He runs a kitchen, Labels Are for Jars, which serves meals every day to hungry and homeless people, most of them Haitian or Dominican. Some of the Red Sox players and wives, including Mike and Bertha Lowell and Sean have served meals there. When Sean was with the Red Sox, he was known as "The Mayor"—a very friendly, positive guy. In fact, the players around the league voted Sean the friendliest guy in baseball. Sean really lived his faith. He told me that his dad had been a priest, and had been at the 1963 March on Washington with the Rev. Dr. Martin Luther King Jr., bringing four busloads from Long Island.

The Mass is still conducted at Fenway Park on Sundays before day games in the wives' room, just off the clubhouse. It is attended by players, ushers, management people, concession workers, visiting players, wives, and broadcasters.

Ernie Harwell, the late Hall of Fame broadcaster for the Detroit Tigers, had a tremendous influence on me. He'd been a Chapel speaker many times. I will always admire his faith so much, especially in his dying days. As I told his son, the Rev. Gray Harwell, Ernie taught us how to live and how to die. He announced publicly that he had bile duct cancer, which very few survive. He had an opportunity to share his faith with thousands and thousands of people. When Ernie passed away in May 2010 at the age of 92, thousands of admirers attended his wake at Comerica Park in Detroit.

I have become good friends with Gray, who ministers to other ministers. Clergymen have issues just like the rest of us. His ministry provides for the needs of the clergy. Ernie sponsored his mission for many years, and still does to this day, even though Ernie is no longer with us.

Ernie was a great example to me, and to many others of how to live the baseball life and remain a person of faith, as Andre has been. Both had been social friends as well. After my visit to Andre's house shortly after his wife and daughter died, Andre and I became much closer. More than anything, I've had some wonderful discussions with Andre, and we've stayed friends for more than 30 years. Our families have been close.

In '78, Jan and I attended Andre and Gail Jones' wedding in Oberlin, Ohio. Gail was one of the gospel-singing Jones Sisters. The ceremony was performed by Gail's father, Rev. Howard Jones, who integrated the Billy Graham Crusade, a wonderful learned gentleman who preached in Oberlin and did many missions.

Even after I went to the Red Sox, Andre and I remained friends, which proved a little awkward when the Indians played against the Red Sox. I hoped that if he was going to hit a home run, it would not be a go-ahead or game-winning home run. But more often than not, he did have the big blow that beat the Red Sox. I remember a couple of homers he hit off Bob Stanley that turned games around.

Every time I go to Cleveland he comes into town for a visit, or I go to his office in Akron where he owns warehouses and transportation depots. His companies provide shipping and storage for companies like Wal-Mart and banks and hospitals in Ohio. He does all the shipping in Ohio, Michigan, and West Virginia for Wal-Mart. In recent years, his supply chain business has expanded into Alabama, Georgia, and Virginia.

I thought it was baseball's loss that Andre wasn't offered a front-office job after his playing days ended in '87. Andre was a great judge of talent, and would have made an excellent general manager. During his playing career he was a bright gentleman and a clubhouse leader who knew how to motivate players. But he studied business and got into several businesses and continued to expand. Today, his company is one of the largest minority-owned businesses in Ohio. He is a real leader in the business world in Northern Ohio. He has a Christian business, where everything is ethical and above-board, just as he was when he played. He once told a great story about having a corked bat. He prayed about it, decided it was wrong, and discarded it.

Andre's brother-in-law was the late Pat Kelly, whose best years were with Earl Weaver's Baltimore Orioles. Pat once told Weaver that he should walk with the Lord. Weaver responded, "I'd rather walk with the bases loaded." Pat had a great ministry and a joyous personality. Unfortunately, he passed away suddenly in '05 at the age of 61.

Andre wrote a wonderful book called *Triumph Over Tragedy* in the early '80s, about the accident that claimed his wife and daughter, his ministry, his subsequent marriage to Gail, and how his faith sustained him.

In '08, Rev. Mark Mann, the chaplain at Colgate, my alma mater, was looking for a speaker. I recommended Andre. We went up to Hamilton, New York, together. Gail sang at a gospel festival and spoke to the female attendees while Andre preached at the Sunday service and spoke with male students individually.

There are no coincidences in life. I have met all these wonderful people for a reason. And I have been put in a position to be able to help many people. It may be as simple as to bring joy to the elderly or shut-ins that so enjoy the sound of a baseball broadcast.

At times, I am asked to make a phone call to wish someone well or recommend a former student or intern for a job. People do take my phone calls, and I consider it part of my calling to help when I can. To whom much has been given, much is expected.

CHAPTER 22

"I Heard It Through the Grapevine"

Teaching

I'VE BEEN TEACHING AT BOSTON'S NORTHEASTERN UNIVERSITY IN THE FALL SEMESTER SINCE 1985. Twice I did the winter term, but that was when they were on the quarter system. Now that they are on the semester system, it's difficult for me to do that. I also taught at Franklin Pierce College in Rindge, New Hampshire—a town so small that there are no stores in the downtown area, just a city hall and a church—from 1996 to 2008, and I've done seminars there since then. Rindge is in southwestern New Hampshire, not far from Winchendon and Gardner, Massachusetts, and Brattleboro, Vermont.

In '96, I taught at Emerson College—which is also in Boston—once a week in the fall and had many wonderful students, most from outside the U.S. I wound up at Franklin Pierce because my friend Lou Gorman, who had been the Red Sox general manager, put me in touch with the school's president, Dr. George Hagerty. Lou was teaching a seminar there and trying to get a sports administration program started at the school.

Dr. Hagerty took a small school, which had been founded in 1962 as a school for underachievers, and took it to great heights. I watched the caliber of the students increase drastically over my 13 years there. At the same time, the facilities at the school improved significantly. The communications department where I taught used to be housed in the basement of the school library. The whole setup was very primitive. Then the Marlin Fitzwater Center for Communication was opened. Fitzwater, the deputy press secretary for President Reagan and press secretary for vice president and then president George H.W. Bush, was a close friend of Dr. Hagerty. The Fitzwater Center's equipment is state of the art.

As part of my class at Franklin Pierce, I spoke about anchoring a news show and doing play-by-play for a sporting event. I had some very good students, including many athletes in my class, such as the captain of the women's basketball team. I believe that she's working in broadcasting now. Many of them were baseball players—perhaps planning for a post-playing career in broadcasting. During my years at Franklin Pierce, about 15 students signed contracts to play pro ball.

Some of my former students are working professionally in broadcasting and related fields. One, Matt Leite, has done independent baseball on radio. He's now the broadcaster for the Hagerstown (Maryland) Suns, the Washington Nationals' Class A club.

I had a wonderful experience at Franklin Pierce. I'd drive up—about a 100 mile drive from my home in Massachusetts—every Tuesday. But I gave it up after Dr. Hagerty left to take a teaching job elsewhere. Also, the drive was just too long to take in the fall, especially recently, as the Red Sox were in the postseason almost every year. But I still did seminars at Franklin Pierce for athletes and students who were considering careers in broadcasting. A separate seminar which I enjoyed was for high school students.

In '85, Paul Kaplan was our first broadcast booth intern/statistician. Paul was a student at Northeastern University, a mile from Fenway Park. I mentioned to him that I'd be interested in teaching a broadcasting course at Northeastern, and I asked him to speak to someone at the school for me. He spoke with the department chair, Carl W. Eastman, known as Pete. He was a great guy and a great promoter of the speech communications department. He thought it was an excellent idea. Pete hired me to teach a course in the fall term on sports broadcasting.

I had many Northeastern basketball players in my class, players whose games I was broadcasting on the New England Sports Network (NESN). Northeastern had a very strong team, and I had most of the team in my class, but not Reggie Lewis, the most famous basketball player in the school's history.

I was very shocked to realize that some of these athletes could barely read. A number were said to be dyslexic, but it was eye-opening how many of these players were in college when they needed remedial reading. College athletes are often exploited. They perform and earn income for their schools, but the schools' only academic goal is to keep them eligible, and so many never are on track for a degree. I believe that big-time college athletes should be paid to play revenue-producing sports.

Other than the sports teams, Northeastern was basically a commuter school. When Northeastern later changed from a commuter school to a residential school, I found that the caliber of the students went up significantly. The admission standards are now much higher and Northeastern is more difficult to get into now. Students in my class at Northeastern come from all over the country.

My students have a lot of advantages. I took my first Northeastern class to a New England Patriots practice during the fall of '85. They got to interview several players. I was a little upset with one student who said to Julius Adams, "Hey, Julius, you got any tickets for the Miami game?" I explained how unprofessional it was to ask a player you are interviewing for tickets. Also, at least at this point, you're a total stranger. Is a player really going to give you a ticket? I had to ream that kid out in front of the class. I don't think he realized how rude and unprofessional he had been. But it was a lesson learned, by him and by the others.

My class attends a Boston Bruins practice every year. The players are great. Hockey players are probably the most cooperative in sports. Nate Greenberg, the Bruins vice president of media relations, graciously had us in and gave each student a media guide. The Bruins' practices are closed to the public, but we watch from ice level. Then we go to the Boston Garden media dining room. A player or coach comes in to address the class and hold a "news conference."

Teddy Donato, who was part of Harvard's national championship hockey team in '89 and is now the longtime hockey coach there, has spoken. So has Bruins broadcaster Dave Goucher, who talked about working first at Boston University—Northeastern's archrival in hockey—then doing minor league hockey games in Wheeling, West Virginia, and Providence before moving up to the Bruins. Dave is considered one of the best in the game. Former Bruins coach Robby Ftorek has spoken, too. The students have to learn about the Bruins to prepare for the mock news conference. We were so happy when the Boston Bruins won the Stanley Cup in 2011. The organization has always been so accommodating.

Lou Gorman would come to my class to speak, and before the class I would pick the top students to have lunch with Lou. He was wonderful and the students learned a lot. Of course the students who were not invited felt slighted. But I couldn't accommodate the entire class at Northeastern's faculty dining center. So we changed it, and brought the whole class to Fenway. The class met either in the media dining room or in one of the function rooms. It works very well because we hear from many of the team's executives.

Larry Luccino, the President and CEO of the Red Sox, is a regular at these classes every year. He brings a goody bag and awards students prizes based on the caliber of their questions. He's very frank in saying that the more flattering the question, the better the prize. The student who asked whether Larry had a good chance of becoming commissioner of baseball when Bud Selig retires was awarded a very nice Red Sox cap. The student who told Luccino that he was a Yankees fan got a Red Sox pacifier.

In early November 2005, I was scheduled to bring my classes from Northeastern and Franklin Pierce to Fenway Park. The speakers were going to be team Larry Luccino; Mike Dee; Dr. Charles Steinberg, the team's vice president of public affairs; and several others. We were due to meet in the main function room down the third base line, but that morning I was informed that the room was going to be used by Theo Epstein for a press conference. We'd have to meet elsewhere. There was construction and renovation going on all over the ballpark, so there really weren't many places our group of about 40 could go. The new Monster Seats had recently opened above the Green Monster. Fortunately, it was a nice day, a little windy, but temperatures in the 50s. So I thought it would be great to take my students up to the Monster Seats. We got permission and that's where we went. The students sat in the second and third rows, and our guest lecturers stood in the first row. The construction noise was a little distracting, but it wasn't uncomfortable. I'm sure that the students who were there will never forget having a class in the Monster Seats at Fenway Park. Today, a ticket for those seats costs about $200.

We have also heard from several of the team's female executives, including Susan Goodenow, the team's vice president of public affairs.

In recent years, a high percentage of students in my class have been women. I enjoy having them in my class, because at that age they are much more disciplined and advanced than the male students—especially the female students who are athletes. They are very organized and driven.

It's important for my students to hear from successful women in sports. Some of the female reporters from NESN have come to the class. Heidi Watney, NESN's current sideline reporter for Red Sox games, and the first runner up in the '02 Miss California pageant, has spoken very frankly to the class.

Another speaker at my class has been Hazel Mae, later with the MLB Network. She's an outstanding broadcaster who is very knowledgeable about baseball as well as other sports. We've also had Tina Cervasio, another NESN Red Sox sideline reporter. She is now with the MSG network covering Madison Square Garden, the New York Knicks, and some baseball.

Sean McDonough, the former Red Sox television broadcaster has spoken, too. He's now with ESPN, doing baseball, college baseball and basketball. Don Orsillo, one of NESN's current Red Sox broadcasters, has also spoken to the class.

Don is a former student of mine. Another former student who came back to speak to the class is Katie Haas. She was in the class early in the decade, then went to work for the Red Sox in the advertising and marketing office. Katie is now the Red Sox director of Florida operations, which includes the spring training site, rehabilitation facilities, and the Sox brand new stadium in Ft. Myers.

I always hire an intern/statistician from the class at Northeastern to work with me in the broadcast booth, giving us drop-in commercials, looking up facts during the game, lining up postgame interviews, and sometimes being a gopher. For years my interns were all male. But for the last three seasons we've had a female student as our broadcast booth intern. Our first female intern was Kainani Stevens. She wrote us a wonderful email explaining why she wanted the job and why she thought she was qualified for it. She got the job and was outstanding in the booth for two years. Then we hired Bethany Singleton, who is also excellent. Over the years, our interns have been very good.

Jeff Idelson interned with us in '87–88. He graduated from Connecticut College in New London, then became an intern with the Red Sox public relations department. After working with us, Jeff went on to become public relations director for the Yankees and for World Cup Soccer. Jeff went on to become vice president for communications at the Baseball Hall of Fame in Cooperstown, and since '08, the president of the Hall of Fame. We're very proud of Jeff. Jeff was just about the best intern anyone could have. He would think of things for us to say before we thought of them. He came up with great facts for us to use during the games, and was very original and innovative. He has continued his excellent work at the Hall of Fame. Bob Feller, my old broadcast partner in Cleveland, loved Jeff. So do the other Hall of Famers with whom he comes in contact.

Students

Don Orsillo took my class and then worked in the booth for two years—one with Ken Coleman and one with Bob Starr and myself. His appetite was legendary. He'd eat two meals in the media dining room, then he'd go to the concession stand behind third base some time during the game. Bob Starr dubbed it the "Don Orsillo Memorial Concession Stand." After graduation, Don went to Pittsfield, Massachusetts, where he did a season of NY-Penn League baseball, receiving $1,600 for the entire season. He did the radio games on the road and the PA announcements at home, because the owner thought that broadcasting the home games on the radio would hurt attendance. When it rained, Don became part of the grounds crew, and pulled the tarp. During the off-season, Don did Springfield Indians hockey in the American Hockey League. Then he went to Binghamton, New York, where he was the voice of the Binghamton Mets (AA) for four years, before moving up to the AAA Pawtucket Red Sox (1996–2000). I recommended Don to PawSox ownership. He worked year-round for the team in the advertising and promotions department, and did a great job. If you're going to broadcast minor league baseball, Pawtucket, Rhode Island, is probably one of the best places to do it because of the outstanding ownership group, led by the late Ben Mondor, who is one of the most generous people in or out of baseball. Ben, general manager Mike Tamburro, and the entire staff have been together for years.

Don filled in on Boston Red Sox TV occasionally in '00, and in '01 took over the NESN telecasts. He has been broadcasting Red Sox games on TV ever since with former Red Sox second baseman Jerry Remy. Don also does some ESPN work in the off-season. Don was a great student and intern, and I am both happy and proud to see that he's done so well.

After Don was a very special young man named Glenn Wilburn, a New York native. He loved Willie Randolph and loved the Yankees, but we hired him anyway. Glenn has become like a member of our family. Glenn did a wonderful job for us for two years. He then moved on to work in the public relations department of the NL office and Major League Baseball in New York. Glenn was the assistant media relations director for the Red Sox for a few years, then left to work for the Montreal Expos, which were being run by the commissioner's office. Since then he's worked for MLB.com and Fox. Glenn came to all our family weddings. We got to know his mother in New York, and we've remained very close.

Several recent interns are working in broadcasting. After working in the broadcast booth at Fenway, Josh Heller moved on to do independent baseball and is now working in the American Hockey League. Dan Nettell has gone on to work as a producer for XM radio.

Another student who took my class is the Reverend Leslie Sterling. Leslie, a professional musician and singer, also worked as an office manager. She loved sports. She collected sound bites for various networks. Leslie was about 30 when she took my class, which is when I got to know her well. As an older student, she was a marvelous influence on her classmates. She raised the achievement level of the entire class. When Sherm Feller, the longtime public address announcer for the Red Sox, passed away before the '94 season, the team asked me whether I knew of any student who might be a good PA announcer. I recommended Leslie Sterling. They brought her in for a tryout on the PA system one day when Fenway was empty. She blew them away—she was so good and so powerful. Her music background helped. Leslie was the PA announcer at Fenway Park for two years, the first woman to hold that job in the AL.

When my son Duke was trying to break into the broadcasting business, I thought so much of Leslie that I sent him to her for voice and elocution lessons. She was a marvelous teacher and Duke loved her.

Leslie thought about leaving after the first year to study for the ministry. She put that off, but a year later she went to the Brattle Street Divinity School near Harvard University. Today, she is an ordained Episcopal priest. Her parish is in Brookline, Massachusetts, not far from Fenway Park. Leslie has remained a special favorite of ours.

One student—Jessica Stoller—worked for *Vogue*. She now runs a New York City fashion consulting firm.

John Ryder was an intern in the mid-90s. He is now an on-air talent at WEEI radio, our flagship station. He hosts a postgame show, a Red Sox review, and a Celtics postgame show.

He was followed by Chris DiPierro, who now has two Stanley Cup rings. Chris is the marketing director for the Boston Bruins, the '11 Stanley Cup Champions, and also worked for the Anaheim Mighty Ducks when they won the Cup.

The list of my interns who have gone on to careers either in the broadcasting industry or professional sports keeps growing.

Students in my class have experiences they simply could not have in a regular classroom, whether at Fenway, or the Boston Garden, or simply hearing from so many sports celebrities.

During my first year of teaching in '85, Howard Cosell was on campus to receive an award from Northeastern's well-known Center for the Study of Sports in Society (which has since moved to the University of Central Florida under the leadership of Richard Lapchik). Among other things, the Center grades sports franchises on their minority hirings.

I was invited to bring my class to hear Cosell's lecture. He was promoting his new book, *I Never Played the Game*. Cosell had just quit *Monday Night Football*. In his book he attacked his former broadcast partners Don Meredith, Frank Gifford, and Al Michaels.

Cosell and I met before his talk, and I told him that I had been listening to him for years, including his Mets pregame broadcasts in '62. I told him that I made my students read his book. His response was vintage Howard Cosell.

"As well you should, young man, as well you should."

CHAPTER 23

"We Are Family"
Balancing Family Life with Baseball Broadcasting

THE KEY INGREDIENTS ARE HAVING A RESPONSIBLE, DEDICATED, AND UNDERSTANDING SPOUSE AND A STRONG MARRIAGE, AND I CERTAINLY HAVE BEEN VERY BLESSED TO HAVE BOTH. In 2011, Jan and I celebrated our 40th wedding anniversary. I have been very fortunate to have Janice as my wife and best friend, and sometimes acting as two parents. It can be very lonely, at times, I know. As a big-league broadcaster, I travel with a party, have a lot of fun on the road, and see lots of friends around the country. But Jan is home alone. It used to be with young children, but now, with our three children grown, many times it is alone. It takes a very understanding person to be able to do that. When you do what I do, you miss a lot because of the travel, usually about 110 days on the road, including spring training. I saw very few of my sons Duke and Tommy's little league baseball games. I did try to see most of their football games, because the Red Sox season had usually ended by then. I coached Katie's youth basketball team, and I went to most of her field hockey games—though I never understood all the rules—but I still missed so much.

I'll never forget getting a call in the booth in Detroit one night that Duke had hit a walk-off home run in a little league game. This was long before cell phones, so getting through to me took quite an effort. That was a great call to get. But usually, when you get a call in the booth on the road, it's not good news—something wrong with the house or a sick child. More often than not, I'm in Kansas City or Baltimore or Oakland at the time.

It takes a great spouse not only to share the responsibility, but to assume so much of my responsibility while I'm away. It also meant that for the most part Jan had to become the family disciplinarian.

During the off-season I tried to make up for lost time. As I mentioned, I coached Katie's basketball team. I went to a lot of football practices and games. But you can't really make up for the time and events you miss while the kids are growing up. The advantage is, I could frequently take my wife and children to work with me. Most people can't do that. This is a perk of my job—being able to share some of the fun things I do with my family. Starting when the kids were old enough, I took each of my children individually on a road trip each season. I used my frequent flier miles. They'd fly by themselves commercially, and I'd meet them. They'd spend a series in a city with me. Tommy went to Texas; Duke went to Seattle. Eventually, they made it to every city in the AL. Duke and Tom would be on the field before the game. Johnny Pesky played pepper with them, or hit fungoes to them. Joe Morgan let them take batting practice in the old Kingdome in Seattle, or in the Rangers' old Arlington Stadium in Texas. The kids ate in the media dining room and watched the game from the booth. If we had a night game or an off-day, we did things in town. We went to Wet 'n' Wild and Six Flags in Texas, baseball museums in Kansas City and Baltimore, and rode the cable cars in San Francisco. The time I spent with them on these trips was wonderful.

Jan stayed home full-time with our young children as we had no relatives nearby to help us out. When Kate was in the fourth grade, Jan began to substitute teach in our hometown. This schedule allowed Jan to be home before Kate got home from school. The boys were old enough to let themselves in the house if I had to leave before Jan got home.

Early on, Jan could not travel with me much because the kids were in school. We tried to schedule the trips so Jan could make as many as she wanted to go on. Jan likes to come to the West Coast once a year. She likes San Francisco and Sausalito. She likes the Crab Cooker, a great seafood place with plastic knives and forks in Newport Beach near Anaheim. Or the Surf and Sand resort which has a beautiful semi-outdoor dining area overlooking the Pacific. Jan always comes to New York when the Red Sox play the Yankees. She can see Duke and his wife, Kiki, and see some Broadway shows, which she loves. Jan goes to Tampa Bay each year because she loves the Renaissance Vinoy in St. Petersburg. We go kayaking at Fort DeSoto, and biking around Snell Island.

Jan has been to every city in the AL with the exception of Arlington, Texas, because she thinks it's too hot. I love the heat. Jan has also experienced the postseason when she could get away.

When the team was in the postseason in the late 1980s and early '90s, we still had little kids at home. So in '88, my father, Dr. Frank, made the trip with me to the Bay Area. Unfortunately, it was an abbreviated visit to Oakland for the last two games of the ALCS, because the Red Sox lost 4–0. Despite the Red Sox losses, my dad enjoyed the trip. Two years later, Jan made the trip to the Bay Area. The Red Sox always had events planned for the wives, such as a boat ride under the Golden Gate Bridge, trips to Sausalito, and shopping trips.

In 2004, Jan came with me to St. Louis for the World Series, even though she was teaching full-time. Fortunately, her principal recognized the unique circumstances, and gave her the time off. She was in St. Louis for Games 3 and 4, as the Red Sox swept the Cardinals.

Having Jan with me in St. Louis as the Red Sox won the World Series for the first time in 86 years was really wonderful. We visited the Gateway Arch, took a riverboat ride up the Mississippi, and we visited Brian and Chrissie Daubach. On the day of Game 4, the final game of the Series, we had lunch at Mike Shannon's Restaurant. Mike's a former St. Louis outfielder, and for 40 years, a radio broadcaster for the Cardinals. Jeff Idelson, my former intern who is now president of the Hall of Fame, and Bill Madden, the Hall of Fame baseball writer for the *New York Daily News*, joined us for lunch. I will always remember what happened that day because it turned out to be so historic.

I thought it was fitting that during Game 4, when the Red Sox won their first World Series since 1918, there was a full lunar eclipse—the first ever during a World Series.

Jan was also with me in Denver in '07 when the Sox swept the Colorado Rockies to win the World Series again. While in Colorado, Jan and I went out to an amphitheater in the beautiful Red Rock area. Jan got to experience a little of the Rocky Mountains. And she was at the party, which the Rockies hosted, before Game 3. We attended the party in the media room after the Red Sox won Game 4 and swept the Series. We flew back together on the team plane, which allowed Jan to be part of the entire experience. I know that these trips don't make up for all the family events, good and bad, that I missed because of my job, but you make adjustments.

For example, our son Tom was scheduled to make his First Holy Communion in 1983, my first year broadcasting for the Red Sox. I was in Winter Haven, Florida, for spring training, getting to know the team, having the team get to know me, and broadcasting some games. We still had not sold our house in Cleveland, where Jan and the kids were living. I could not fly home for this important event in Tom's life, but I certainly did not want to miss this event. Thanks to special dispensation, Tom made his First Communion at the outdoor Mass we had every Saturday next to the swimming pool at the Holiday Inn in Winter Haven. A local priest celebrated Mass, and Jan, Duke, Kate, and I were all there. To this day, many people come up to me and say, "I was there when your son made his First Communion right by Paddy O'Shea's Bar at the Holiday Inn in Winter Haven."

My children have had the opportunity to develop very close relationships with some of the people I met through my job. All three of my children are very close with former Red Sox manager Joe Morgan, who remains one of our closest friends. Joe and his wife, Dotty, took a great interest in their baseball activities and in their lives in general.

Former Red Sox general manager Lou Gorman, who passed away in '11, and I used to do a pregame show in his office every day. Duke, Tommy, and Kate occasionally came with me, either together or individually. Lou was wonderful with them. He'd give them souvenirs, candy, cookies, whatever he could find. He was "Uncle Lou" to the kids, and he explained the inner workings of baseball to them. I think this helped Duke in his career as a sports reporter, because—unlike my own early career—he had no fear, no intimidation factor, upon meeting a major league player. He had been exposed to these athletes his whole life. Duke, who played baseball in college for Stonehill, took batting practice with the Red Sox in the Metrodome in Minneapolis.

Future Hall of Famer Kirby Puckett watched him and coached him. Duke was on the field at Fenway Park with Tony Peña, who worked him out and loved his throwing arm. My children were able to take advantage of my job; but I still missed a lot of their events along the way. I tried to compensate for time and events missed, and hoped that they more or less would balance out. I'm not sure they ever did.

Johnny Pesky took special interest in all three of our children. He hit countless fungoes to Duke and Tom and played pepper with them on road trips. When Duke and Kiki got married in '99, we did not invite Johnny to the wedding, figuring it would be an imposition since the wedding was in Springfield, Massachusetts, two hours away. We didn't want him to feel obligated to come. Johnny was hurt and he let me know it. We made sure that Johnny and his wife, Ruthie, were sent an invitation to Tom and Rachel's wedding in '00.

When we drove up to the wedding reception hall on the Holy Cross campus in Worcester, after Tom and Rachel's wedding, Johnny and Ruthie were the first people we saw. Johnny later told people, "I shamed the old man into it. I should have been at Duke's wedding. I hit him more ground balls."

The only time I took time off from work was for each of my children's high school graduations and weddings. I took two days off for Duke's wedding and two days for Tommy's wedding. The only other games I've missed have been for my mother-in-law's funeral and weddings for my sister Hope and my brother Charlie.

My children's college graduations all happened to be on dates when I could go to the graduation and still make the Red Sox game. I remember a night game in New York after Tom graduated from Holy Cross in Worcester, Massachusetts. When Duke graduated from Stonehill in Easton, Massachusetts, we had an afternoon game at Fenway—which I made, too. When Kate graduated from Boston College on a Monday, the Red Sox were off, so I didn't have to miss that game either.

My children had the opportunity to travel with me and to do things that most kids do not get to do. Sometimes, I invited them to bring a friend, who also experienced this unusual life. I think the activities and experiences that they had compensated somewhat for the times I was not there.

I'm glad I didn't travel for basketball in the baseball off-season. When I broadcast basketball, it was home games for Boston University and Northeastern University on New England Sports Network (NESN), so I never had to leave Boston. I reserved the winter to be at home with my family. Jan and I put three children through college, so my decision not to broadcast much in the winter was hard on the pocketbook, but I still think it was the right decision.

Anybody who is contemplating a career as a baseball broadcaster needs a very strong spouse. You're on the road 110 days a year, and it puts a strain on your family. I am very lucky to have Jan. She has been unbelievable. She worked, first part-time as a reading tutor, and then with her own classroom as a teacher when our kids were in high school. Jan was born to teach. She particularly loved to teach reading. She's a wonderful teacher who developed a very close relationship with her students and their parents.

Jan had her first classroom at the age of 19 as part of a program for outstanding young students at St. Patrick's School in Youngstown, Ohio, earning less than $4,000 a year. I would take her third-grade students out for kickball when we were dating, but had to rely on her for help when I had difficulty controlling them.

After our children were grown she did a special program of tutoring, which meant shorter days but every day. Finally, Jan decided to apply for a full-time job and taught second and third grade for several years. Teaching is a difficult schedule when you're married to a baseball announcer. The school day is 8:00 AM to 3:00 PM or so—but Jan rarely left school at 3:00 PM—and I had to leave for Fenway at 3:00 PM for a night game. Most nights, Jan would be asleep when I came home. Jan worked September to June, but had the summer off. I worked March to October and had the winter off. Our mutual vacations were Thanksgiving, Christmas, Martin Luther King Weekend, and February vacation week!

I take great pride when parents tell me how much Jan has meant to their children and their learning experience in school. Jan also tutored players' children during spring training after retiring as a full-time teacher.

My brothers and sisters and extended family also got a chance to experience what I do. My brothers Frank and Charlie were both athletes. Frank, now a dermatologist, went into practice with our father, also Frank and also a dermatologist. My brother Frank went to Hopkins Grammar School, the old prep school in New Haven, where he pitched a no-hitter. Frank later pitched for Yale.

My brother Charlie was a quarterback at Hopkins, then went to Yale, where he was the ace of the pitching staff. To this day, he is the only Yale pitcher to beat Harvard twice in one year. (For some reason, during those years, Harvard usually had a better baseball team.) He was also the backup quarterback to Stone Phillips, later an NBC news personality. Today, Charlie is a plastic surgeon in Hartford, Connecticut, specializing in the repair of cleft palates for young people.

Frank has been to two Red Sox Fantasy camps, and he's going again in '12. He runs triathlons and is still very athletic at age 57. Charlie once pitched batting practice for the Cleveland Indians when I was broadcasting for them in 1979, when he was a medical student at Columbia. In Yankee Stadium in '79, Charlie pitched batting practice for the "extra men"—the non-starters. He nearly hit Cliff "Heathcliff" Johnson. He put the first pitch behind Johnson's head. I thought, "I finally got my dream job of broadcasting in the big leagues, and my brother's going to get me canned because he drilled one of our players." Some of the other

Indians players enjoyed watching the 6'4" Cliff dance. But after that, Charlie threw well and Dave Garcia, an Indians coach and later manager, complimented me on Charlie's pitching. He had a good sinker. I only saw Charlie pitch one game, and that was at Rollins College Tournament in Winter Park, Florida, against Northwestern, where he lost 1–0.

My father loved listening to me broadcast the Red Sox games. He had his earpiece in wherever he went. In fact, he once went to an opera at the Schubert Theater in New Haven, where many great shows started, and he had his earpiece in during the opera. At one point, it fell out or got disconnected, and my broadcast blared during the opera.

Like my dad, my Uncle Charlie never missed a pitch. Charlie was like a second dad to us when we were young. He lived two blocks away. Uncle Charlie had Red Sox license plates and a Red Sox watch. Uncle Charlie—a curveball in baseball slang—was very generous to us in many ways. My mother still listens to the games regularly, as do my five sisters: Carolyn, Cherie, Pam, Emily, and Hope, and their children, who often connect with me on my baseball travels.

While I missed a lot of Mother's Days, Father's Days, and little league games, I kept my family involved by long distance. And while my children were, I'm sure, disappointed for the many times I wasn't home, they were able to take advantage of some of the perks of my job.

CHAPTER 24

"Teach Your Children Well"
What Baseball Taught My Children

I THINK MY THREE CHILDREN LEARNED LESSONS ABOUT DIVERSITY BECAUSE OF MY WORK IN BASEBALL. The best example is my friendship with Deacon Jones, who played for the Chicago White Sox; was the hitting coach for the Houston Astros and San Diego Padres, where he tutored Tony Gwynn; and scouted for the Baltimore Orioles. Deacon's father really was a deacon in his church.

Deacon grew up in White Plains, New York, and is a member of the White Plains High School Hall of Fame. He was recruited to play football by Ohio State's legendary football coach Woody Hayes, who sat in Deacon's living room. But Deacon had the courage to tell him that he was going to play baseball. He didn't want to risk ruining his athletic career by playing college football. He went to Ithaca College, where he was an athletic star. (He's in its Hall of Fame, too.)

After his junior year at Ithaca, he worked out for the White Sox. Manager Marty Marion asked him what he wanted for a bonus. He replied that he wanted $5,000, which he'd get if he played one year. Deacon also said that he wanted a car like Marion's—a Cadillac. White Sox general manager Frank Lane told Marion, "Give him your car." Marion did. Deacon was signed and played very well for the Savannah/Lynchburg White Sox in the Sally League. As a major leaguer, he hit one home run for the White Sox, but a shoulder injury limited his career. (These were the days before the designated hitter.) He played winter ball in Puerto Rico where one of his teammates was the great Roberto Clemente. Since he couldn't throw right-handed, he taught himself to throw left-handed. He continued to play in the minors before he began his career as a minor league manager, a hitting instructor, and then a scout.

In 1951, Deacon became the first African American to be the American Legion Player of the Year. In the '50s and '60s he endured racism in the south. He told my children about being chased by Klansmen, having a gun pulled on him in the Savannah bus station, having to eat on the bus in southern towns where the restaurants wouldn't serve African Americans and how a franchise actually moved because of the courage of Deacon and his wife, Tiki.

They were playing in Savannah. Deacon's best friend and teammate was Don Buford, who went on to have an excellent 10-year major league career with the White Sox and the Orioles. The ballpark in Savannah had segregated seating, so that blacks could not sit with whites. One night, Tiki and Don Buford's wife couldn't take it anymore, so they sat with the other wives in the section behind home plate. Deacon and Buford looked up from the field to see what was going on, and they gestured to their wives to move. But no, their wives indicated that they were staying. And they did. There were no incidents, except that the team's owners got very nervous, and asked them if they'd move. They refused. The team owners feared that team sponsors would withdraw their support. They did. The team picked up and moved to Lynchburg, Virginia. (Deacon asked, "Why Lynchburg? That's not a good name for a town for us to move to.")

Deacon told my kids these stories, and I think that hearing them firsthand, from somebody who lived through these experiences, had a tremendous impact on their own perspective.

One of my closest friends when I lived in Solon, Ohio, was Leonard Schur, a Cleveland lawyer who kept kosher, even at the ballpark. He was an Indians season ticket holder who regularly took my three kids to sit with him in the front row at Municipal Stadium. But they had to abide by his rules: bring your own snacks. Only one trip to the concession stands for one item. No bathroom trips until the fifth inning.

Leonard was a great baseball guy who taught me the value of talking to scouts, something he always tried to do for information on players. Leonard also reviewed my contract with the SportsExchange, the Cleveland Cable channel, and negotiated the sale of our Solon home when we moved to New England.

Baseball has allowed my family to forge diverse friendships and we have benefitted greatly from baseball's multiculturalism. Duke was especially close with

Tony Peña, who loved his throwing arm. Tony would have him on the field at Fenway, and worked with Duke on making the throw from catcher to second base. (Duke was a catcher on the Stonehill College team before switching to pitching in his junior year.) Tony, always very demonstrative, was not only a great teacher, he was very encouraging and enthusiastic with Duke.

I think that being with all of these people in a social situation—Deacon Jones, Tony Peña, Leonard Schur, Andre Thornton, and his son, Andy, who was very close with Duke when we lived in Ohio—had a profound effect on my kids' thinking and their sense of fairness in dealing with people of different ethnicities and different races than they might have encountered in the suburbs where we lived.

Kate wrote this when she was in high school.

Ode to Baseball
By
Kate Castiglione

"It breaks your heart. It is designed to break your heart. The game begins in the spring, when everything else begins again, and it blossoms in the summer filling the afternoons and evenings, and then as soon as the chill rains come out it stops and leaves you to face the fall alone. You count on it, rely on it to buffer the passage of time, to keep the memory of sunshine and high skies alive, and then just when the days are all twilight, when you need it most, it stops."

This poem, "The Green Fields of the Mind," describes my love for the game. It was written by A. Bartlett Giamatti, former commissioner of baseball. It is read every year by my all-time favorite baseball announcer, Joe Castiglione, to close the season for the Boston Red Sox.

For most, baseball is the national pastime, for others it is just another game, but for me it is a way of life. Call me obsessive, call me a fanatic, call me what you wish. But please be sympathetic in your judgments, for I blame my environment and my upbringing for instilling in me somewhat of a craze for the game.

Every dad reads his little girl a bedtime story each night. My dad, being the fun dad that he is, did the same. However, his bedtime story was a little different than most.

My bedtime stories were usually nine innings long. While most kids fell asleep to "…and they lived happily ever after," I fell asleep to something like "two on, two out in the bottom of the sixth, the Red Sox are in the lead three to nothing as Wade Boggs steps up to the plate."

I never could stay awake long enough to hear the end, but Dad always filled me in the next day at breakfast or over the phone, depending if the Sox were home or away. Every night I asked God to make the Red Sox win their game. I love listening to the Red Sox on the radio, only now I can stay awake for the whole, entire game. While most little girls were playing with Barbie dolls, I was keeping the scorecard for the Red Sox games.

Every Sunday, I went to work with my dad. For two hours I would sit and watch batting practice before the game, hoping my "boyfriend" Ellis Burks would notice me and sign my Hello Kitty autograph book for the third time.

When the game started, my eyes were glued on the field. I knew every player, their number, and position. I was the official pitch counter of Red Sox radio, or so I was told. I had my own little clicker and kept track of every pitch that was thrown for my dad. Sometimes he'd even let me recite the disclaimer over the radio. I even started to receive my own fan mail at Fenway.

Most families sit down to eat dinner together at the same time each and every evening. We of course do the same, only sometimes my dad can't make it because the Red Sox have an away game and dinner at my house is never eaten at the same time. I think we're the only family that lets baseball determine dinnertime. When my dad is home, my mom always says "listen to the game and be home an hour and a half after it ends when your father gets home from work." So you see, even if I didn't like baseball, I would still be forced to listen to it if I wanted to eat dinner. If the game goes into extra innings—forget about it—I am going to starve.

Vacations take on a whole new meaning in my house. For example, last fall I went to Toronto because it was the only ballpark in the AL I had not yet visited.

With interleague play now (that is, the NL playing the AL), I get to visit a new bunch of cities. Last summer, the Red Sox family trip was to Atlanta, my first NL ballpark. My ultimate goal is to visit every ballpark

in both the American and National League. My dad has traveled so much
with baseball and as a result he has made friends all over the country.
Because of these friends, my family and I have had the opportunity to
do so many wonderful things, such as flying a helicopter into Mt. St.
Helens and getting a personalized tour of the Secret Service facility in
Washington, D.C.

I have learned so much from the game of baseball. For one, it has
taught me that money does not make happiness. We all know that
baseball players are paid a great deal of money, but what most of us fail
to realize is that they are forced to be apart from their family and friends
for nine months out of the year. People (fans in particular) cheer for them
only when they are doing well and bash them when they are in a slump.
Even million-dollar ballplayers need acceptance. Baseball has also taught
me to appreciate my family. My dad goes to spring training in Florida for
a month every March and travels through October. I get to go away with
him a lot, but there are times when I really miss him and there are times
when he can't be there for me, and it definitely hurts both of us. But
it has made me appreciate the time that I do spend with him so much
more. Baseball has taught me that absence does make the heart grow
fonder.

I still love going to the Red Sox games with my dad and listening to
them on the radio. However, I have since retired from my position as
the official pitch counter of Red Sox radio and my fan mail has ceased.
As I have grown older, the game of baseball has taken on a whole new
meaning in my life. It is no longer just a game to me but rather a field
of opportunities. I am just now beginning to realize all the wonderful
things that baseball has enabled me to experience. Because of the game, I
have been able to travel all throughout the country. I have met so many
glamorous people, and best of all, it has enabled me to spend so much
time with my father. Whether it be in person, or listening to his voice on
the radio, he always seems to be with me.

I can't imagine a life without baseball, a summer without travel, or a
dad with a nine-to-five job. Hopefully, now, you can all understand my
obsession with the game a little more.

Perhaps you think that I am a little crazy, but at least now you can
clearly see that I have been warped by my environment, and that I have

been raised to be a fanatic. Nevertheless, I'd like to take this moment to personally thank the game of baseball for making my life so complete. Baseball has been very, very good to me, and I can't help but to love the game.

CHAPTER 25

"Tell Her No"
No-Hitters I Have Called

A BASEBALL ADAGE SAYS THAT YOU NEVER KNOW WHAT YOU'RE GOING TO SEE AT THE BALLPARK. It's absolutely true. Every game is different. You might see something today that you've never seen before.

Who knew that on a chilly Tuesday night against Seattle (April 29, 1986), Roger Clemens would be the first pitcher to strike out 20 batters in a nine-inning game? Or that 10 seasons later, in a game between two teams going nowhere but home, before a small crowd at Tiger Stadium (September 18, 1996), Clemens would again strike out 20?

I've seen a few inside-the-park home runs—one of the most exciting plays in the game—triple plays, monster home runs, hidden ball tricks, and Daniel Nava hitting the first pitch of his career for a home run.

The worst thing I ever saw was pitcher Bryce Florie getting hit in the right eye at Fenway Park by a comebacker off the bat of Ryan Thompson, a reserve Yankee outfielder, on September 8, 2000. Florie collapsed, writhing in agony. Even as he lay prone on the pitcher's mound, his legs continued to twitch. Florie suffered retina damage, three fractures to his eye socket, and a nasal fracture. Florie, a 30-year-old from Charleston, South Carolina, in his seventh big league season, tried to come back in '01, but the injury pretty much ended his career.

I've been fortunate to see 10 no-hitters in my career. I broadcast six and saw four others. A no-hitter is generally sort of a fluke in that you need a lot of luck to get one. As a broadcaster, I feel obliged to let the audience know that the pitcher has a no-hitter going as the game moves on. The old superstition of not mentioning the fact that this is a no-hitter would be unfair to the listeners, especially those who just tuned in. Also, there is no way that I have ever had any control from the broadcast booth over whether a batter gets a hit or makes an out.

I saw Bob Gibson's no-hitter on August 14, 1971, at Pittsburgh. He struck out Willie Stargell for the third time to end the game. I "broadcast" the last two innings on my tape recorder from a booth.

I saw the last two outs of Dick Bosman's perfect game (July 19, 1974, Indians vs. A's) and did a report for NBC after the game.

I saw the last out of Dennis Eckersley's no-hitter for Cleveland over the Angels on May 30, 1977. I did postgame interviews after the game.

I also saw Len Barker throw a perfect game (Indians vs. Blue Jays, May 15, 1981), but I didn't broadcast it. I was doing a postgame talk show on WWWE, the Indians' flagship station.

The six no-hitters I called:

1. Dave Righetti of the Yankees no-hit the Red Sox on July 4, 1983, in New York. Before an Independence Day crowd of 41,000, Righetti struck out Wade Boggs to end the game on a 95-degree day in the Bronx.

2. Chris Bosio of the Mariners threw a no-hitter against Boston at the Kingdome in Seattle on April 22, 1993. There were only 13,600 at the Kingdome. Bosio walked the first two batters—an inauspicious beginning for a no-hitter—but then Mike Greenwell hit into a double play, and that was it for Red Sox baserunners. With two out in the ninth inning, Omar Vizquel, a likely Hall of Famer, barehanded a ground ball by pinch-hitter Ernie Riles and threw to first for the final out. Vizquel could have used his glove instead of styling, but he was good enough to pull it off.

3. Hideo Nomo, Red Sox, April 4, 2001, 3–0 over Baltimore Orioles at Camden Yards. Brian Daubach hit two home runs and Troy O'Leary caught the final out in left field.

4. Derek Lowe, Red Sox, April 27, 2002, 10–0 over Tampa Bay in Boston. Jason Tyner grounded out to second baseman Rey Sanchez for the final out.

5. Clay Buchholz, Red Sox, September 1, 2007, 10–0 over Baltimore Orioles in Boston. Nick Markakis took a curveball for a called strike three to end the game.

6. Jon Lester, Red Sox, May 19, 2008, 7–0 over Kansas City in Boston. A totally dominating performance.

Acknowledgments

Joe Castiglione

There are many people to thank. First, of course, my wife, Jan, and my three children: Duke, Tommy, and Kate. It would have been impossible for me to live my dream as a baseball broadcaster for 33 years without the loving and supportive family with which I have been blessed. And my parents, Frank and Pam, who were so supportive of my broadcasting career as soon as they thought that it could really happen.

Thanks to my agent, Steve Freyer, who has been very supportive and has done a great job for me. It's very reassuring to have an agent you can really trust who goes to bat for you during contract negotiations.

I am grateful to the many fans in Red Sox Nation who have listened to our broadcasts over the years. The feedback that I have received has been overwhelmingly supportive, and I am most grateful.

The media relations directors and their staffs, especially Glen Geffner, John Blake, Pam Ganley, and most of all Dick Bresciani. Dick was the team's media relations director for three decades and is now the Red Sox historian. Dick and his wife, Joanne, have been friends of Jan and mine for 30 years. He is probably the most knowledgeable person I've ever known regarding Red Sox history, as well as specifics on games and people.

Dick is a member of the Red Sox Hall of Fame, the University of Massachusetts Hall of Fame, the Cape Cod League Hall of Fame, and the New England Chapter of the National Italian-American Sports Hall of Fame. Nobody deserves these honors more.

The Red Sox traveling secretaries, including Jack Rogers, a prince of a man and probably the best that ever lived. He was always so gracious and helpful with the media. Jack and his wife, Ellie, were also wonderful with Jan and my children. Steve August, and Jack McCormick, traveling secretaries who always made our travel run so smoothly.

My engineers, especially Doug Lane, who has worked on our broadcasts since 1996, all of my partners throughout my career, and the players who have been so cooperative over the years.

I've worked with a number of managers. A good relationship between broadcasters and managers is essential for information and to help us do our jobs. Likewise, the coaches who provide so much knowledge and friendship.

The baseball writers. We really rely on the newspaper and Internet writers for information. They do a very thorough job. I'm indebted to them.

My mentors. Lloyd Walsh, the voice of Colgate football at WRUN, who gave me my first professional experience and has been a great mentor to me in my career.

The late Bill O'Donnell, broadcaster for the Baltimore Orioles from 1966 until his death in 1982. We met in Syracuse. Bill always advised me about broadcasting jobs in baseball, and was extremely helpful in critiquing my demo tape.

Ken Coleman. My seven years with Ken were wonderful. He mentored me. He's the reason I was hired in Boston. Ken recommended me for the job in Boston and always encouraged me after I was hired. Ken talked me up in public, as did Johnny Pesky. They were both very supportive, especially in my first few years in Boston. Ken and Johnny helped me get established and earn the respect of others because they both thought so highly of me.

Ken and I socialized on the road. We ate together, traveled together, and we had drinks together. After every road trip, when we got back to Fenway Park in the middle of the night, I drove Ken home to Cohasset. This was something I did because I wanted to. Also, it would have been difficult for Ken to park his car at Fenway Park without damaging it. (Ken was not the greatest driver in the world.) We bonded almost as soon as we met. Our paths to Fenway Park were very similar. He's a New Englander. I'm a New Englander. He worked in Cleveland. I worked in Cleveland. He did the Browns and the Indians. I anchored TV and did the Indians. Both of us eventually came to the Red Sox.

Ernie Harwell and all the management people at WPLM: Jack Campbell and his wife, Jane Day. Sadly, Jane—probably the nicest boss anyone could have—

passed away in 1990. Plus the people at American Radio and Entercom and all the management people there who let me do my job.

Douglas B. Lyons

I'd like to thank Joe for including me again in his second book. I'd also like to thank my brother, Jeffrey—a baseball fan almost since birth, and a devout Red Sox fan—for introducing me to Joe and his family. I know why Jeff refers to Joe as the fifth Lyons brother.

Whenever I meet somebody who works in professional baseball, I always introduce myself as a friend of Joe Castiglione. This never fails to elicit a smile for at least three reasons: 1.) Joe knows everybody. 2.) Everybody likes Joe Castiglione. 3.) Most people remember a kindness Joe has done for them over the years—introduced them to somebody they wanted to meet, put them in contact with somebody, aided a benefit or a charity—or just had the pleasure of spending time with Joe.

As a writer, Joe is very easy to work with. Joe writes in full paragraphs, and all of his sentences parse. As soon as we started working on this book, Joe knew, chapter by chapter, how the book would be organized. Joe has an incredible memory for details—which restaurant he went to, whom he sat with, or who was on base, the name of the pitcher (and where he's from), and the weather at 10-year-old games. And when you've seen more than 5,000 Red Sox games, there's a lot to remember.

I suppose that anybody could write an account of what the Red Sox did during a particular time frame. But Joe adds much more than just the narrative of who came to bat, who got a hit, and who struck out. Whom did he have dinner with the night before? Where did they go to church? Where did they go kayaking? Which historic site did they take a detour to? Was Jan with him? What did he think of the new stadium with its new broadcast booth? What is the broadcaster for the other team like?

People used to say that listening to a game was "just like being at the ballpark." If Joe Castiglione is broadcasting the game, or telling you about it, it's much better.